Breaking
the Political
Glass Ceiling

Women in American Politics series, edited by Karen O'Connor

Madam President: Women Blazing the Leadership Trail
Eleanor Clift and Tom Brazaitis

Breaking the Political Glass Ceiling: Women and Congressional Elections
Barbara Palmer and Dennis Simon

Breaking the Political Glass Ceiling

Women and Congressional Elections

Barbara Palmer

and

Dennis Simon

Routledge
Taylor & Francis Group
New York   London

Published in 2006 by
Routledge
Taylor & Francis Group
270 Madison Avenue
New York, NY 10016

Published in Great Britain by
Routledge
Taylor & Francis Group
2 Park Square
Milton Park, Abingdon
Oxon OX14 4RN

Printed in the United States of America on acid-free paper
10 9 8 7 6 5 4 3 2 1

International Standard Book Number-10: 0-415-95087-2 (Hardcover) 0-415-95088-0 (Softcover)
International Standard Book Number-13: 978-0-415-95087-9 (Hardcover) 978-0-415-95088-6 (Softcover)
Library of Congress Card Number 2005024675

Library of Congress Cataloging-in-Publication Data

Palmer, Barbara, 1967-
   Breaking the political glass ceiling : women and congressional elections / Barbara Palmer and Dennis Simon.
         p. cm. -- (Women in American politics)
   Includes bibliographical references and index.
   ISBN 0-415-95087-2 (hb : alk. paper) -- ISBN 0-415-95088-0 (pb : alk. paper)
   1. Women in politics--United States. I. Simon, Dennis Michael. II. Title. III. Series.

HQ1236.5.U6P35 2006
324.973'092082--dc22   2005024675

Taylor & Francis Group
is the Academic Division of Informa plc.

Visit the Taylor & Francis Web site at
http://www.taylorandfrancis.com

and the Routledge Web site at
http://www.routledge-ny.com

Contents

For their years of understanding, support, and encouragement

To Mary Ann and Otto Palmer

Barbara Palmer

To Debbie, Jonathan, and Jennifer Simon
Valeria and Gary Simon and the memory of Michael Simon
Joan Roach and the memory of John Roach

Dennis Simon

Preface

This project began casually, with the academic equivalent of a water cooler conversation. In the fall of 1998, we were colleagues in the Department of Political Science at Southern Methodist University. Dennis Simon was teaching a course on congressional elections. He divided the House and Senate elections among the members of his class and required them to gather data on the party, background, and gender of the candidates. In looking over their work, he noticed that there were fourteen races in which a woman ran against another woman. At the drinking fountain one day, he mentioned these races to Barbara Palmer, whose expertise included women and politics, and asked whether she found it surprising. Our discussion of this "tidbit" about the 1998 midterm elections raised numerous questions about women in the electoral arena and congressional elections generally. Thus began a six-year project that has included conference papers and journal articles, and has resulted in this book. We brought together two perspectives on politics in the United States and familiarity with two different bodies of literature. This project has been truly collaborative.

In the spring of 1999, the Research Council at Southern Methodist University awarded us a grant to begin the study. We used the funds primarily to hire research assistants to help in gathering and compiling what, in retrospect, turned out to be a staggering amount of data on House and Senate elections. We wish to thank those assistants who were recruited from Barbara's Women and Politics class at Southern Methodist University: Zhelia Bazleh, Diana Dorough, Cynthia Flores, Mandy Gough, Brooke Guest, Vanessa Hammond, Bernard Jones, Kristi Katsanis, Emily Katt, Albany Mitchell, Sheri Rogers, Heather Scott, Jessica Sheppard, Jennifer Sumrall, Andrea Swift, Natalie Thompson, Brenda Tutt, Amy Williams, and Kari Young. We owe a special expression of gratitude to those students who not only coded data but also "came back for more" to help us clean it and enter it into spreadsheets: Lindsay Abbate, Erin Echols, Elizabeth Myers, and Steve Schulte. We suspect that their experience in "doing real political science" was a deciding factor in their choice to attend law school. We also would like to thank those students who worked with Barbara at American University, especially Amy Baumann, Meredith Hess, Cameo Kaisler, and Laura Pautz. David Brown, dean of the Washington Semester Program at American University, provided much-needed summer funds that allowed Barbara to travel back to Dallas to work on this project. Christine Carberry, of Southern Methodist University, was both expert and meticulous in preparing the index for this volume. We are grateful to her for unearthing a number of errors and omissions in the text. Our gratitude is also extended to Angela Chnapko and Amy Rodriguez at Taylor & Francis for their encouragement and guidance during the preparation, editing, and publication of the book.

We wish to thank all the panelists and discussants who offered critiques of our work over the years and helped us to improve it. Debts of gratitude are also owed to our colleagues. At Southern Methodist University, we regularly vetted our ideas with Brad Carter, Valerie Hunt, Dennis Ippolito, Cal Jillson, Joe Kobylka, Harold Stanley, and Matthew Wilson. We also had frequent conversations with Carole Wilson of the University of Texas at Dallas. In addition, we would like to thank Karen O'Connor, director of the Women and Politics Institute at American University. Their comments, questions, and encouragement proved most valuable, and we are grateful for their gift of collegiality. Susannah Shakow and Coke Stewart of Washington, D.C. provided much-needed proofreading and a fresh perspective to our work.

1
Why So Few, and Why So Slow?

In 1974, the central question posed by Jeane Kirkpatrick in her book, *Political Woman*, was "Why, when women in increasing numbers are asserting themselves, training themselves, seeking equal rights, equal opportunities and equal responsibilities in every aspect of American life, have so few [entered] the political arena?"[1] The central question that motivates our book is why, after thirty additional years of women asserting themselves, training themselves, and seeking equal rights, equal opportunities, and equal responsibilities, is the integration of women into Congress taking so long? Are women ever going to break the "political glass ceiling"?

A Snapshot: The Women of 1956

In 1956, sixteen women were elected to Congress, fifteen in the House and one in the Senate. The nation had elected President Dwight Eisenhower to a second term of office with 57.4 percent of the popular vote. Eisenhower's electoral appeal, however, was not sufficient to capture control of Congress. The Democrats enjoyed a 234–201 majority in the House of Representatives and a smaller, 49–47, majority in the Senate.[2] The national political agenda was crowded that year. President Eisenhower would address an international crisis triggered in late 1956 by the British-French-Israeli invasion of the Suez Canal. The successful launch of Sputnik by the Soviets added to the anxiety about the ongoing Cold War and sparked a debate about the quality of education in the nation. The debate would ultimately lead to the National Defense Education Act in 1958. In September 1957, the effort to desegregate Central High School would force President Eisenhower to send federal troops to Little Rock, Arkansas.

---

[1] Jeane Kirkpatrick, *Political Woman* (New York: Basic Books, 1974), ix.
[2] Alaska and Hawaii were not yet states, so the total number of senators was ninety-six.

The 85th Congress (1957 session) is noteworthy for two additional reasons. First, the election of 1956 was a high-water mark in the number of women elected to the House. Second, the 85th Congress enacted the Civil Rights Act of 1957, the first civil rights legislation passed by Congress since the Reconstruction era. Fourteen of the fifteen women in the House voted for the act, with Representative Iris Blitch (D-GA) casting the lone "nay" vote among them.

Nine of the women in the House were Democrats and six were Republicans. Senator Margaret Chase Smith (ME), the only woman in the Senate, was a Republican. Only one woman, Representative Martha Griffiths (D-MI), was a lawyer. Six were widows initially elected to succeed their deceased husbands. The most senior woman was Republican Edith Nourse Rogers of Massachusetts, a widow first elected in 1925; in 1957, she began serving her seventeenth term. Next in seniority was Republican Frances Bolton of Ohio, a philanthropist and, like Rogers, a widow. Bolton, first elected in 1940, began serving her tenth term. Another widow was West Virginia Democrat Maude Kee, who succeeded her husband, John. When Maude retired in 1964, her son, James, won the election to replace her.[3]

Many of these women would distinguish themselves as policy leaders in the House. Representative Martha Griffiths (D-MI) was a key force in passing the Civil Rights Act of 1964 and later became known as the "mother of the Equal Rights Amendment."[4] Representative Leonor Sullivan (D-MO) was a cosponsor of the Equal Pay Act of 1963 and an early advocate of consumer protection.[5] Representative Edith Green (D-OR) "left her mark on nearly every schooling bill enacted during her twenty years on Capitol Hill" and was the author and principle advocate of Title IX of the Educational Amendments of 1972.[6] Representative Gracie Pfost (D-ID), who became known as "Hell's Belle," was an opponent of private power companies and fought for federal intervention to manage the project planned for the Hell's Canyon branch of the Snake River.[7]

The Rules of the Game

In spite of the tremendous contributions of these women, that only fifteen were elected to the House in 1956 provides a vivid example that women had "a very small share, though a very large stake, in political power."[8] For women, entry into the inner world of politics was largely blocked. Specifically, women who were interested in politics faced numerous barriers, including cultural norms and gender stereotypes that limited their choices, little access to the

---

[3] Karen Foerstel, *Biographical Dictionary of Congressional Women* (Westport, Conn.: Greenwood Press, 1999), 144–45. Altogether, the Kee family held the seat from 1933 to 1973.
[4] Foerstel, 1999, 109–11.
[5] Foerstel, 1999, 263–65.
[6] Foerstel, 1999, 104.
[7] Foerstel, 1999, 218.
[8] Kirkpatrick, 1974, 3.

"pipeline" or the hierarchy of political offices, and the politics of congressional redistricting.

Cultural Norms: A "Man's Game"

In the 1950s, women were socialized to view politics as a man's game, a game that was inconsistent with the gender roles to which women were assigned. As Kirkpatrick explained:

> Like men, women gain status for effective, responsible performance of culturally sanctioned roles. Any effort to perform roles assigned by the culture to the opposite sex is likely to result in a loss of status on the sex specific status ladder. The values on which women are expected to concentrate are those of affection, rectitude, well-being; the skills relevant to the pursuit of these values are those associated with nurturing, serving, and pleasing a family and community: homemaking, personal adornment, preparing and serving food, nursing the ill, comforting the downcast, aiding and pleasing a husband, caring for and educating the young. It is assumed furthermore that these activities will consume all a women's time, that to perform them well is both a full time and a life time job.[9]

Women attending college in the 1940s, for example, reported being cautioned about appearing too smart and earning top grades, because displays of intelligence endangered their social status on campus. Women were also reminded, typically by their parents and brothers, that pursuing a career would reduce their prospects for marriage and motherhood.[10] In 1950, only 23.9 percent of bachelor's degrees were awarded to women.[11] Traditional sex roles were widely accepted by men and women. In 1936, a Gallup Poll asked respondents whether a married woman should work if she had a husband capable of supporting her; 82 percent of the sample said, "No."[12] A similar question appeared in an October 1938 poll; 78 percent disapproved of married women entering the workforce. This included 81 percent of male respondents and 75 percent of female respondents.[13] Prior to World War II, the proportion of married women who worked outside the home was 14.7 percent. Labor shortages during the war drew married women in the workforce; by 1944, the proportion increased to 21.7 percent. In 1956, 29.0 percent of married women worked outside the home.[14] Working outside the home and pursuing a professional career represented a rejection of tradition, socialization, and conformity.

---

[9] Kirkpatrick, 1974, 15.
[10] Mirra Komarovsky, "Cultural Contradictions and Sex Roles," *American Journal of Sociology* 52 (1946): 184–89.
[11] National Center for Education Statistics, http://nces.ed.gov (accessed August 1, 2005).
[12] *Gallup Poll, 1935–1971* (Wilmington, Del.: Scholarly Resources, 1973), 39.
[13] *Gallup Poll*, 1973, 131.
[14] U.S. Bureau of the Census, *Historical Statistics of the United States* (Washington, D.C.: U.S. Department of Commerce, Bureau of the Census, 1975), 133.

Also accepted was the norm that politics was the domain of men. A 1945 Gallup Poll reported that a majority of men and women disagreed with the statement that not enough "capable women are holding important jobs" in government.[15] In the 1950s, voter turnout among men was ten percentage points higher than among women.[16] One survey found that, compared to men, women were less likely to express a sense of involvement in politics; women had a lower sense of political efficacy and personal competence than men.[17] The political scientists conducting the survey reported that women who were married often refused to participate in the survey and referred "interviewers to their husbands as being the person in the family who pays attention to politics."[18] Moreover, these cultural norms about women and politics were slow to change. Indeed, as late as 1975, 48 percent of respondents in a survey conducted by the National Opinion Research Center agreed that "most men are better suited emotionally for politics than are most women."[19]

Against this cultural backdrop, it comes as no surprise that a "woman entering politics risks the social and psychological penalties so frequently associated with nonconformity. Disdain, internal conflicts, and failure are widely believed to be her likely rewards."[20] Entering the electoral arena was, therefore, an act of political and social courage. The example of Representative Coya Knutson (D-MN) poignantly illustrates that women with political ambitions were often punished. Knutson first ran for the House as a long shot in 1954, defeating a six-term incumbent Republican. During her campaign in the large rural district, she played the accordion and sang songs, in addition to criticizing the Eisenhower administration's agricultural policy. In 1958, Knutson was running for her third term. In response to Knutson's refusal to play along with the Democratic Party in their 1956 presidential endorsements, party leaders approached her husband, Andy, an alcoholic who physically abused her and her adopted son, to help sabotage her reelection campaign. At the prompting of party leaders, Andy wrote a letter to Coya, pleading that she return to Minnesota and give up her career in politics, complaining how their home life had deteriorated since she left for Washington, D.C. He also accused his wife of having an affair with one of her congressional staffers and threatened a $200,000 lawsuit. This infamous "Coya, Come Home" letter gained national media attention, and her Republican opponent ran on the slogan "A Big Man for a Man-Sized Job." She was defeated by fewer than 1,400 votes by Republi-

---

[15] *Gallup Poll,* 1973, 548–49.

[16] Angus Campbell et al., *The American Voter* (Chicago: University of Chicago Press, 1960), 485.

[17] Campbell et al., 1960, 489–90.

[18] Campbell et al., 1960, 485.

[19] William Mayer, *The Changing American Mind* (Ann Arbor: University of Michigan Press, 1992), 394.

[20] Kirkpatrick, 1974, 15.

can Odin Langin.[21] She was the only Democratic incumbent to lose that year.

Serving in political office could also be extremely unpleasant. Women in Congress often had to fight for access and positions, such as committee assignments, that would have rightfully been given to them had they been men.[22] For example, in 1949, Representative Reva Bosone, a Democrat from Utah, requested a seat on the House Interior Committee. When she approached Representative Jere Cooper (D-TN), the chair of the Ways and Means Committee who had the final say over assignments, he responded, "Oh, my. Oh, no. She'd be embarrassed because it would be embarrassing to be on the committee and discuss the sex of animals."[23] She shot back and said, "It would be refreshing to hear about animals' sex relationships compared to the perversions among human beings."[24] When Shirley Chisholm (D-NY) came to Washington, D.C., in 1968, she asked to be assigned to the Committee on Education and Labor. She was a former teacher with extensive experience in education policy while serving in the New York Assembly. Education was extremely important to her poor, black, Brooklyn district. The Democratic Party leadership in Congress, however, assigned her to the Agriculture Committee and the Subcommittee on Forestry and Rural Development. Outraged, she refused the assignment and took her case to Speaker of the House John McCormack (D-MA). He told her she should be a "good soldier," put her time in on the committee, and wait for a better assignment. Chisholm responded, "All my forty-three years I have been a good soldier. . . . The time is growing late, and I can't be a good soldier any longer."[25] She protested her committee assignment on the House floor, stating that "it would be hard to imagine an assignment that is less relevant to my background or to the needs of the predominantly black and Puerto Rican people who elected me," and was reassigned to the Veterans Affairs Committee.[26] It was not her first choice, but Chisholm did note, "There are a lot more veterans in my district than trees."[27] In 1973, Representative Pat Schroeder (D-CO) did receive an assignment on

---

[21] Chuck Haga, "'Come Home,' Coya Dies," *Minneapolis Star Tribune*, October 11, 1996, 1A; Leonard Inskip, "A Revival of Sorts for Minnesota's Knutson," *Minneapolis Star Tribune*, February 4, 1997, 11A; and Foerstel, 1999, 152–53. Another woman would not be elected to the House from the State of Minnesota until Democrat Betty McCollum in 2000.

[22] Sally Friedman, "House Committee Assignments of Women and Minority Newcomers, 1965–1994," *Legislative Studies Quarterly* 21 (1996): 73–81.

[23] Karen Foerstel and Herbert Foerstel, *Climbing the Hill: Gender Conflict in Congress* (Westport, Conn.: Praeger Press, 1996), 95.

[24] Fortunately, Cooper laughed and put her on the committee, Foerstel and Foerstel, 1996, 96.

[25] Shirley Chisholm, *Unbought and Unbossed: An Autobiography* (New York: Houghton Mifflin, 1970), 82–83.

[26] Chisholm, 1970, 84.

[27] After her speech on the House floor, several members told her that she had just committed political suicide; Chisholm, 1970, 84. She eventually did serve on the Education and Labor Committee and on the powerful House Rules Committee at the end of her congressional career; Marcy Kaptur, *Women of Congress: A Twentieth-Century Odyssey* (Washington, D.C.: CQ Press, 1996), 149.

the committee of her choice, Armed Services, but the chair, F. Edward Hebert, a seventy-two-year-old Democrat from Louisiana, made it clear he did not want a woman on his committee. Hebert was also outraged that session because a newly elected African American, Representative Ron Dellums (D-CA), was assigned to his committee. Hebert announced that "women and blacks were worth only half of one 'regular' member," so Schroeder and Dellums were forced to share a chair during committee meetings.[28] An apt summary of the congressional ethos facing female members was provided by Representative Florence Dwyer (R-NJ), who served her first term in the 85th Congress (1957 session): "A Congresswoman must look like a girl, act like a lady, think like a man, speak on any given subject with authority and most of all work like a dog."[29]

Entry Professions and the Pipeline

One of the most prevalent explanations for the slow integration of women into Congress is "the pipeline theory." In American politics, there is a hierarchy of public office that functions as a career ladder for elected officials. A local office often serves as a springboard into the state legislature that, in turn, provides the requisite experience to run for the U.S. House of Representatives. Both the state legislature and the U.S. House serve as avenues to statewide office, the most prominent of which are governorships and the U.S. Senate. Each successive office has a larger territorial jurisdiction, a larger constituency, and an increase in salary and prestige.[30] Before one can even enter this hierarchy, however, there are particular professions in the private sector that traditionally lead to political office, such as law and business. Although members of Congress come from a wide variety of career backgrounds, the most common by far is law. Those practicing in these professions typically form the "eligibility pool" of candidates for office. The pipeline theory maintains that once more women are in the eligibility pool, they will run for state and local office and then eventually "spill over" into Congress.

---

[28] Pat Schroeder, *Twenty-four Years of House Work and the Place Is Still a Mess* (Kansas City, Mo.: Andrews McMeel, 1999), 41. Schroeder explained that she got the seat on the Armed Services Committee in the first place because of the pressure put on Hebert by Representative Wilbur Mills (D-AR), the head of the Committee on Committees. Normally, Hebert would have been able to veto Mills's decision to put Schroeder on the committee, but Mills pushed hard for Schroeder. Earlier that year, Mills was found "frolicking" in the Tidal Basin near the Jefferson Memorial with a stripper, Fannie Fox. Mills's support for Schroeder's appointment to the committee was an apparent attempt to appease his wife; Schroeder, 1999, 40. In January 1975, the House Democratic Caucus adopted numerous reforms, including a vote by secret ballot for committee chairs. In an act of poetic justice, Hebert lost and was removed as chair; *Congress and the Nation, 1973–1976* (Washington, D.C.: CQ Press, 1977), 13–14.

[29] Foerstel, 1999, 79.

[30] See for example Donald Matthews, *U.S. Senators and Their World* (Chapel Hill: University of North Carolina Press, 1960); Joseph Schlesinger, *Ambition and Politics: Political Careers in the United States* (Chicago: Rand McNally, 1966); David Canon, *Actors, Athletes and Astronauts* (Chicago: University of Chicago Press, 1990); and Wayne Francis and Lawrence Kenny, *Up the Political Ladder: Career Paths in U.S. Politics* (Thousand Oaks, Calif.: Sage, 2000).

As table 1.1 reveals, very few of the fifty-five women elected to the House between 1918 and 1956 advanced to Congress through this traditional pipeline. The primary reason for this is that for most of American history, women were barred from entering many of the professions in the eligibility pool; the pipeline was blocked.[31] In 1956, only 3.5 percent of law degrees were awarded to women. Harvard Law School, for example, did not even admit women until 1950 and, despite skyrocketing applications, held the admissions rate for women between 3.0 and 4.0 percent until the 1970s.[32] Prior to 1970, less than 5 percent of lawyers were women.[33] Of the fifty-five women elected to the House between 1918 and 1956, only seven were lawyers.

Very few of these women had prior experience in lower-level political office. Six women had won election to local office, and nine had served in

Table 1.1 A Profile of the Fifty-five Women Elected to the House between 1918 and 1956

Background	Number of Women	Percent
Lawyer	7	12.7
Prior Elective Office Experience		
Elected to local office	6	10.9
Elected to state house of representatives	9	16.4
Elected to state senate	1	1.8
Elected to statewide office	1	1.8
Other Political Experience		
Served in appointed administrative office	10	18.2
Served in party organization	14	25.4
Lateral Entry		
Widows	21	38.2
No prior elective office experience	6	10.9

---

[31] See for example Irene Diamond, *Sex Roles in the State House* (New Haven, Conn.: Yale University Press, 1977); Barbara Burrell, *A Woman's Place Is in the House: Campaigning for Congress in the Feminist Era* (Ann Arbor: University of Michigan Press, 1994); Susan Carroll, *Women as Candidates in American Politics* (Bloomington: Indiana University Press, 1994); M. Margaret Conway, Gertude Steurnagel, and David Ahern, *Women and Political Participation* (Washington, D.C.: CQ Press, 1997); Nancy McGlen and Karen O'Connor, *Women, Politics and American Society*, 2nd ed. (Upper Saddle River, N.J.: Prentice Hall, 1998); and M. Margaret Conway, *Political Participation in the United States*, 3rd ed. (Washington, D.C.: CQ Press, 2000).

[32] Cynthia Fuchs Epstein, *Women in Law*, 2nd ed. (Chicago: University of Illinois Press, 1993).

[33] Epstein, 1993, 4.

their state house of representatives. Representative Iris Blitch (D-GA) was the only woman to serve in the state senate and the only woman elected to both the lower and upper chambers of a state legislature. Democratic Representative Chase Going Woodhouse served Connecticut as Secretary of State and is the only woman of the fifty-five who had been elected to statewide office. Prior to pursuing a political career, she was an economics professor.[34]

Because the pipeline was largely off-limits, women relied on other routes to gain experience.[35] As table 1.1 shows, ten of the fifty-five women, 18.2 percent, held administrative appointments, mostly at the local level, and fourteen, 25.4 percent, worked in some capacity for their political party. But even as volunteers in party organizations, women faced barriers. They were regularly confined to "expressive roles," while men assumed "instrumental roles;"[36] women hosted social events and were assigned "menial tasks associated with secretarial work," while men worked at recruiting candidates and managing campaigns.[37] Moon Landrieu, former mayor of New Orleans and father of U.S. Senator Mary Landrieu (D-LA), described this division of labor as "women do the lickin' and the stickin' while men plan the strategy."[38] In the late 1960s, Representative Patsy Mink (D-HI) pushed the Democratic National Committee to put more women in party leadership and policy-making positions. She was confronted by another committee member, Edgar Berman, Vice President Hubert Humphrey's personal physician, who claimed that "if we had a menopausal woman President who had to make the decision of the Bay of Pigs," she would be "subject to the curious mental aberrations of that age group."[39] Mink demanded, and got, Berman's resignation from the committee. In response, he claimed he had been "crucified on the cross of women's liberation" and that her anger was "a typical example of an ordinarily controlled woman under the raging hormonal imbalance of the periodical lunar cycle."[40]

Because of such attitudes, the women who were elected to the House frequently gained their seats through "lateral entry," not through elective office or the party hierarchy. As table 1.1 reports, twenty-one of the fifty-five women elected to the House between 1916 and 1956 were congressional widows; they ran for the House seats held by their deceased husbands. Six other women won their seats without the benefit of holding prior elective or party office. Occasionally, these women capitalized upon their "celebrity status" to launch

---

[34] Foerstel, 1999, 281.

[35] See for example Kirkpatrick, 1974; Susan Welch, "Recruitment of Women to Public Office," *Western Political Quarterly* 31 (1978): 372–80; and Raisa Deber, "The Fault Dear Brutus: Women as Congressional Candidates in Pennsylvania," *Journal of Politics* 44 (1982): 463–79.

[36] Diane Fowlkes, Jerry Perkins, and Sue Tolleson Rinehart, "Gender Roles and Party Roles," *American Political Science Review* 73 (1979): 772–80; and Edmond Constantini, "Political Women and Political Ambition: Closing the Gender Gap," *American Journal of Political Science* 34 (1990): 741–70.

[37] Conway, Steurnagel, and Ahern, 1997, 95.

[38] Conway, Steurnagel, and Ahern, 1997, 95.

[39] Foerstel and Foerstel, 1996, 27.

[40] Foerstel and Foerstel, 1996, 27.

a successful campaign for office. In other words, they relied on prior name recognition and acclaim they had earned outside the political arena.[41] For example, prior to running for the House, Clare Boothe Luce (R-CT; see figure 1.1) was a writer for *Vogue* and *Vanity Fair*. In 1932, at the age of twenty-nine, she was named managing editor of *Vanity Fair*. A collection of her articles satirizing the social life of New York City was published in *Stuffed Shirts*.[42] She left the magazine two years later to work as a playwright and had several of her plays produced on Broadway, including *The Women*, *Kiss the Boys Goodbye*, and *Margin for Error*.[43] In 1935, she married Henry Luce, a founder and editor of *Time* magazine. Together, they developed *Life* magazine, which began publication in November 1936. In 1938, Luce's stepfather, Albert Austin (R-CT), won a seat in the House representing the 4th District of

Fig. 1.1 Representative Clare Boothe Luce was first elected to the House in 1942, having never run for office before. Photo courtesy of the Library of Congress.

---

[41] Canon, 1990.

[42] Clare Boothe Luce, *Stuffed Shirts* (New York: Liveright, 1933).

[43] These plays were published by Random House in 1937, 1939, and 1940.

Connecticut. Two years later, Austin was defeated by Democrat LeRoy Downs. In 1942, having never run for political office, Luce won the Republican nomination and then defeated Downs.[44]

Helen Gahagan Douglas (D-CA; see figure 1.2) was a contemporary of Luce. At age twenty-one, she made her Broadway debut in *Dreams for Sale*, a play that won its author, Owen Davis, a Pulitzer Prize. A Broadway critic called her "ten of the twelve most beautiful women in the world."[45] Douglas also pursued a career as an opera singer. In 1931, she married the well-known and popular actor, Melvyn Douglas, and the couple left New York to pursue film careers in Hollywood. Helen appeared in one film. In the 1935 release entitled *She*, she played Queen Hash-A-Mo-Tep of Kor, a beautiful five-hundred-year-old queen of a lost arctic city who can only die if she falls in love.[46] The film lost $180,000 at the box office. According to critics, Douglas lacked "screen presence."[47] In Hollywood, Douglas became active in politics and testified before Congress on "the plight of migratory farm workers."[48] Her testimony attracted the attention of First Lady Eleanor Roosevelt. At Roosevelt's urging, Douglas became a candidate for Congress in 1944 when the retirement of Democrat Thomas Ford created an open seat in the 14th District of California. She won the election with 51.5 percent of the vote and was reelected in 1946 and 1948 by more comfortable margins. In 1950, Douglas won the Democratic nomination for the open Senate seat in California but was defeated by Republican Richard Nixon. As a member of the House, Douglas worked hard to emphasize her competence, in part, by "consciously playing down her beauty under conservative garb and hair style."[49] During the 79th Congress (1945 and 1946 sessions), Douglas and Luce were colleagues in the House. Both of them had to contend with press coverage that tended to exaggerate personal rivalry between them.[50]

This attitude toward women who became involved in politics is reflected in the concluding chapter of *Political Life*, published in 1959 by Robert Lane, a political science professor at Yale. He explains:

---

[44] In 1944, she was elected to a second term, defeating Democrat Margaret Connor by less than 1 percent of the vote. Luce declined to run again in 1946. After an eight-year hiatus from politics, Luce campaigned for Dwight Eisenhower in 1952. Thereafter, she became a fixture in Republican national politics. She served as ambassador to Italy from 1953 to 1957, co-chaired the 1964 campaign for U.S. Senator Barry Goldwater (R-AZ), and served two stints on the Foreign Intelligence Advisory Board (1973–1977 and 1982–1987). Just before her death in 1987, she was awarded the Presidential Medal of Freedom by President Ronald Reagan; Foerstal, 1999, 165–67.

[45] Leonard Pitt, "Mrs. Deeds Goes to Washington," *Reviews in American History* 21(1993): 477–81, 477. See also Ingrid Winther Scobie, *Center Stage: Helen Gahagan Douglas, A Life* (New York: Oxford University Press, 1992); Foerstel, 1999, 73–75; and "Helen Gahagan Douglas: A Life," http://www.ou.edu/special/albertctr/archives/exhibit/hgdbio.htm (accessed June 13, 2005).

[46] *Internet Movie Data Base*, http://imdb.com/title/tt0026983/ (accessed June 13, 2005).

[47] *Internet Movie Data Base*, http://imdb.com/title/tt0026983/ (accessed June 13, 2005).

[48] Pitt, 1993, 478.

[49] Sara Alpern, "Center Stage: Helen Gahagan Douglas, a Life," *American Historical Review* 98 (1993): 967–68.

[50] Alpern, 1993, 967.

Fig. 1.2 Representative Helen Gahagan Douglas first ran for the House in 1944, after being encouraged by First Lady Eleanor Roosevelt. Photo courtesy of the Library of Congress.

Broadly speaking, political affairs are considered by the culture to be somewhat peripheral to the female sphere of competence and proper concern. . . . [I]t is too seldom remembered in . . . American society that working girls and career women, and women who insistently serve the community in volunteer capacities, and women with extra-curricular interests of an absorbing kind are often borrowing their time and attention and capacity for relaxed play and love from their children to whom it rightfully belongs.[51]

---

[51] Robert Lane, *Political Life* (Glencoe, Ill.: Free Press, 1959), 354–55. Lane goes on to intimate agreement with Abram Kardiner, who attributes the rise in juvenile delinquency and homosexuality to the feminist movement in his book, *Sex and Morality* (Indianapolis, Ind.: Bobbs-Merrill, 1954).

John Lindsay, the mayor of New York City from 1966 to 1973, put it more bluntly: "Whatever women do, they do best after dark."[52] Thus, it should come as no surprise that many women who entered politics had very different career paths than their male counterparts.

The Politics of Redistricting

Potential female candidates for House seats also faced a more subtle barrier associated with the geography of congressional districts: malapportionment that favored rural districts. Prior to the early 1960s, most districts in the United States were malapportioned, in other words, most districts did not have equal populations.[53] According to the 1950 U.S. Census, if districts had been apportioned with equal populations, they would have approximately 349,000 residents.[54] The actual population of congressional districts, however, varied widely. In 1950, eighty-nine districts had less than 300,000 residents, and twenty-eight districts had less than 250,000 residents. There were also eighty-nine districts with populations exceeding 400,000, and twenty-eight with populations exceeding 450,000.[55]

This malapportionment created widespread disparities in representation that favored rural America. In essence, votes in less populated districts were "worth more" than the votes in highly populated districts. For example, the most populous constituency to elect a woman in 1956 was the 3rd District of Oregon, Democrat Edith Green's district. The 3rd District, with a population of 471,537, was a geographically small district that included the City of Portland. In contrast, the rural 4th District of Texas, represented by Democratic Speaker of the House Sam Rayburn, or "Mr. Sam," had 186,043 people. The value of an individual vote in the Texas 4th was over two-and-a-half times the value of an individual vote in Oregon's 3rd. In addition to diluting the voting power of minority groups residing in urban areas, the impact of this rural bias

---

[52] Conway, Steuernagel, and Ahern, 1997, 95.

[53] After decades of dismissing malapportionment as a "political question," in 1962, the U.S. Supreme Court ruled in *Baker v. Carr* that a challenge to the apportionment of seats in the Tennessee General Assembly was a justiciable issue. The standard established by this landmark case is often described as the "one person, one vote" rule and held that disparities in population across legislative districts were unconstitutional. Once implemented, the decision reduced the dominance of representatives of underpopulated rural districts in many state legislatures. In 1964, the Supreme Court announced its decision in *Wesberry v. Sanders*, a case that challenged the congressional district boundaries in Georgia. Here, the Court applied the precedent from *Baker* and held that "construed in its historical context, the command of Article I, Section 2, that Representatives be chosen 'by the People of the several States' means that as nearly as is practicable one man's vote in a congressional election is to be worth as much as another's," 376 U.S. 1, 7.

[54] Calculation of this target population excludes those at-large seats that have a statewide constituency and those states that are guaranteed one representative regardless of population (e.g., Vermont).

[55] Dennis Simon, "Electoral and Ideological Change in the South: The Case of the U.S. House of Representatives, 1952–2000" (paper presented at the Southern Political Science Association Annual Meeting, January 2004, New Orleans).

was to limit the number of urban districts, the kinds of districts in which the women of the 1950s were successful. In 1956, the median urban population of districts electing men was 58.2 percent. Twelve women had won their party's nomination but were defeated in the general election; the median urban population in those twelve districts was 54.0 percent. In contrast, the median urban population in those fifteen districts that had elected women was 87.1 percent. Most of the successful female candidates came from large cities: in addition to Green, Representative Frances Bolton (R-OH) was from Cleveland, Marguerite Church (R-IL) from Chicago, Kathryn Granahan (D-PA) from Philadelphia, Edna Kelly (D-NY) from New York City, and Leonor Sullivan (D-MO) from St. Louis. This suggests that women fared much better in urban districts. Malapportionment, however, constricted the number of these districts.

There were other apportionment issues that affected the electoral fate of women as well. Prior to the Supreme Court's decision in *Wesberry v. Sanders* in 1964, it was not unusual for a state gaining a seat in the reapportionment process to elect the new member at large for one or two elections until the state legislature got around to redrawing the district lines and eliminated the at-large seat. Of the fifty-five women elected between 1916 and 1956, eight were elected as at-large representatives. Only two, Representatives Isabella Greenway (D-AZ) and Caroline O'Day (D-NY), served more than one term in the House. Two women, Representatives Jeannette Rankin (R-MT) and Winnifred Stanley (R-NY), left the House after redistricting dissolved their at-large seats.

After the 1960 U.S. Census and the Supreme Court's decisions in *Baker v. Carr* (1962) and *Wesberry*, states began a wave of redistricting in the 1960s, and several other women who were first elected between 1916 and 1956 fell victim to reapportionment. Some states lost seats and existing districts had to be dissolved, as was the case for Representative Kathryn Granahan's district (D-PA). As "compensation," Democratic leaders in Pennsylvania persuaded President John F. Kennedy to nominate Granahan for the post of U.S. treasurer.[56] In some cases, redistricting forced two incumbents to compete for a single seat. In 1968, to comply with *Wesberry*, Ohio enacted a redistricting plan that pitted Republican Representative Frances Bolton, who was seeking her sixteenth term in the House, against Democratic incumbent Charles Vanik. He defeated Bolton with 54.7 percent of the vote. Redistricting also forced incumbents of the same party to compete against each other. The 1968 redistricting plan in New York ended the career of Representative Edna Kelly when she had to run against fellow Democrat Emanuel Celler, chair of the House Judiciary Committee. In addition to enforced sex roles that limited their choices and the denial of access to the political pipeline, the success of some female candidates was often thwarted in the process of redistricting.

---

[56] Her signature was on every dollar bill issued during her tenure as U.S. treasurer; Foerstel, 1999, 100.

The Plan of the Book and Our Data

Our overview of the barriers faced by women in the mid-twentieth century reveals why so few were elected to the House and the Senate. The social and political culture was not amenable to female politicians. The preparatory professions and paths to public office were blocked. The geographic composition of House districts and the manipulation of those districts were additional challenges. Much has changed in American politics and culture. Our analysis is designed to examine the pace of women's integration into the electoral system since the 1950s. Chapter 2 provides an overview of the number of women running in primaries, winning primaries, and winning general elections for the House and Senate from 1956 to 2004. We also discuss the historical development of careerism in Congress and the near invincibility of incumbents as factors that have influenced the pace of female participation in the national electoral arena. In other words, careerism and incumbency provide the foundation for the "political glass ceiling."

We developed a data set that includes all elections to the U.S. House of Representatives from 1956 through 2004. Our major source for this "master file" is the *America Votes* series. For each district in each election year, we recorded the number of female candidates running for the Democratic and Republican nominations, the total number of candidates seeking each party's nomination, whether a woman won the Democratic or Republican nomination, and the outcome of the general election.[57] For each district, we also recorded the party and sex of the incumbent, whether the incumbent was seeking reelection, and the incumbent's share of the two-party vote in the prior election. Identifying the sex of candidates was done by examining the names listed in each district in the primary and general elections provided by *America Votes*. Occasionally, the sex of the candidate was not obvious from the name. While the most common questionable names were Pat, Lee, Terry, Leslie, and Robin (including Robin Hood), we also encountered the exotic Simone (no last name) and Echo in California.

---

[57] In gathering these data, there are several special cases. The states of Connecticut, Utah, and Virginia employ a mixed system of conventions and primaries to nominate their congressional candidates. The nominating conventions are held first, with primaries scheduled only if there is a significant challenge to the designated convention nominee. In instances where there is no primary, we coded the gender of the nominees only because the number of candidates seeking the nomination at the convention is unknown. Louisiana is yet another special case. The state employs an open primary system in which candidates, regardless of party, run in a single primary. If a candidate wins an absolute majority of the primary vote, the candidate is elected to the House and there is no general election. For Louisiana, we coded the number of Democrats and Republicans (women and total) running in the initial primary. In instances where there was a general election, we followed the same conventions used with other states, noting, of course, instances in which the general election involved two candidates from the same party. Finally, there are states that have a primary runoff system. In these states, a candidate must win over fifty percent of the primary vote to obtain the party nomination. If no candidate wins over 50 percent, there is a runoff primary between the top two finishers. The winner of this runoff then becomes the party nominee. Our coding records the number of candidates (women and total) in the initial primary and the gender of the ultimate nominees.

Other puzzlers included Kish, Avone, Twain, and Mattox. To investigate these unknowns, we consulted relevant editions of the *Almanac of American Politics* and the *Congressional Quarterly Weekly Report.* Quite often, the coverage in these sources provided information about the sex of the party nominees. For the more recent period (approximately 1974 onward), we conducted a Nexis search of newspaper coverage. In almost every case, we were able to find media coverage that revealed the sex of the candidates. Finally, if these methods provided no information, the name was excluded from our count of candidates. The total number of exclusions was less than 2 percent of all candidate names. Applying these procedures to electoral data from 1956 through 2004, we coded 10,866 House elections involving over 33,500 candidate names, and 862 Senate elections involving over 4,100 candidate names.

In chapters 3 and 4, we turn to the question of political ambition and strategic behavior among women. Our focus in chapter 3 is the congressional widow. We explore why some widows simply served out the term of their deceased husbands while others chose to pursue congressional careers. Our analysis shows that there are systematic differences between these two groups of widows, including their ages when they first ran, their level of independent political experience, the region where they ran, and the era in which they were first elected to the House. To perform the analysis, we gathered biographical information on all women who served in the House between 1917 and 2005 from the *Biographical Directory of the American Congress*;[58] the *Biographical Directory of Congressional Women*;[59] *Congressional Women: Their Recruitment, Integration, and Behavior,* 2nd ed.;[60] and various editions of the *Almanac of American Politics.*[61] In addition to identifying whether a female member of the House was a widow, the database includes her party, her state, her congressional district, the date she was first elected to the House, her age when she was first elected to the House, her history of prior officeholding, and the number of terms she served in the House.

In chapter 4, we continue our study of political ambition and ask why some women pursue a career in the House while others leave the security of their seat and run for higher office. Our analysis shows that when faced with the opportunity to run for the Senate, women respond to the same strategic considerations as men. These considerations include the size of the state, the length of the representative's House career, whether the representative is a risk taker, and the probability of winning the Senate seat. For this analysis,

---

[58] We use the 1971 and 1997 editions (Washington, D.C.: CQ Press) as well as the online version, http://bioguide.congress.gov/biosearch/biosearch.asp.

[59] Foerstel, 1999.

[60] Irwin Gertzog, *Congressional Women: Their Recruitment, Integration, and Behavior,* 2nd ed. (Westport, Conn.: Praeger Press, 1995).

[61] Information on the most recent widows was also compiled through various issues of *CQ Weekly,* from Lexis-Nexis searches, and from the Center for American Women and Politics.

we created a database where the unit of analysis is the opportunity of female incumbents in the House to run for the Senate from 1916 to 2002. The data are built from both our master file and our biographical file. We then use our analysis to speculate about the female House members who may make a run for the Senate and the female senators who may make a run for the presidency. Together, chapters 3 and 4 suggest that women who pursue careers in the House or run for the Senate have exhibited the same forms of ambition and behave in the same strategic manner as their male counterparts.

We then turn, in chapter 5, to the competitive environment faced by House incumbents seeking reelection and explore whether this environment is the same for men and women. Here, we rely upon our master file to perform an analysis that covers the period from 1956 to 2004.

We found that while female House incumbents are reelected at rates slightly higher than male House incumbents, these women face a more competitive environment. In other words, beneath the apparent equality of incumbency reelection rates, women have to work harder to keep their seats. We also show that the presence of a female incumbent draws more women into the electoral arena.

Our results in chapter 5 show that female candidates tend to cluster in particular districts. Chapter 6 is designed to investigate why. Our analysis shows that districts that elect women have distinctive features. In effect, there are "women-friendly" districts. We develop an "index of women-friendliness" and use it to examine electoral competition in swing and open districts. To conduct this phase of our analysis, we supplemented our master file with demographic data from the *Congressional District Data Set*[62] and *Congressional District Demographic and Political Data.*[63] Both databases are drawn from the U.S. Census. For the 1972–2000 period, we integrated twelve demographic measures representing the political geography of congressional districts into our master data file.

Chapter 7 summarizes our results and discusses the implications. Using the demographic data we compiled for 2002 and 2004, we assess the political fortunes of women in the upcoming election cycles given the redistricting regime in place until 2010, and provide a list of the nation's "best" and "worst" districts for women candidates. We ultimately conclude that while incumbency serves as the primary barrier for female candidates and has substantially slowed the integration of women into Congress, there is more to the story. Open seats can provide opportunities for women, but not all open seats are equally likely to elect women. In fact, a substantial proportion of congressional

---

[62] Created by Professor Scott Adler, http://socsci.colorado.edu/~esadler/districtdatawebsite/CongressionalDistrictDatasetwebpage.htm.

[63] Created by Professor David Lublin, http://www.american.edu/dlublin/research/data/data.html.

districts are still highly unlikely to elect female candidates. As it turns out, many of the districts that are the most likely to elect women candidates are currently held by male members of Congress. Thus, the "political glass ceiling" is a function of incumbency and district-level factors that have kept the integration of women into Congress at an achingly slow pace.

2

The Political Glass Ceiling

In the history of Congress, 203 women have served in the House, 130 Democrats (64.0 percent) and seventy-three Republicans (36.0 percent); and thirty-three women have served in the Senate, twenty Democrats (60.6 percent) and thirteen Republicans (39.4 percent). Only three states have been represented by two women senators serving simultaneously: California, Maine, and Washington.[1] One-third of all the women to serve in Congress are current members. In the 109th Congress (2005 session), there were sixty-six women in the House and fourteen women in the Senate, making Congress 14.9 percent female. Why is the integration of women into Congress taking so long? When will we have a Congress in which half the members are women?

The first woman to serve in Congress, Representative Jeannette Rankin (R-MT; see figure 2.1), was elected to the House in 1916, before women even had the constitutional right to vote. Rankin was, however, active in the suffrage movement, and largely thanks to her efforts, Montana gave women the right to vote in 1914. Rankin became a candidate for the House two years later after her brother encouraged her to run. He became her campaign manager. She ran because "there are hundreds of men to care for the nation's tariff and foreign policy and irrigation projects. But there isn't a single woman to look after the nation's greatest asset: its children."[2] Four days after taking her oath of office, she cast a vote that would cost her reelection. With fifty-five other members, she voted against the United States entering World War I. Two years later, with her vote against the war seen as a liability and her at-large district dissolved, she did not seek reelection to the House and instead ran for the

---

[1] Center for American Women and Politics, *Women in the U.S. Senate 1922–2005* (New Brunswick, N.J.: Rutgers University, 2005), http://www.rci.rutgers.edu/~cawp/Facts/Officeholders/senate.pdf (accessed June 15, 1005).

[2] Quoted from Karen Foerstel, *Biographical Dictionary of Congressional Women* (Westport, Conn.: Greenwood Press, 1999), 225.

Fig. 2.1 Representative Jeannette Rankin, the first woman to ever serve in Congress, ran in 1916 at the age of thirty-six. Photo courtesy of the Library of Congress.

Senate. She lost the Republican primary, but ran in the general election as a National Party candidate, coming in a distant third. During her term in the House, Rankin cosponsored the constitutional amendment granting women's suffrage, but it failed to pass the Senate in that session. Because she was not reelected in 1918, she was not a member of Congress when the amendment finally passed in 1920. She became actively involved in the peace movement and secretary for the National Consumers League, lobbying for child labor laws along with minimum-wage and maximum-hour legislation. In 1940, at the age of sixty, Rankin ran again for the House and won. But on December 8, 1941, the day after the bombing of Pearl Harbor, she cast the only vote against the United States' declaration of war against Japan. Once again, she decided not to run for reelection and continued her work as a peace activist.[3] Rankin completed her House service as the only representative to oppose American entry into World War I and World War II.[4]

---

[3] Foerstel, 1999, 226–27. See also Kaptur, *Women of Congress: A Twentieth-Century Odyssey* (Washington, D.C.: CQ Press, 1996).

[4] For the next three decades after Rankin's initial victory, one or two women would typically be elected to the House. From 1940 to 1954, four or five women regularly served in the House during a given Congress.

The first woman to serve in the Senate was Rebecca Latimer Felton (D-GA), who was appointed in 1922 and served for two days, the shortest Senate career in history. Felton was also a strong advocate of women's rights and was especially interested in the plight of rural women, although at one point she did support lynching blacks "as a warning against suspected rapists."[5] After Felton's brief appearance, it would be ten years before another woman would serve in the Senate. Senator Hattie Caraway (D-AR) was first appointed in 1931 after the death of her husband and then was reelected twice. In her bid for her third term, she was defeated in the primary by J. William Fulbright, who would hold the seat for the next three decades and chair the Senate Foreign Relations Committee. During her tenure, she earned the nickname "Silent Hattie" because of her rare speeches on the Senate floor. She explained, "I haven't the heart to take a minute away from the men. The poor dears love it so."[6] Caraway was given the same desk on the Senate floor that Felton had used and remarked, "I guess they wanted as few of them contaminated as possible."[7] Caraway served almost her entire thirteen-year career as the only woman in the Senate.[8]

After these pioneers, the slow integration of women began. The growth in female candidates since 1916, however, has not been a slow, steady climb. Using our original data from 1956 to 2004, we show that consistent increases in the number of female candidates did not begin until the early 1970s. Since 1970 and for the next two decades, the number of women in the House would increase by one or two in a given election cycle. In the Senate, the integration was even slower. But in 1992, the "Year of the Woman," a record number of women candidates ran and won, doubling the number of women in the House and tripling the number of women in the Senate. Since then, the typical increase in the number of women in the House has been four or five. What explains these trends? Our analysis in this chapter focuses on the power of incumbency. House and Senate incumbents are virtually unbeatable. They face little competition, and those who do face competition are likely to win in a "blow out." We show that the phenomenon of long-term career incumbents, however, is relatively recent. For the first one hundred years of congressional history, most members of Congress did not serve more than one or two terms. This changed in the early part of the twentieth century, just as the first women began running. Our analysis thus illustrates the development of the political glass ceiling: the growth of careerism occurred just as women were entering the national political arena. And by the time social attitudes about the role of

---

[5] Foerstel, 1999, 87–89.
[6] Foerstel, 1999, 51.
[7] Foerstel, 1999, 51.
[8] During her tenure in the Senate, two other women would briefly serve after being appointed after the deaths of their husbands; Center for American Women and Politics, *Women in the U.S. Senate 1922–2005*, 2005.

women began to change in the 1970s, the power of incumbency was well established. The political glass ceiling was firmly in place.

The Integration of Women into the House

Gaining a seat in Congress involves three distinct steps: (1) seeking the nomination of a party, which in the vast majority of instances means running in a primary; (2) winning the primary; and (3) winning the general election. All candidates, whether they are incumbents, challengers, or running in an open seat, must go through these steps in every election cycle. In essence, these are critical steps in the career pipeline discussed in chapter 1. Figure 2.2 provides an overview of the integration of women into the House from 1956 to 2004, showing the number of women running in primaries, winning primaries, and winning the general election.

Women and Elections to the House

As noted in chapter 1, the first year included in our data, 1956, marked a high point in the number of women candidates; it would not be reached again until 1972. In 1956, fifty-three women ran in primaries, twenty-nine women won primaries, and fifteen were elected to the House. By 1968, this dropped to forty women running in primaries, nineteen women winning primaries, and ten winning election to the House. One female House member commented, "There are three times as many whooping cranes as congresswomen. . . . While many things are being done to protect the rare, long-legged bird, nobody seems concerned about our being an endangered species."[9] These declines seem especially surprising given the events of the early 1960s. Women's rights were not a priority for President John F. Kennedy, but in 1961, he did create the Commission on the Status of Women and appointed former First Lady Eleanor Roosevelt to be its chair.[10] In 1963, Betty Friedan's *The Feminine Mystique* brought "the problem that has no name" to the attention of millions of American women, and she toured the country talking about her book.[11] In 1964, Congress passed the landmark Civil Rights Act

---

[9] Quoted from Karen Foerstel and Herbert Foerstel, *Climbing the Hill: Gender Conflict in Congress* (Westport, Conn.: Praeger Press, 1996), 25.

[10] It has been suggested that he created the commission in part because of pressure from labor unions that thought it would "siphon off pressure for an Equal Rights Amendment"; Jane Mansbridge, *Why We Lost the ERA* (Chicago: University of Chicago Press, 1986), 9–10. See also Cynthia Harrison, *On Account of Sex: The Politics of Women's Issues, 1945–1968* (Berkeley: University of California, 1988); Flora Davis, *Moving the Mountain: The Women's Movement in America since 1960* (New York: Simon & Schuster, 1991). In 1963, the commission released a report, *American Woman*, which provided an extensive account of the discrimination of women and made recommendations regarding paid maternity leave, federally subsidized child care, and more equitable divorce settlements; Davis, 1991, p. 37.

[11] Davis, 1991.

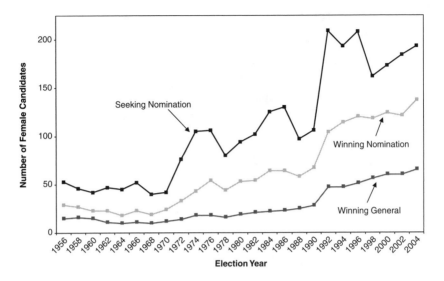

Fig. 2.2 Women and elections to the House.

that banned segregation and discrimination in employment.[12] On September 7, 1968, a group of women lead by Jo Freeman and Shulamith Firestone protested the Miss America pageant in Atlantic City, New Jersey, and received national news coverage; this would be "the first time the mass media gave headline coverage to the new feminist movement."[13] At the same time, however, the integration of women into the House was slowing down.

These trends would change, however, in 1972. The early 1970s mark the beginning of a new era in the number of female candidates in House elections.[14] Between 1970 and 1974, the number of women running in primaries jumped from 42 to 105, the number of women winning primaries increased from 24 to 43, and the number of women winning the general election went from 12 to 18. The timing of this new era coincides with the dawn of the Women's Movement, marking the beginning of changing attitudes toward

---

[12] The word "sex" as an illegal category of discrimination was added at the last minute by Representative Howard Smith (D-VA). The prevailing wisdom is that he did this in order to make the bill too radical and ensure its failure; Davis, 1991, 38–45. But the female members of Congress took the amendment very seriously, and this strategy to kill the legislation was ultimately unsuccessful. In 1966, the executive director of the Equal Employment Opportunity Commission, Herman Edelsberg, publicly stated that he had no intention of enforcing the provision. As far as he was concerned, "[M]en were entitled to female secretaries"; quoted from Jo Freeman, *The Politics of Women's Liberation* (New York: David McKay Co, 1975), 54.

[13] Judith Hole and Ellen Levine, *Rebirth of Feminism* (New York: Quadrangle Books, 1971), 123. The press coverage itself is an interesting study of the media's ability to frame issues and influence perception. At the protest, demonstrators had set up a "freedom trashcan" and were encouraged to throw in things that represented traditional images of femininity, including high heels, curling irons, girdles, and bras. The coverage of the protest suggested that the women actually burned bras, leading to the term "bra-burners"; Hole and Levine, 1971, 123–24, 228–30.

women as candidates and officeholders. "[L]ike most social movements, the women's movement seemed to burst onto the political scene with little warning."[15] As Jo Freeman explained, "Within the short space of a few months the movement went from a struggling new idea to a national phenomenon."[16] In 1970, new women's rights organizations were forming at a rate faster than anyone could count.[17] Membership in the National Organization for Women exploded from 3,000 in 1970 to 50,000 in 1974.[18] *Ms. Magazine* was launched in 1972. Practical politics was emphasized as well. Organizations dedicated to recruiting and electing women to public office were created for the first time. In July 1971, Bella Abzug, Shirley Chisholm, Gloria Steinem, and Betty Friedan started the National Women's Political Caucus at a conference attended by over 300 women. In 1974, the Women's Campaign Fund was created to provide financial support directly to women candidates, to help women network with other powerful political action committees (PACs), and to make connections with political consultants.[19] Thus, a new financial base for women candidates was established to increase their viability.

Other important events also took place during these years. The issue of abortion achieved national prominence, as *Roe v. Wade* was argued before the U.S. Supreme Court in 1971 and reargued in October 1972. The decision handed down in March 1973 struck down a restrictive Texas law and "prompted extensive, long-lasting national debate."[20] In 1971, the Court also reached its landmark decision in *Reed v. Reed* and for the first time ruled that discriminatory treatment based on sex was a violation of the Equal Protection Clause.[21] That same year, the national Democratic Party approved the recommendations of the McGovern-Fraser Commission, a panel assigned the task of reforming the delegate selection rules. After adopting these reforms, the proportion of female delegates to the Democratic National Convention increased from 13 percent in 1968 to 40 percent in 1972.[22] Watergate and

---

[14] When viewed historically, 1972 represents a "critical moment." It is analogous to the 1963–1964 period in the politics of race in the United States; Edward Carmines and James Stimson, *Issue Evolution: Race and the Transformation of American Politics* (Princeton, N.J.: Princeton University Press, 1989). See Dennis Simon and Barbara Palmer, "Gender, Party, and Political Change: The Evolution of a Democratic Advantage," APSAnet eSymposium, "An Open Boundaries Workshop: Women in Politics in a Comparative Perspective." *PS Online* 37 (2004): http://www.apsanet.org/imgtest/EvolutionDemocraticAdvan-Palmer.pdf (accessed July 15, 2005).

[15] Ann Costain, *Inviting Women's Rebellion: A Political Process Interpretation of the Women's Movement* (Baltimore: Johns Hopkins University Press, 1992), 1.

[16] Freeman, 1975, 150.

[17] Freeman, 1975, 147–48.

[18] Davis, 1991, 108.

[19] Linda Witt, Karen Paget, and Glenna Matthews, *Running as a Woman: Gender and Power in American Politics* (New York: Free Press, 1995), 136–137.

[20] Karen O'Connor, *No Neutral Ground: Abortion Politics in an Age of Absolutes* (Boulder, Colo.: Westview Press, 1996), 3.

[21] Karen O'Connor, *Women's Organizations' Use of the Courts* (Lexington, Mass.: Lexington Books, 1980).

[22] Stephen Wayne, *The Road to the White House, 2000: The Politics of Presidential Elections* (Boston: St. Martin's Press, 2000), 120.

opposition to the Vietnam War mobilized women activists. In 1970, Bella Abzug, founder of Women Strike for Peace, organized Democrats in New York to oppose American foreign policy in Vietnam and also decided to run for Congress. On the day she was sworn in, she introduced a bill demanding that President Nixon withdraw American forces from Vietnam.[23]

The 93rd Congress (1972 session) passed the largest number of bills on the "women's agenda" in congressional history, including Title IX of the Education Amendments.[24] One of the most galvanizing episodes of this period was the congressional debate over the proposed Equal Rights Amendment. Consideration of the amendment began on August 10, 1970. Representative Martha Griffiths (D-MI) organized an effort to use the discharge petition, a rarely used parliamentary maneuver, to wrest control of the resolution from the hostile chair of the House Judiciary Committee, Representative Emanuel Celler (D-NY), and bring it to the floor for debate.[25] The effort was successful, and the amendment passed in the House by a vote of 352–15. It was then "amended to death" in the Senate, including, among other things, a provision exempting women from military service and allowing school prayer. As a result, no final vote was taken on the ERA in the 1970 session of the Senate. However, the proponents of the ERA were successful in the 93rd Congress (1971 session), when a new version of the ERA was introduced. Attempts to amend the resolution failed, and bipartisan majorities voted to send the ERA to the states for ratification in March 1972.[26]

These events produced a substantial spike in the media coverage of women's issues in the early 1970s.[27] In effect, these developments constituted a declaration that politics was no longer an arena primarily reserved for men. For the next two decades, the number of women in Congress began a slow, steady climb, until an astonishing turn of events in 1992. As figure 2.2

---

[23] Two years later, the New York legislature eliminated Abzug's district in their new redistricting plan. She chose to run in a primary in a neighboring district against another incumbent Democrat, Bill Fitts Ryan. Ryan won, but two months before the election, he died. Abzug then was selected by the county Democratic Party to replace him. Ryan's widow had also unsuccessfully sought the seat; Foerstel and Foerstel, 1996, 31.

[24] Costain, 1992, 10.

[25] During Celler's House career, he was a champion for the civil rights of blacks. However, during the battle over the Civil Rights Act of 1964, he opposed the addition of women to the list of groups protected in Title VII; the amendment to add women to Title VII was a maneuver by Representative Howard Smith of Virginia, chairman of the House Rules Committee and an opponent of the bill, to divide its supporters; Steven Gillon, *That's Not What We Meant to Do: Reform and Its Unintended Consequences in Twentieth-Century America* (New York: W.W. Norton, 2000), 122. Celler was instrumental in keeping the proposed Equal Rights Amendment bottled up in committee for most of the 1960s, and his opposition ultimately led to his primary defeat by Elizabeth Holtzman.

[26] Mansbridge, 1986. See also Janet Boles, *The Politics of the Equal Rights Amendment* (New York: Longman, 1979); and Nancy McGlen et al., *Women, Politics, and American Society*, 3rd ed. (Upper Saddle River, N.J.: Prentice Hall, 2002).

[27] Using the *New York Times*, Costain's analysis shows a significant increase in both the number of issues covered and the number of reports for 1970, 1971, and 1972; see especially chapter 4.

illustrates, there was a dramatic spike in the number of women candidates. Often referred to as the "Year of the Woman," 1992 saw an unprecedented number of women running for office; 209 women ran in primaries, 104 women won primaries, and 47 women were elected to the House.[28] Only twenty-three of these women were incumbents. Twenty-four new women were sworn in on January 5, 1993, doubling the number of women in the House.[29]

Initially, there were few who thought that 1992 would become the tremendous victory for women that it did. The ousting of Saddam Hussein's army from Kuwait in the Gulf War of 1990 and early 1991 dominated news coverage. It was assumed that the success of President George Bush, foreign affairs, and military issues would be the top concerns on the political agenda during the election. This changed in the fall of 1991, when President Bush nominated Clarence Thomas, former chair of the Equal Employment Opportunity Commission, to fill a vacancy on the U.S. Supreme Court created by the death of Justice Thurgood Marshall. During the confirmation hearings, it was revealed that Thomas was accused of sexually harassing Anita Hill, an attorney working for the commission when Thomas served as chair. Many women were outraged as they watched the live broadcast of the hearings and saw the all–white male Senate Judiciary Committee badger Hill. Hill became "a symbol of women's status in American life and, in particular, their exclusion from the halls of power."[30] For the first time, the hearings brought national attention to the issue of sexual harassment. Moreover, as the economy slumped, the political agenda fundamentally changed; issues such as education and health care, issues generally associated with women, were now the major problems on the minds of voters.[31]

The Thomas-Hill hearings not only inspired women to run for office; they also inspired them to open their checkbooks. In 1990, PACs that supported women candidates contributed $2.7 million. In 1992, this increased to $11.5 million.[32] Female candidates also did particularly well among voters. Surveys taken in the spring and summer of 1992 showed that male and female voters believed that increasing the number of women in office would benefit the country.[33] Many women ran as "outsiders," which gave them a substantial

---

[28] The partisan split was thirty-five Democrats and twelve Republicans.

[29] After the swearing-in, Representative Henry Hyde (R-IL) remarked that with all the new women in Congress, the House floor was beginning to look "like a mall"; quoted from Foerstel and Foerstel, 1996, 112.

[30] Witt, Paget, and Matthews, 1995, 1.

[31] Witt, Paget, and Matthews, 1995. According to a Gallup Poll released on September 17, 1992, 27 percent of the issues mentioned by respondents when asked about the most important problem facing the country were "compassion issues," such as poverty, homelessness, health care, and education. Additionally, 7 percent of the responses cited dissatisfaction with government, ethics, and moral decline; *Gallup Poll* (Wilmington, Del.: Scholarly Resources, 1992), 160.

[32] Clara Bingham, *Women on the Hill* (New York: Times Books, 1997), 70.

advantage with the anti-incumbency mood of the electorate that particular year.[34] An exit poll indicated that voters actually preferred female candidates to male candidates.[35] As one journalist explained, "[T]he farther away a woman was from power, the better her position to attain it."[36] Reactions to these events crystallized into the most spectacular success female candidates have ever seen.

The following election cycle, 1994, stood in sharp contrast. Dubbed the "Year of the Angry White Male," the number of women in the House remained the same.[37] This stagnancy, however, masked several cross-cutting trends. The number of women running in primaries dropped, but the number of women winning primaries increased; in other words, women were more likely to win their primaries in 1994 than they were in 1992. Eleven new women were elected to the House, a higher number than usual, but eight female incumbents were defeated, six of whom had just been elected in 1992. As one journalist noted, "Marjorie Margolies-Mezvinsky was gone in less time than it takes to say 'Marjorie Margolies-Mezvinsky.'"[38] Margolies-Mezvinsky, a Democrat from Pennsylvania sometimes referred to as the "3-M Woman," won her first election to the House in 1992 by a margin of only 1,373 votes in a district that was solidly Republican.[39] Her defeat in 1994 is attributed to her vote for President Bill Clinton's budget plan. She had actually voted against Clinton's preliminary budget proposals three times and knew that voting for the budget would be "political suicide."[40] She promised Clinton, however, that she would not let the budget fail and would vote "yes" if hers would be the deciding vote. It was. Just after she cast her vote at the last minute, the Republicans on the House floor chanted, "Bye-bye Marjorie!"[41] She lost her reelection bid by 10,000 votes.[42]

The Year of the Angry White Male got its name in part because of the substantial increase in the gender gap among voters. Since the 1980s, approximately 52 percent of men consistently identified with the Republican Party. In

---

[33] Carole Chaney and Barbara Sinclair, "Women and the 1992 House Elections," in *The Year of the Woman: Myths and Reality*, ed. Elizabeth Adell Cook, Sue Thomas, and Clyde Wilcox (Boulder, Colo.: Westview Press, 1994), 127.

[34] Kathy Dolan, "Voting for Women in the 'Year of the Woman,'" *American Journal of Political Science* 42 (1998): 272–93.

[35] Elizabeth Adell Cook, "Voter Reactions to Women Candidates," in *Women and Elective Office: Past, Present and Future*, eds. Sue Thomas and Clyde Wilcox (New York: Oxford University Press, 1998), 59.

[36] Bingham, 1997, 28.

[37] Witt, Paget, and Matthews, 1995, 285.

[38] Quoted from Foerstel and Foerstel, 1996, 53.

[39] Foerstel and Foerstel, 1996, 53.

[40] Bob Woodward, *The Agenda: Inside the Clinton White House* (New York: Simon and Schuster, 1994), 300.

[41] Woodward, 1994, 300–2.

[42] Foerstel, 1999, 172. See also Marjorie Margolies-Mezvinsky, *A Woman's Place: The Freshmen Women Who Changed the Face of Congress* (New York: Crown, 1994).

1994, 62 percent of men voted Republican.[43] In addition, the issues on the national agenda changed from education and health care to crime, which hurt many women candidates.[44] The same anti-incumbency mood that helped women win in 1992 made it difficult for them to retain their seats, as they were now perceived as "insiders."[45] For the first time in four decades, Republicans took control of the House and the Senate. That year, Republican women did very well. Of the eleven women first elected to the House, seven were Republicans. All eight of the female incumbents who lost were Democrats.[46] Many pundits felt that a more accurate label for the election would be the "Year of the Republican Woman."[47]

Although the number of women running in primary elections took a dive in 1998, the next several election cycles saw relatively steady growth in the number of women candidates. In 2004, a record number of women, 137, won their primaries. Three female incumbents retired, and eight new women were elected, for a net gain of five. All fifty-seven of the female incumbents who ran for reelection won. Sixty-six women served in the House during the 109th Congress (2005 session).

The Integration of Women into the Senate

Prior to 1970, only a handful of women ran in Senate primaries, even fewer won their primaries, and hardly any won Senate seats in a general election.[48] For many of the women who have served in the Senate, the political career pipeline was not the route they took. While House seats that become vacant due to unscheduled retirements must be filled by a special election, Senate seats that become vacant can be initially filled by gubernatorial appointment. Then a special election is held in the next election cycle to fill the remainder of the term. Fifteen of the thirty-three women who have served in the Senate were interim appointments made by governors. Eight of the fifteen were appointed after the death of their husbands. Among these Senate widows, four did not seek service beyond their initial appointment: Jocelyn Burdick (D-ND), Vera Bushfield (R-SD), Muriel Humphrey (D-MN), and Rose Long (D-LA).[49] Maurine Neuberger (D-OR), because of the timing of her husband's death, simultaneously ran in both a special election to serve

---

[43] Witt, Paget, and Matthews, 1995, 298.

[44] Foerstel and Foerstel, 1996, 50–51.

[45] Foerstel and Foerstel, 1996, 52.

[46] In addition to Margolies-Mezvinsky, four other first-term female Democrats were defeated in 1994: Lynn Schenck (CA), Karen Shepherd (UT), Leslie Byrne (VA), and Maria Cantwell (WA).

[47] Foerstel and Foerstel, 1996, 48.

[48] For a complete list of all the women who served in the Senate, see Center for American Women and Politics, *Women in the U.S. Senate 1922–2005*, 2005.

[49] Long's husband, the notorious former Governor of Louisiana Huey Long, was assassinated after being in the Senate for only three years. Rose was not the first choice of Governor O. K. Allen, but he died before he could make the appointment. Allen's successor selected Rose to avoid infighting in the Democratic Party. Long resigned after her husband's term expired; Foerstal, 1999, 163.

out the remaining two months of her husband's 1960 term and in the general election for the full term that began in January 1961. She did not seek reelection in 1966.[50]

Three widows attempted to retain their seats and ran in the special elections to complete the remainder of their terms. Only one, Senator Hattie Caraway (D-AR), was successful; after her initial appointment in 1931, she was reelected twice. The other two were not successful. Maryon Allen (D-AL) was initially appointed by Governor George Wallace to the Senate in June 1978 after the death of her husband, Senator James Allen. While it was assumed she would not try to keep the seat, she decided that she would run in the special election that fall to fill the remaining two years of her husband's term.[51] She lost the primary.[52] Her defeat is partially attributed to an interview she did for the Style Section of the *Washington Post* that ran in July. The article described her as a "small, fragile, delicate-looking . . . southern lady," and also noted that she was "startlingly honest."[53] In the interview, Allen said, "I learned one thing in politics. The hardest thing to do is keep your mouth shut. I never have before. Sometimes I just want to scream at some of these people and say 'you goddam idiot.'"[54] She responded to speculation that the wife of Governor Wallace, Cornelia, might run for governor herself by stating that "the Wallaces should shut up. It would be the Christian thing to do."[55] Halfway through the interview, Allen asked to borrow a mirror to retouch her lipstick and said that "without a mirror I always end up with lipstick halfway up my nostril."[56] She called the management style of the Carter administration "dumb," noted that conservative activist Phyllis Schlafly was "about as feminine as a sidewalk drill," and described the chief justice of the Alabama Supreme Court, Howell

---

[50] Maurine and her husband, Richard Neuberger (D-OR), were a 1950s version of the political "power couple." When they wed, she was a teacher and he was a journalist. Their partnership included collaborating on magazine articles as well as electoral campaigns. Maurine was the manager of her husband's successful campaign for the Oregon Senate in 1948. Two years later, she was elected to the state house of representatives. In 1954, she managed her husband's successful campaign for the U.S. Senate and left the Oregon legislature to work in his Washington, D.C., office. Following his election to the Senate, Richard wrote an article for *Harper's* entitled "My Wife Put Me in the Senate"; Foerstel, 1999, 201–3.

[51] Foerstel, 1999, 21.

[52] This particular election was unusual in Alabama politics because there were three statewide elections. In addition to Allen's seat, there was an open race for governor since Governor Wallace was term-limited, and the other Senate seat was open after the retirement of Senator John Sparkman. In Allen's Democratic primary race, she was defeated in a runoff election by Donald Stewart, who was originally among the candidates seeking nomination for the seat vacated by Sparkman. In June 1978, Stewart switched races rather than run against Alabama Supreme Court Chief Justice Howell Heflin, finished second to Allen in the initial primary, won the runoff in what was called a "stunning upset," and defeated Republican James Martin to win the seat; Bill Peterson, "Alabama Senate 'Sleeper' Catches Political Experts Dozing," *Washington Post*, October 3, 1978, A2. See also Michael Barone, Grant Ujifusa, and Douglas Matthews, *Almanac of American Politics, 1980* (New York: E. P. Dutton, 1979), 2–3.

[53] Sally Quinn, "Maryon Allen: The Southerngirl in the Senate," *Washington Post*, July 30, 1978, K1.

[54] Quinn, 1978, K1.

[55] Quinn, 1978, K1.

[56] Quinn, 1978, K1.

Heflin, as "cuter than Warren Burger," and Robert Byrd, then majority leader of the Senate, as "just a little power nuts and everybody knows it."[57]

The other widow who pursued reelection, Jean Carnahan, became senator after "one of the most unusual elections in U.S. history."[58] Mel Carnahan, the Democratic candidate and governor of Missouri, was killed in a plane crash three weeks before the November election in 2000. It was too late to remove his name from the ballot. Democratic Party leaders convinced Jean to accept the lieutenant governor's appointment if Mel won. He did, making him the first deceased candidate to win a Senate election.[59] He defeated incumbent Republican Senator John Ashcroft, who was later appointed attorney general by President George W. Bush. Two years later, when Jean had to run in a special election to complete the remainder of the term, she was defeated by Republican Representative Jim Talent.

Seven women were appointed after other unscheduled vacancies. Dixie Graves (D-AL), for example, benefited from her husband's political position while he was alive. As the governor of Alabama, Bibb Graves appointed her to complete the term of Senator Hugo Black, who resigned from his Senate seat to become an associate justice on the U.S. Supreme Court.[60] Three women obtained Senate seats due to the death of another senator. Senator Felton, the first woman, was appointed at the age of eighty-seven after the death of Senator Thomas Watson (D-GA). The governor who appointed Felton called her "a noble Georgia woman now in the sunset of a splendid, useful life."[61] Senators Eva Bowring (R-NE) and Hazel Abel (R-NE) completed the term of Senator Dwight Griswold (R-NE). Griswold won his Senate seat in 1952 in a special election to fill a vacancy created by the death of Senator Kenneth Wherry (R-NE). Griswold himself died two years later, and the governor of Nebraska, Robert Crosby, asked Bowring if she would be interested in the appointment in the spring of 1954. She almost turned it down, explaining that she was already serving as the vice chair of the Nebraska Central Republican Committee and herding cattle on her 10,000-acre ranch.[62] She reconsidered, noting that "I've been saying for years that women should get into politics, and so when I got the chance, I just didn't feel I could turn it down."[63] Nebraska election law, however, required her to give up the seat two months before the end of the session and that a special election be held. Bowring decided not to run in the special election. Abel ran, facing a field of fourteen men, and won. She criss-crossed the state in an air-conditioned Cadillac,

[57] Quinn, 1978, K1.

[58] "Carnahan, Jean," in *CQ's Politics in America 2002, the 107th Congress* (Washington, D.C.: CQ Press, 2001), http://library.cqpress.com/elections/pia107-0453058594 (accessed July 9, 2005).

[59] "Carnahan, Jean," 2001.

[60] Foerstel, 1999, 102.

[61] Foerstel, 1999, 87.

[62] Foerstel, 1999, 35.

[63] Quoted from Foerstel, 1999, 35.

earning the nickname "Hurricane Hazel."[64] Although she only served the two months left in the unexpired term, she said, "To me it was more than a short term in the Senate. I wanted Nebraska voters to express their approval of a woman in government."[65] Two other women were appointed to the Senate after the death of another senator, Gladys Pyle (R-SD) and Vera Bushfield (R-SD), but they did not take their seats because the Senate was out of session.

Of these seven women, only one sought to retain the seat, but she was ultimately unsuccessful. In June 1996, Kansas Governor Bob Graves, a moderate Republican, appointed Sheila Frahm, another moderate Republican, to fill the vacancy caused by the resignation of Senator Bob Dole when he became the Republican nominee for president after his thirty-year career in the Senate. Frahm had served as the majority leader in the state senate and as lieutenant governor. In the special primary to fill the remainder of Dole's term, held a few months after her appointment, Governor Graves and Senator Nancy Kassebaum (R-KS) endorsed Frahm. Her opponent, one-term House member Sam Brownback, mobilized the Christian Coalition and criticized her pro-choice position and refusal to endorse term limits. His negative ads targeting Frahm gave him a reputation for "being comfortable with sleaze."[66] The race was characterized as "high noon" between the moderate and conservative blocks of the Republican Party.[67] Although polls showed Frahm with a commanding two-to-one lead three months before the primary, Brownback defeated her, 55 to 42 percent, and then went on to defeat another woman, Democrat Jill Hocking, to win the seat.[68] One campaign observer commented, "I've not seen anything so heated and pointed in Kansas politics in the 25 years I've lived here."[69]

In 1948, Senator Margaret Chase Smith (R-ME), after a nine-year career in the House, became the first woman to be elected to the Senate in her own right. Her House career, however, began after her husband died. In 1930, at the age of thirty-three, she married Clyde Smith, who was fifty-four years old. In 1936, Clyde Smith was elected to the House as a Republican representing the 2nd District of Maine. Margaret worked on his staff; she answered constituent mail, wrote his speeches, and researched legislation. She was also part of the leadership hierarchy in the Republican Party of Maine. Just before his death in April 1940, Clyde Smith asked the voters in his district to elect his "partner in public life."[70] She won with almost three times the vote her

---

[64] Foerstel, 1999, 17.

[65] Quoted from Foerstel, 1999, 17.

[66] Guy Gugliotta, "In a Republican Redoubt, Doubts on Senate Hopeful: Conservative in Tight Race for Kansas Seat," *Washington Post*, October 29, 1996, A8.

[67] Robert Novak, "Showdown in Kansas a Major Test for GOP," *Chicago Sun-Times*, August 6, 1996, 21. See also William Welch, "Ideology Rocks the Vote in Kansas," *USA Today*, August 2, 1996, A13.

[68] Welch, 1996, A13.

[69] Dirk Johnson, "Race for Dole's Senate Seat Provokes Ideological Split," *New York Times*, August 5, 1996, A11.

[70] Foerstel, 1999, 254.

husband received in his last election. After being elected to the Senate in 1948, she served for twenty-four years, most of it as the lone woman. She departed the Senate fearful that "there is no indication another qualified woman is coming in."[71]

Women and Elections to the Senate

As figure 2.3 shows, the trends in the number of women running in primaries, winning primaries, and winning Senate seats match the trends in the House for the most part.[72] The Senate numbers, however, are much smaller than those of the House. From 1958 to 1968, the number of women running in Senate primaries did double, but the number of women winning their primaries remained constant. After Senator Smith's election in 1948, the only woman to join her for any length of time was Maurine Neuberger (D-OR), who served for one term.[73] After Senator Smith retired in 1973, there were no women in the Senate until Muriel Humphrey (D-MN) was appointed in 1978 to complete the term of her deceased husband, Senator Hubert H. Humphrey (D-MN).

The real increase in the number of female Senate candidates began in the late 1970s and early 1980s. EMILY's List, a PAC that raises money for

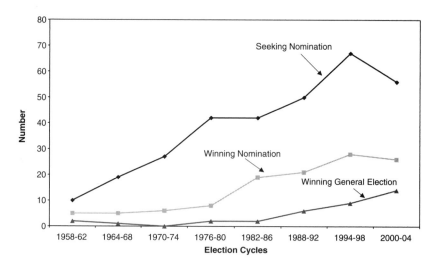

Fig. 2.3 Women and elections to the Senate.

---

[71] Foerstel, 1999, 256.

[72] The data are grouped into six-year periods. For each period, the membership of the Senate is divided into three groups (Class 1, Class 2, and Class 3). In each election cycle, one class—essentially one-third of the membership—stands for reelection. The six-year period we use thus represents the time span required for the entire membership of the Senate to stand for reelection.

[73] Smith had personally encouraged Neuberger to run; Foerstel, 1999, 201. Three other women did briefly serve with her: Eve Bowring (R-NE) for seven months and Hazel Abel (R-NE) for two months in 1954, and Elaine Edwards (D-LA) for three months in 1952.

pro-choice female Democrats, supplied candidates with much-needed funds. The creation of EMILY's List was fostered by Harriett Woods' experience when she ran for Senate in Missouri in 1982. Woods had twenty years of political experience on the city council and in the state senate. Even though no male candidates initially expressed interest, Democratic Party leaders told her, "We have to find a man for the job."[74] At the last minute, a lobbyist with no prior political experience filed, but Woods won the primary. Very late in the general election campaign, she received a "token contribution" from the national party.[75] To raise more money, Woods started calling other women, including philanthropist Ellen Malcolm, and raised $50,000, but it was not enough. She lost the general election to John Danforth by less than 1 percent. Woods and Malcolm realized that the $50,000 was "too little, too late," and founded EMILY's List (EMILY is an acronym for "Early Money Is Like Yeast")[76] to provide women with money early in their campaigns when they needed it most. The first race they funded was Representative Barbara Mikulski's 1986 bid for the Senate in Maryland; they raised $250,000 for her primary.[77] Mikulski became the first Democratic woman elected to the Senate in her own right. In the 2004 election cycle, EMILY's List raised over $34 million.[78]

The Year of the Woman also had a notable impact on the number of women in the Senate, with the number of female senators increasing from two in 1990 to six in 1992. The Thomas-Hill hearings, in particular, inspired women to run. Patty Murray, for example, a first-term state senator in Washington, was so angered by the way the fourteen white males on the Judiciary Committee treated Hill that she decided to run for the Senate herself.[79] She challenged first-term Democratic Senator Brock Adams in the primary. The *Seattle Times* called her "the longest of long shots."[80] She received no support from the party or even EMILY's List. But then media reports revealed that Adams sexually harassed and molested eight women. One of his former congressional aides publicly accused him of drugging her drink and taking advantage of her. Adams announced that he would not seek reelection.[81] Throughout her campaign, Murray referred to Anita Hill and became known as the "mom in tennis shoes." After she won the Democratic primary, her Republican opponent, Rod Chandler, mocked her by carrying around a pair of sneakers.[82] By all appearances, Chandler should have cruised to victory: he was

---

[74] Quoted from Witt, Paget, and Matthews, 1995, 137.

[75] Witt, Paget, and Matthews, 1995, 138.

[76] Quoted from Witt, Paget, and Matthews, 1995, 138.

[77] Witt, Paget, and Matthews, 1995, 139.

[78] Federal Election Commission, http://herndon1.sdrdc.com/cgi-bin/cancomsrs/ (accessed July 15, 2005).

[79] Bingham, 1997, 28–29.

[80] Quoted from Bingham, 1997, 35.

[81] Bingham, 1997, 37.

[82] Bingham, 1997, 43.

outspending Murray two to one, had a great deal of campaign experience after five terms in the House, and was a former television anchor man. During their second televised debate, he hammered away at a shaky Murray. But instead of a closing statement, he sang a song made famous by Roger Miller: "Dang me, dang me. They ought to take a rope and hang me—hang me from the highest tree. Woman would you weep for me?" He continued singing the song, telling the tale of a philanderer who leaves his wife and child. The audience sat in stunned silence. Murray replied, "That's just the kind of attitude that got me into this race, Rod." She won with 54 percent of the vote.[83]

The number of women running in Senate primaries peaked in 1992, when twenty-eight women ran. In 2004, twenty-three women ran in primaries, with ten women winning their party's nomination. Of these ten women, the five incumbents won,[84] but the two women challenging incumbents, Nancy Farmer (D-MO) and Doris R. Haddock (D-NH), both lost. Three women ran in open seats against male opponents: Betty Castor (D-FL), Denise Majette (D-GA), and Inez Tenenbaum (D-SC). The closest of these three races was Betty Castor's campaign against Republican Mel Martinez, the former secretary of Housing and Urban Development (HUD). Martinez ran an ad insinuating that Castor was against the "war on terror." He attacked her for refusing to suspend Professor Sami Al-Arian while she was president of the University of South Florida. Al-Arian was suspected of having ties to Islamic Jihad and was accused of financing terrorism.[85] The Florida Leadership Council, a PAC, attacked Castor's handling of Al-Arian in a newspaper ad asking, "Who would Osama bin Laden prefer?"[86] Castor countered with her own ads, calling Martinez "unprincipled and nasty."[87] She attacked him for authorizing federal grants for nursing homes to refurbish rooms with La-Z-Boy furniture while he was secretary of HUD; after Martinez left HUD, he became a member of La-Z-Boy's Board of Directors.[88] Martinez won with 49.4 percent of the vote to Castor's 48.4 percent.[89] In the 109th Congress (2005 session), there were fourteen women in the Senate.

---

[83] Democrat Lynn Yeakel was another Senate hopeful in 1992 and challenged incumbent Republican Senator Arlen Specter in Pennsylvania. One Democratic Party official flippantly remarked to the press that all she had going for her was that she "had breasts." Claire Sargent, who was running for the U.S. Senate in Arizona, quipped, "It's about time we voted for senators with breasts. After all, we've been voting for boobs long enough"; quoted from Witt, Paget, and Matthews, 20.

[84] Barbara Boxer (D-CA), Blanche Lincoln (D-AR), Barbara Mikulski (D-MD), Lisa Murkowski (R-AK), and Patty Murray (D-WA).

[85] William March and Keith Epstein, "Bile Flows as Tight Senate Race Heads to End," *Tampa Tribune*, October 29, 2004, 1.

[86] March and Epstein, 2004, 1.

[87] Jim Rutenberg, "An Idea, with 4 Words, That Was Supposed to Soothe the Tone of Ads but Did Not," *New York Times*, October 30, 2004, 15.

[88] Steve Bousquet and Anita Kumar, "Castor, Martinez Keep Senate Race Attacks Coming," *St. Petersburg (Fla.) Times*, October 29, 2004, 5B.

[89] Martinez became the first Cuban American to be elected to the Senate; Allison North Jones and Ellen Gedalius, "Martinez 'Humbled to Be' U.S. Senator," *Tampa Tribune*, November 4, 2004, 5.

In sum, our data show that the integration of women into Congress has not been marked by slow, steady growth. In fact, during the 1960s, the number of women running and winning declined. It was not until the early 1970s that relatively consistent increases in the number of women candidates began and continued for the next twenty years. In 1992, there was a dramatic increase in the number of women running in primaries, winning primaries, and winning the general election. In contrast, 1994 saw no net gain in the number of women in Congress. Since then, however, the rate at which women are being integrated into Congress has actually been higher. What explains these trends? While every election cycle features a unique campaign environment, is there a general pattern that can help to explain why there are still so few women in Congress?

The Power of Incumbency

Today, one of the central features of American elections is incumbency.[90] Once candidates win an election and become members of Congress, they have substantial advantages when they run for reelection. For example, incumbents have access to the franking privilege. Since the First Continental Congress in 1775, members of Congress had the right to send mail to every one of their constituents for free; in place of a stamp, they use their signature. The idea was that this would facilitate communication between representatives and their constituents. Members also discovered, however, that this could also help their reelection campaigns. While reforms in the 1990s have substantially reduced abuse, the use of the frank typically doubles during election years. Representative Bill Frenzel (R-MN) commented that newcomers to Congress are taught three rules for getting reelected: "Use the frank. Use the frank. Use the frank."[91] In the 2002 election cycle, use of the franking privilege gave incumbents a $31 million dollar advantage over their challengers.[92]

In addition, simply by virtue of being a member of Congress, incumbents have more name recognition than challengers. At least half of the people who voted in the last election can recognize the incumbent, while challengers are typically unknown. In the early stages of a campaign, television ads repeatedly mention the candidate's name in an effort to increase recognition.[93] Unless a major scandal develops, the local press is unlikely to provide any coverage of challengers at all, and if they are covered, the stories are usually about how they have no chance of winning. Many newspapers have a policy that if a challenger is running uncontested in the primary, they will not provide

---

[90] See for example Gary Jacobson, *The Politics of Congressional Elections*, 4th ed. (New York: HarperCollins, 1997); and Paul Herrnson, *Congressional Elections: Campaigning at Home and in Washington* (Washington, D.C.: CQ Press, 1998).

[91] Quoted from Roger Davidson and Walter Oleszek, *Congress and Its Members*, 9th ed. (Washington, D.C.: CQ Press, 2004), 145.

[92] Davidson and Oleszek, 2004, 146.

[93] Herrnson, 2004, 216.

any coverage of the candidate until after the primary. If a state's primary is not until September, this means that the challenger only has six weeks to get press coverage.[94] Meanwhile, the incumbent is getting coverage of their legislative accomplishments in Washington.[95] As one political consultant explained, press coverage of incumbents and challengers is so unequal that "the local press is the unindicted co-conspirator" in perpetuating the invincibility of incumbents.[96]

Incumbents also have the added advantage of having a well-established "money machine" at their disposal. Many candidates, regardless of whether they are incumbents, find fundraising not only time consuming but also humiliating. Rather than face his fourth reelection campaign, Senator John Glenn (D-OH) retired in 1998, commenting that "I'd rather wrestle a gorilla than ask anybody for another fifty cents."[97] Running for office requires the creation of a fundraising network, a network that can be used over and over again when candidates run for reelection. The experience that incumbents have in asking people for money makes it easier for them to raise more money. In addition, PACs, a major source of campaign dollars, are much more likely to give to incumbents; in fact, incumbents receive six times the PAC contributions that challengers do.[98] It is also not uncommon for incumbents to have money left from their previous campaigns; this provides the base for building substantial "war chests" to scare off future challengers. As a result, incumbents are able to outspend their challengers by substantial margins. For example, in the 2004 election cycle, House incumbents raised an average of $1.1 million, while their challengers typically raised less than $200,000. Senate incumbents raised an average of $8.6 million, while their challengers raised $970,000; incumbents outspent their opponents by a ratio of nine to one.[99]

As a result, incumbents are virtually assured reelection. As table 2.1 shows, for the last fifty years, incumbent House members have a 95.3 percent success rate. In fact, only once in the last fifty years has their reelection rate dipped below 90 percent; in the Democratic landslide of 1964, it dropped to 88.6 percent.[100] Four years later, however, the rates peaked at 98.8 percent. In 2004, only 7 of 349 House incumbents lost.[101] Not only do House incumbents enjoy

---

[94] Herrnson, 2004, 228–29.

[95] Edward Sidlow, *Challenging the Incumbent: An Underdog's Undertaking* (Washington, D.C.: CQ Press, 2004).

[96] Herrnson, 2004, 228.

[97] Quoted from Davidson and Oleszek, 2004, 69.

[98] Davidson and Oleszek, 2004, 74.

[99] *2004 Election Overview: Incumbent Advantage*, http://www.opensecrets.org/overview/incumbs.asp?cycle=2004 (accessed June 15, 2005). See also Norman Ornstein, Thomas E. Mann, and Michael Malbin, eds., *Vital Statistics on Congress* (Washington, D.C.: CQ Press, 1998).

[100] In 1964, 39 of 161 Republican incumbents were defeated. Among Democrats, only 5 of 225 incumbents lost their general election races.

[101] Four of the male Democrats were from Texas and were the targets of a partisan gerrymander following the 2002 election. If these four incumbents are eliminated, the incumbency reelection rate for 2004 was 98.9 percent.

Table 2.1 Incumbents and Elections to the House by Redistricting Period

Redistricting Period	Incumbents Running Who Are Reelected (%)	Incumbents Reelected with a Safe Margin (%)	Incumbents with No Primary Opponent (%)	Incumbents Renominated (%)	Incumbents with No Major Party Opponent (%)	Incumbents Who Get a "Free Pass" (%)
1956–1960	93.2	79.0	73.4	98.8	20.1	13.0
1962–1970	93.6	83.5	68.4	98.6	13.4	7.9
1972–1980	94.1	85.3	66.4	98.5	14.6	8.1
1982–1990	96.7	89.9	70.5	99.4	18.1	12.4
1992–2000	95.4	86.9	71.8	98.6	13.6	9.3
2002–2004	98.7	95.0	76.1	99.5	18.4	12.8
Overall	95.3	86.6	71.1	98.8	16.4	10.1

a high rate of reelection, but over time they have also increasingly won by larger margins. During the 1950s, 79.0 percent of incumbents were reelected with more than 55 percent of the two-party vote. Fifty years later, 95.0 percent of incumbents were reelected with more than 55 percent of the two-party vote. In other words, incumbents have grown more secure electorally; almost all of them come from safe seats.

Table 2.1 also reveals that House elections are uncompetitive, particularly primaries. In an average election year, nearly 70 percent of incumbents have no opponent in the party primary. They are virtually assured renomination. Since 1956, only 1.1 percent of incumbents lost a primary challenge. On the rare occasion when incumbents lose a primary, it is usually because they are running against another incumbent in the wake of redistricting.[102] In 2002, for example, Michigan lost a House seat. The state legislature redrew the lines, pitting two Democratic incumbents against each other, Representatives Lynn Rivers and John Dingell. In a primary that split the party, Rivers received the support of women's groups, environmentalists, and gun-control advocates, while Dingell relied on a coalition made up of unions, the auto industry, business lobbyists, and the National Rifle Association. He won with 59 percent of the vote.[103] In 2003, the state legislature in Texas did an unprecedented second round of redistricting after partisan control of the state house of representatives changed. Although the Texas case is unusual, it highlights the importance of redistricting for incumbents. Eleven of seventeen Democratic incumbents lost over half of the constituents who elected them in 2002. One incumbent changed parties, one retired, and one lost his primary.[104] Four more were defeated in the general election.[105]

In addition to facing little or no competition in their own primaries, it is not uncommon for incumbents to run uncontested in the general election. Historically, over 16 percent of House incumbents face no opponent in the general election. While this phenomenon dropped from its peak in 1956–1960, it increased to 18.4 percent in the two most recent election cycles. In every election cycle, there is a substantial minority of incumbents who have no competition in the general election. For obvious reasons, the most desirable state of affairs for any incumbent is the "free pass"—facing no competition in both the primary and general election. As the last column of table 2.1 shows, between 1956 and 2004, the proportion of "free passes" averaged just over 10 percent of those incumbents seeking reelection. In three of six instances, including the elections of 2002 and 2004, the proportion exceeds

---

[102] Herrnson, 2004, 50.

[103] "Dingell, John D.," in *CQ's Politics in America 2006, the 109th Congress* (Washington, D.C.: CQ Press, 2005), http://library.cqpress.com/congress/pia109-Dingell-John-D (accessed July 15, 2005).

[104] They were Ralph Hall, Jim Turner, and Chris Bell, respectively; Ronald Keith Gaddie, "The Texas Redistricting, Measure for Measure," in *Extensions: Congressional Redistricting*, ed. Ronald Peters (Norman: University of Oklahoma, 2004), 19–24.

[105] They were Max Sandlin, Nick Lampson, Charles Stenholm, and Martin Frost; Gaddie, 2004, 24.

12 percent.[106] What this shows is that a substantial minority of House incumbents have no competition at all.

While reelection rates are still high, Senate seats are more competitive than House seats. As table 2.2 shows, Senate incumbents are, on average, reelected 84.7 percent of the time. A substantial proportion also come from safe seats, although there is much more variability. In the late 1970s, less then half of the Senate incumbents won with more than 55 percent of the two-party vote. Twenty years later, more than three-quarters of all senators won with more than 55 percent of the two-party vote, the most in congressional history. There has been an even more dramatic change in the number of Senate incumbents facing primary challenges. During the initial six-year cycle in our analysis, 1958 to 1962, only 38.3 percent of incumbents had no primary opposition, suggesting there was substantial competition, especially when compared to the rates for the House. In the last three cycles, (2000, 2002, 2004) 62.2 percent of incumbents had no primary opposition; in other words, today most senators run unopposed for renomination by their party. Regardless of the level of primary competition, senators, like House members, are virtually assured of renomination, winning 96.4 percent of their primaries. With the exception of the mid-1990s, there have always been a good number of senators who run unopposed in the general election. Free passes, however, are relatively uncommon and do not approach the level found in House elections.

Tables 2.1 and 2.2 suggest, then, that voters are extremely reluctant to oust a House or Senate incumbent. Occasionally, scandal will make incumbents vulnerable. For example, in April 2001, Chandra Levy, an intern working in Washington, D.C., disappeared. Eventually, a connection was made between Levy and seven-term Representative Gary Condit (D-CA). Condit initially refused to cooperate with police, and the story became a media frenzy. He appeared on *Prime Time Live* and on the cover of *People* magazine with his wife, denying that he was anything but friends with Levy. After four months, Condit admitted to police that they had a sexual relationship.[107] Although the police never considered him a suspect, the damage was done. He lost his 2002 primary to Dennis Cardoza, 53 to 39 percent.[108]

---

[106] There is evidence that the "free pass" is disproportionately southern. For example, between 1956 and 1960, 44.0 percent of House elections in the South involved a "free pass"; in non-southern congressional districts, the proportion was 2.4 percent. In the elections of 2002 and 2004, the proportion in the South was 25.5 percent, and in the non-South, 9.5 percent. In the South, the beneficiaries of these passes have changed. Between 1956 and 1960, 98.7 percent (147/149) of the "free passes" in the South went to Democrats. In the elections of 2002 and 2004, 63.3 percent (38/60) of the passes went to southern Republicans.

[107] Allan Lengel and Petula Dvorak, "Condit Offers Long-Awaited Comment Tonight," *Washington Post*, August 23, 2001, A18.

[108] Cardoza actually worked on Condit's first House campaign and on his congressional staff. Later, when Cardoza served in the California State Assembly, he hired Condit's son and sister to work on his staff; http://nationaljournal.com/pubs/almanac/2004/people/ca/rep_ca18.htm (accessed July 15, 2005). Levy's remains were found over a year after she disappeared in Rock Creek Park; Allan Lengel, "Discovery May Alter Questions for Condit," *Washington Post*, May 24, 2002, A22.

Table 2.2 Incumbents and Elections to the U.S. Senate

Election "Class"	Incumbents Running Who Are Reelected (%)	Incumbents Reelected with a Safe Margin (%)	Incumbents Facing No Primary Opponent (%)	Incumbents Renominated (%)	Incumbents with No Major Party Opponent (%)	Incumbents Who Get a "Free Pass" (%)
1958–1962	84.7	61.2	38.3	98.8	8.2	3.6
1964–1968	89.0	63.4	34.6	91.1	7.3	0.0
1970–1974	83.5	59.5	42.5	94.0	5.1	2.0
1976–1980	65.3	48.6	35.9	91.0	5.6	1.0
1982–1986	85.2	71.6	54.2	100.0	1.1	1.0
1988–1992	89.3	70.2	51.8	98.8	7.1	2.9
1994–1998	91.8	67.1	53.5	98.6	0.0	0.0
2000–2004	88.9	77.8	62.2	98.8	8.6	5.9
Overall	84.7	65.2	46.7	96.4	5.4	2.2

In many cases, however, scandal has remarkably little effect on incumbents. Eight-term Representative Jim Moran (D-VA) has long had a reputation for being controversial. In 1995, Moran had to apologize to Representative Randy Cunningham (R-CA) after he shoved him off the House floor and into a cloakroom.[109] In 2002, with over two dozen credit cards and $700,000 worth of debt, Moran received a home-refinancing loan from MBNA, the largest loan the company made that year, at a lower interest rate than industry standards suggested. Four days later, Moran cosponsored a bankruptcy bill that MBNA spent millions lobbying for.[110] In March 2003, he appeared at an antiwar event and stated, "If it were not for the strong support of the Jewish community for this war with Iraq, we would not be doing this."[111] Several Jewish members of the House encouraged him to resign.[112] Despite this behavior, Moran defeated his Republican opponent, Lisa Marie Cheney, winning 62 percent of the two-party vote in 2004, the seventh of eight campaigns in which he was elected with more than 60 percent of the vote. Beyond Moran, "one of the most colorful figures" to serve in Congress is former nine-term Democratic Representative Jim Traficant from Ohio, well known for his colorful suits and bad hairpiece.[113] He once voted for Republican Representative Dennis Hastert for speaker of the House; in response, Democratic Party leaders refused to give Traficant any committee assignments.[114] In 2000, despite an investigation for violating tax laws and accepting illegal gifts, he cruised to reelection, winning 68.7 percent of the two-party vote. Shortly afterwards, he was indicted on ten counts of bribery, tax evasion, and obstruction of justice.[115] During the trial, he represented himself. He admitted he took money from mobsters, but claimed he did it to get evidence against them, and argued that the investigation of him was a "government vendetta."[116] After he was convicted in 2001 on all ten counts, he refused to resign his House seat and ran for reelection as an independent; he vowed to become the first person

---

[109] Jim Geraghty, "Moranic Record," *National Review Online*, March 12, 2003, http://www.nationalreview.com/comment/comment-geraghty031203.asp (accessed July 15, 2005).

[110] Even more incredible, Moran gave a speech on the House floor in support of the bankruptcy bill, stating, "Some people are taking these credit cards in, they sign up, they max it out, whatever they can charge. . . . They pile up debt, and then they get themselves relieved from paying off their debt, and oftentimes they can go right back to doing it all over again. It needs to be fixed." Jo Becker and Spencer Hsu, "Credit Firm Gave Moran Favorable Loan Deal," *Washington Post*, July 7, 2002, A1.

[111] Chris Jenkins and R. H. Melton, "Contrite, Combatative Moran on the Ropes; Congressman Fights to Survive," *Washington Post*, March 16, 2003, A1.

[112] Jenkins and Melton, 2003, A1.

[113] "Traficant, James A., Jr.," in *CQ's Politics in America 2002, The 107th Congress* (Washington, D.C.: CQ Press, 2001), http://library.cqpress.com/congress/pia107-0453055393 (accessed July 15, 2005).

[114] "Traficant, James A., Jr.," 2001.

[115] "Traficant, James A., Jr.," 2001.

[116] "Traficant, James A., Jr.," 2001; and Steven Patrick, "Traficant Refuses to Go Quietly Despite Calls for His Resignation," *CQ Weekly*, April 13, 2002, 962.

elected to Congress from a prison cell.[117] The House voted to expel him.[118] Even in jail, he received 15 percent of the vote and had a 30 percent approval rating.[119]

Open Seats in Elections to the House and Senate

Given the tremendous odds against defeating an incumbent, it would appear that the primary opportunity for turnover is open seats. And there is some evidence that women are more likely to run in open seats and win.[120] In fact, the election to draw the most women candidates was a 1996 Democratic primary for Maryland's 7th District, a safe Democratic black-majority district that covered large sections of Baltimore. Representative Kweisi Mfume (D-MD) resigned in February to become the head of the NAACP, and the state decided to combine the primary for the special and general election. The stampede of candidates included five Republicans and twenty-seven Democrats. Six of the Democrats were women. Elijah Cummings, the speaker pro tem for the Maryland House of Representatives, was the strongest candidate and locked up the primary with 37 percent of the vote. His closest competitor was Reverend Frank Reid, from a large African American church. State Senator Delores Kelley came in third, with 10 percent of the vote.[121] Kelley, also African American, had been in the state legislature since 1991. After her congressional primary loss in 1996, she held on to her state senate seat and eventually became chair of the Joint Committee on Fair Practices and the Joint Committee on the Port of Baltimore.[122]

As figure 2.4 shows, while the number of open Senate seats in an election cycle has remained relatively stable at eight, the number of open House seats has fluctuated substantially over the fifty years of our analysis. Once again, the most prominent feature of figure 2.4 is the spike in open House seats in 1992, the election cycle that produced the dramatic increase in the number of women running and winning election to Congress. That year,

---

[117] Jack Torry, "From His Cell, Traficant Still a Force in Election," *Columbus Dispatch*, November 2, 2002, 1A.

[118] Ruth Brady and Donna Cassata, "Ohio's Convicted Rep. Traficant May Campaign from Prison," *CQ Weekly*, August 3, 2002, 2110.

[119] Torry, 2002, 1A.

[120] See for example Barbara Burrell, "Women Candidates in Open-Seat Primaries for the U.S. House: 1968–1990," *Legislative Studies Quarterly* 17 (1992): 493–508; Robert Bernstein, "Might Women Have the Edge in Open-Seat House Primaries?" *Women and Politics* 17 (1997): 1–26; and Melinda Mueller and Barbara Poole, "A New Year of the Woman? Women Candidates for U.S. House Seats in 2004" (paper presented at the Southern Political Science Association Annual Meeting, January 2005, New Orleans).

[121] "New Member Profile: Elijah E. Cummings, D-Md. (7)," *CQ Weekly*, April 20, 1996, 1070.

[122] http://mdarchives.state.md.us/msa/mdmanual/05sen/html/msa12170.html (accessed June 5, 2005). The winner of the Republican primary was Kenneth Kondner, a dental technician. After the primary, Cummings beat Kondner in the special election and then again in the regularly scheduled general election in November.

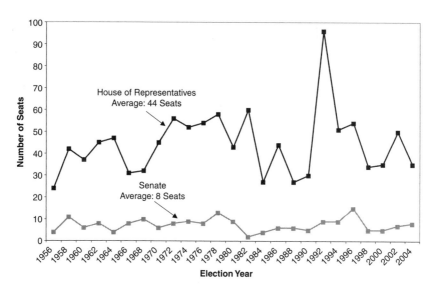

Fig. 2.4 Open seats in elections to the House and Senate.

states had just redrawn their district lines following the 1990 U.S. Census. Typically, redistricting induces a few incumbents to retire rather than face reelection in a redrawn district with a substantial proportion of new constituents; nineteen House seats were reallocated from states losing population in the Northeast and Midwest to states growing in population in the South and West.[123] In addition, 1992 was the last year that members could take advantage of a loophole in campaign finance regulations allowing them to convert leftover campaign funds to personal use; twenty representatives were eligible to take over $500,000 with them if they retired that year.[124] The House check-writing scandal also created an unusually high number of open seats. In 1991, the General Accounting Office discovered that the House bank, run by the sergeant-at-arms, reported 8,331 bounced checks. The bank covered the checks of 269 representatives with no penalties or interest.[125] Many of the worst offenders, such as Representative Dennis Hertel (D-MI), who had 547 overdrafts, decided to retire.[126] Ultimately, seventy-seven incumbents who had overdrafts retired or were defeated in primaries or general elections.[127] These events created ninety-one open House seats in 1992.

---

[123] *CQ's Guide to 1990 Congressional Redistricting* (Washington, D.C.: CQ Press, 1993), 1.

[124] Janet Hook, "Will the Flood of Retirements Arrive in 1992? Maybe Not," *CQ Weekly,* January 12, 1991, 72.

[125] Phil Kuntz, "Uproar over Bank Scandal Goads House to Cut Perks," *CQ Weekly,* October 5, 1991, 2841.

[126] Representative Ron Dellums (D-CA) had the most: 851; Kuntz, 1991, 2841.

[127] Phil Kuntz, "Overdrafts Were a Potent Charge," *CQ Weekly,* November 7, 1992, 3575.

Consequently, the Year of the Woman was largely a function of women taking advantage of this remarkable number of opportunities.[128] It was "the perfect storm," an election cycle that featured a unique combination of factors: a campaign environment that favored women candidates, a mobilizing event in the Thomas-Hill hearings, and an unusually high number of open seats. Consequently, it is unlikely that anything like the increases in women's success that happened in 1992 will occur again. Ultimately, our analysis thus far shows that there is not much genuine competition in American congressional elections. Incumbents, especially in the House, have very little opposition and are virtually invincible. As former Representative Clem Miller (D-CA) explained, "[F]ew die and none resign."[129]

The Rise of Careerism

It is important to keep in mind, however, that the pursuit of long-term congressional careers is a twentieth-century phenomenon. High reelection rates and low retirement rates are associated with the development of professionalized legislatures.[130] In contrast to "amateur" or "citizen" legislatures, where membership turnover is high, professionalized bodies have a variety of identifiable characteristics that further the careerist aspirations of their members.[131] There is a division of labor through a committee system with fixed jurisdictions. In addition, there are formal rules and informal norms that govern member behavior. Within committees, for example, the norm of specialization encourages the development of substantive expertise. Position in the committee hierarchy is determined largely by seniority. Given this, the importance of continuous service becomes obvious: influence in the policy-making process and prestige among colleagues are among the payoffs for the

---

[128] Barbara Burrell, *A Woman's Place Is in the House: Campaigning for Congress in the Feminist Era* (Ann Arbor: University of Michigan Press, 1994); Susan Carroll, *Women as Candidates in American Politics* (Bloomington: Indiana University Press, 1994); Chaney and Sinclair 1994; Clyde Wilcox, "Why Was 1992 the 'Year of the Woman'? Explaining Women's Gains in 1992," in *The Year of the Woman: Myths and Reality,* ed. Elizabeth Adell Cook, Sue Thomas, and Clyde Wilcox (Boulder, Colo.: Westview Press, 1994); Elizabeth Adell Cook and Clyde Wilcox, "Women Voters in the Year of the Woman," in *Democracy's Feast: Elections in America,* ed. Herbert Weisberg (Chatham, N.J.: Chatham House, 1995); Ronald Keith Gaddie and Charles Bullock, "Congressional Elections and the Year of the Woman: Structural and Elite Influences on Female Candidates," *Social Science Quarterly* 76 (1995): 749–62; Neil Berch, "The 'Year of the Woman' in Context: A Test of Six Explanations," *American Politics Quarterly* 24 (1996): 169–93; and Georgia Duerst-Lahti, "The Bottleneck: Women Becoming Candidates," in *Women and Elective Office: Past, Present and Future,* ed. Sue Thomas and Clyde Wilcox (New York: Oxford University Press, 1998).

[129] Clem Miller, *Member of the House: Letters of a Congressman,* ed. John Baker (New York: Scribner, 1962), 93.

[130] Nelson Polsby, "The Institutionalization of the U.S. House of Representatives," *American Political Science Review* 52 (1968): 124–43; Samuel Kernell, "Toward Understanding 19th Century Congressional Careers: Ambition, Competition, and Rotation," *American Journal of Political Science* 21 (1977): 669–93; H. Douglas Price, "Congress and the Evolution of Legislative Professionalism," in *Change in Congress,* ed. Norman Ornstein (New York: Praeger, 1975); and Jonathan Katz and Brian Sala, "Careerism, Committee Assignments, and the Electoral Connection," *American Political Science Review* 90 (1996): 21–33.

successful careerist. Reelection becomes the most immediate goal, and a necessary condition, for long-term service. Thus, the mindset of the careerist "is not just how to win next time, but how to win consistently."[132] Incumbents run for reelection over and over because they want to. For the first one hundred years of Congress, however, most members of Congress did not want to run for reelection.

Figure 2.5 presents, for the years from 1800 to 1992, the proportion of House members who retired after one or two terms and the proportion of House members who served more than five terms.[133] There are three distinct eras: a period characterized by short careers in the House from 1800 to 1860, a transition era between 1862 and 1914, and a period of substantial growth in careerism beginning in 1916.

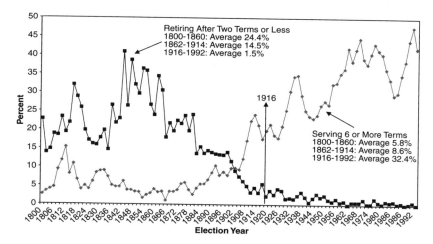

Fig. 2.5 Careerism in the House.

---

[131] Many state legislatures meet only periodically for short sessions and provide, at best, a modest salary for members. For example, the Texas Legislature meets every other year for 140 days and pays only $600 a month. Of necessity, Texas legislators have other jobs; interview by the authors with Lauren Hutton, press secretary for Texas State Senator Tommy Williams, June 4, 2005. In contrast, for the 109th Congress (2005 session), rank-and-file House members earned $158,100 annually; http://usgovinfo.about.com/library/weekly/aa031200a.htm (accessed June 16, 2005). There is evidence that until the 1970s, women were more likely to serve in part-time, less professionalized legislatures; David Hill, "Political Culture and Female Representation," *Journal of Politics* 43 (1981): 159–68.

[132] Richard Fenno, *Congress at the Grassroots: Representational Change in the South, 1970–1998* (Chapel Hill: University of North Carolina Press, 2000), 8.

[133] In constructing this figure, we relied upon Elaine Swift, Robert Brookshire, David Canon, Evelyn Fink, and John Hibbing, comps., *Database of Congressional Historical Statistics*, Interuniversity Consortium for Political Research Study 3371 (Ann Arbor, Mich.: Interuniversity Consortium for Political Research, 2004). The 6th Congress in 1800 was the first to convene in Washington, D.C. Here, our data end in 1992 because this was the last year provided by the Swift et al. data set.

Careerism in the House

From 1800 to 1860, nearly one-fourth of all members retired from the House after serving one or two terms; only 5.6 percent served for more than five terms. During these years, it was understandable why long careers were rare. First, there were the physical conditions. The city of Washington, D.C., was not a pleasant place. It was hot, humid, and undeveloped, and "epidemics of fever were chronic."[134] Congress itself could be equally unpleasant—crowded, noisy, smelly, and occasionally violent. One of the most notorious examples was in 1856, when Representative Preston Brooks (D-SC) beat Senator Charles Sumner (R-MA) senseless with a cane on the Senate floor because of their differing views on the issue of slavery.[135] Duels were not uncommon.[136] The norms of comity and reciprocity had yet to arise.[137] There were few social or cultural diversions in the city, no museums, and no monuments, and cows grazed in front of the White House.[138] In fact, the presence of politicians in Washington seemed to act "as a magnet for society's idle and society's unwanted: people sick in mind or body, imagining conspiracies against them."[139] Long-term service was not pursued, largely because it removed most members from both their private occupations and their homes. A political career meant "estrangement from wives and children" and potentially "financial ruin."[140] Second, in the later part of this era, the rise of strong party organizations actually discouraged careerism in the House. Nominations to run for the House were a product of local party conventions, and in many areas of the country, parties adopted a practice of office rotation to prevent infighting.[141] In 1846, for example, Abraham Lincoln was nominated by the Whig Party convention in the 7th District of Illinois after the incumbent of his party declined renomination. After serving for one term, Lincoln stepped aside and ended his career in the House.[142]

---

[134] James Sterling Young, *The Washington Community 1800–1828* (New York, Columbia University Press, 1966), 42. See also "The Battle for America's Front Yard," *National Geographic*, June 2004, 70.

[135] Roger Davidson and Walter Oleszek, *Congress and Its Members*, 5th ed. (Washington, D.C.: CQ Press, 1996), 32.

[136] Joanne Freeman, *Affairs of Honor: National Politics in the New Republic* (New Haven, Conn.: Yale University Press, 2001).

[137] Donald Matthews, *U.S. Senators and Their World* (Chapel Hill: University of North Carolina Press, 1960); and H. Douglas Price, "Congress and the Evolution of Legislative Professionalism," in *Change in Congress*, ed. Norman Ornstein (New York: Praeger, 1975).

[138] "The Battle for America's Front Yard," 2004, 70.

[139] Young, 1966, 25.

[140] To reduce this separation and to escape the hot summers in the capital city, Congress adapted its work schedule to the planting and harvest cycle. The 7th Congress, elected in 1800, did not convene until December 7, 1801. The session adjourned in time for the planting season on May 3, 1802. The last congressional session before the onset of the Civil War, the 2nd Session of the 36th Congress, began on December 3, 1860, and ended on March 3, 1861; Young, 1966, 52–53.

[141] Robert Struble, "House Turnover and the Principle of Rotation," *Political Science Quarterly* 94 (1979): 649–67. See also Kernell, 1977, 685–88.

[142] Struble, 1979, 659–60.

The post–Civil War years were an era of transition. From 1862 to 1914, there was a noteworthy decline in early retirements, dropping from a high of 30.5 percent to a low of 5.5 percent. On average, the retirement rate declined from 24.4 percent in the prior era to 13.7 percent. The proportion of members serving lengthy careers in the House increased as well. Initially, the increase was gradual, from 1.1 percent in 1864 to 9.8 percent in 1900, and then became more rapid, peaking in 1910 at 24.1 percent.[143] Emerging national issues, coupled with the legislative agenda forwarded by Presidents Theodore Roosevelt and Woodrow Wilson, made Congress a "more authoritative locus of public policy."[144] As a result, the "job of [a] congressman became more important and probably more prestigious, and the hardships became more endurable."[145] In addition, two Progressive era reforms made it easier for incumbents to pursue a career. First, the direct primary, adopted by numerous states between 1905 and 1910, reduced the influence of local party elites in the nomination of candidates for the House.[146] Second, the introduction of the Australian ballot paved the way for candidate-centered campaigning and the cultivation of a "personal vote."[147] Both of these changes helped to open a path to Congress for entrepreneurial and careerist-oriented candidates.

The last era, from 1916 forward, was marked by substantial growth in careerism.[148] On average, nearly one-third of the House membership served for more than five terms. During the 102nd Congress (1991–1993), nearly half the members, 47.6 percent, were long-term incumbents. The average proportion of members retiring after one or two terms dropped below 2.0 percent. The average length of service for House members in the 109th Congress

---

[143] This measure is a product of two factors: the desire to serve a lengthy career and success at the ballot box. Thus, fluctuations in this measure are, in part, a reflection of partisan gains and losses in House elections.

[144] Kernell, 1978, 674.

[145] Kernell, 1978, 674.

[146] This innovation essentially shifted an incumbent's "primary constituency" from party leaders, the practitioners of office rotation in many states, to the party rank and file; David Brady, Kara Buckley, and Douglas Rivers, "The Roots of Careerism in the U.S. House of Representatives," *Legislative Studies Quarterly* 24 (1999): 489–510.

[147] Under the old system, the "party strip ballot" was a single sheet of paper, often produced and distributed by the local party, that provided only the party's chosen candidate for each office. The names of rival candidates within the party were not included. In many states, voters simply deposited the "party strip" in the ballot box. The character of these ballots not only encouraged straight ticket voting, but also "limited the relevance of any individual candidate's personal reputation for the voter's choice"; Katz and Sala, 1996, 22. In contrast, the Australian ballot listed all candidates running for each office; while a straight ticket option was often maintained, voters now had the ability to express their preference office by office. See for example Jerrold Rusk, "The Effect of the Australian Ballot on Split Ticking Voting: 1876–1908," *American Political Science Review* 64 (1970): 1220–38; and Bruce Cain, John Ferejohn, and Morris Fiorina, *The Personal Vote: Constituency Service and Electoral Independence* (Cambridge, Mass.: Harvard University Press, 1987). Between 1888 and 1910, forty-three of the forty-eight states adopted the Australian ballot; Katz and Sala, 1996, 25.

[148] The installation of air conditioning in the Capitol in the 1930s is often credited with not only making Washington a more comfortable place to be but also actually prolonging the session; Davidson and Oleszek, 2004, 34.

(2005 session) was just over four terms.[149] In contrast to the first one hundred years of congressional history, individuals retiring after a short period of service became a rarity. This growth in careerism and incumbency had a substantial impact on how the modern Congress operates. It has influenced the structure of the committee system,[150] the committee assignments sought by members,[151] the wave of internal reforms adopted by the House in the 1970s,[152] how members strategically allocate their time, and the way members campaign for reelection.[153]

Recognizing the development of a professionalized Congress with a career-oriented membership is essential for understanding the context in which women emerged as candidates and officeholders. The timing of this development is of particular importance. The movement of women into the electoral arena began in an era when careerism and incumbency rates were climbing to historic highs. In effect, our analysis documents the formation of the political glass ceiling; it was created just as the first women ran for Congress. It was firmly in place by the 1970s, when the number of women seeking election to the House began to steadily increase. Women began entering the electoral arena in an era when the opportunities for success were the lowest.[154]

Conclusion

One of the most compelling explanations for the lack of women in Congress is the power of incumbency.[155] For both genders, crossing the threshold from challenger to officeholder is extremely difficult. Thus, women have a hard time winning seats in Congress not because they are women, but because of incumbency—and most incumbents are men. Since the 1950s, over 95 percent of incumbents seeking reelection were successful. It is important to keep in mind, however, that long congressional careers, especially in the House, are a twentieth-century phenomenon. In fact, it is quite striking that careerism

---

[149] Mildred Amer, *Membership of the 109th Congress: A Profile* (Washington, D.C.: Congressional Research Service, 2004) 4, http://www.senate.gov/reference/resources/pdf/RS22007.pdf (accessed June 19, 2005).

[150] Polsby, 1968.

[151] Richard Fenno, *Congressmen in Committees* (Boston: Little Brown, 1973); and Christopher Deering and Stephen Smith, *Committees in Congress*, 3rd ed. (Washington, D.C.: CQ Press, 1997). See also Katz and Sala, 1996.

[152] Normal Ornstein, ed., *Congress in Change: Evolution and Reform* (New York: Praeger, 1975).

[153] David Mayhew, *Congress: The Electoral Connection* (New Haven, Conn.: Yale University Press, 1974); Morris Fiorina, *Congress: Keystone of the Washington Establishment*, 2nd ed. (New Haven, Conn.: Yale University Press, 1989); and Fenno, 2000.

[154] See also Kristi Andersen and Stuart Thorson, "Congressional Turnover and the Election of Women," *Western Political Quarterly* 37 (1984): 143–56; and R. Darcy and James Choike, "A Formal Analysis of Legislative Turnover: Women Candidates and Legislative Representation," *American Journal of Political Science* 30 (1986): 237–55.

[155] See for example Burrell, 1994; Carroll, 1994; R. Darcy, Susan Welch, and Janet Clark, *Women, Elections, and Representation*, 2nd ed. (Lincoln: University of Nebraska Press, 1994); and Barbara Palmer and Dennis Simon, "Breaking the Logjam: The Emergence of Women as Congressional Candidates," in *Women and Congress: Running, Winning, and Ruling*, ed. Karen O'Connor (Binghamton, N.Y.: Haworth Press, 2001).

peaked at almost exactly the same time that women first began running for Congress. Just as women were entering the political arena, success in that arena became more difficult. As a result, the phenomenon of incumbents seeking and winning reelection over the long term was firmly entrenched well before social attitudes and gender stereotypes began to change in the 1970s.

There is no doubt that incumbency plays a fundamental role in candidate strategy: the likelihood of success influences decision to become a candidate.[156] Women do not typically offer themselves up as "sacrificial lambs"—running without any hope of winning—any more often than men do.[157] Logically, then, open seats are thought to be the main avenue of access for women. The problem with open seats, of course, is that there are so few of them in a given election cycle. As a result, if women wait for an opportunity to run in an open seat, they may be waiting for a long time. If the average incumbent is now serving four terms, that means the seat is open once every decade. As Melissa Martin, a candidate for northern Virginia's 8th District, explained, "Timing is everything."[158] What we have shown in this chapter is that careerism and the power of incumbency are the foundations for understanding the slow integration of women into Congress. But, as the rest of our analysis will explore, the political glass ceiling is not merely a function of incumbency. Decisions to enter the electoral arena are the products of political ambition, opportunity, and strategic considerations. Once the decision to run is made, success in the electoral arena depends upon the competitive environment in a district, as well as the political geography of the constituency.

---

[156] See for example Wilma Rule, "Why Women Don't Run: The Critical and Contextual Factors in Women's Legislative Recruitment," *Western Political Quarterly* 34 (1981): 60–77; Rosalyn Cooperman and Bruce Oppenheimer, "The Gender Gap in the House of Representatives," in *Congress Reconsidered*, 7th ed., ed. Lawrence Dodd and Bruce Oppenheimer (Washington, D.C.: CQ Press, 2001); and Palmer and Simon, 2001.

[157] Irwin Gertzog and Michele Simard, "Women and 'Hopeless' Congressional Candidacies: Nomination Frequency, 1916–1978," *American Politics Quarterly* 9 (1991): 449–66; Darcy, Welch, and Clark, 1994; and Richard Fox, *Gender Dynamics in Congressional Elections* (Thousand Oaks, Calif.: Sage, 1997); but see Lester Seligman, "Political Recruitment and Party Structure: A Case Study," *American Political Science Review* 5 (1961): 77–86; M. Kent Jennings and Norman Thomas, "Men and Women in Party Elites: Social Roles and Political Resources," *Midwest Journal of Political Science* 12 (1968): 462–92; Peggy Lamson, *Few Are Chosen* (Boston: Houghton Mifflin, 1968); and Raisa Deber, "The Fault Dear Brutus: Women as Congressional Candidates in Pennsylvania," *Journal of Politics* 44 (1982): 463–79.

[158] Interview with Barbara Palmer, Washington, D.C., February 11, 2004. Martin ran for the House for the first time in 2004 as a Republican in a district held by seven-term incumbent, Democrat Jim Moran. Another first-time female candidate, Lisa Marie Cheney, won the district Republican convention and went on to run against Moran in the general election. She lost, 60 to 37 percent.

3

When Women Run for Office
Discrete versus Static Ambition

Why does anyone, male or female, decide to run for political office? Your personal life is fair game for the press. The financial costs are sizeable. You have to ask people for money, and, in some instances, you may have to go into a great deal of personal debt. There are emotional costs as well. Campaigns are grueling, often focused on the personal and trivial, and potentially humiliating. And after all that, you could lose.

Why individuals choose to subject themselves to such experiences is probably best understood by the observation that "ambition lies at the heart of politics."[1] Elective politics is not attractive to everyone. It draws into its arena only those who are willing to demonstrate, in a very public manner, the desire to gain political office. By virtue of being candidates, individuals make a declaration of their ambition for political power and authority. A variety of goals—acquiring personal power and influence, serving communities and constituencies, influencing the content of public policy—can fuel this desire.[2] In spite of the distasteful elements of campaigns, there are, in each election cycle, thousands of people whose political ambition is intense enough that they publicly demonstrate it by choosing to become candidates for political office.

Until relatively recently, the stereotype of the early woman in Congress was the "bereaved widow" who was a "reluctant placeholder" for a deceased husband: "[F]or women aspiring to serve in Congress, the best husband [was] a dead husband."[3] Even women who were not "congressional widows" and won

---

[1] Joseph Schlesinger, *Ambition and Politics: Political Careers in the United States* (Chicago: Rand McNally, 1966), 1.

[2] See for example Richard Fenno, *Congressmen in Committees* (Boston: Little Brown, 1973).

[3] Diane Kincaid, "Over His Dead Body: A Positive Perspective on Widows in the U.S. Congress," *Western Political Quarterly* 31 (1978): 96–104.

election in their own right were often lumped into this category. As a result, the earliest quantitative studies of political ambition had very little to say about women as office seekers. This silence was largely a function of numbers. Joseph Schlesinger's landmark 1966 study, *Ambition and Politics*, includes all elections from 1914 to 1958. Only 155 of 9,508 (1.6 percent) House elections during this period featured a victorious female candidate.[4] Between 1947 and 1957, there were only 3 women among the 180 members examined in Donald Matthews's seminal study, *U.S. Senators and Their World*.[5] To the extent that they even mention female officeholders, neither of these works concluded that women lacked political ambition. Rather, the relative absence of women as officeholders was attributed to the "hoary rule that politics is a man's game,"[6] where "opportunities to advance have been best for white Anglo-Saxon Protestant males."[7] The exclusion of women, as suggested in chapter 1, was a product of cultural norms about gender roles and restrictions on women's ability to enter both the preparatory professions and the hierarchy of political offices. As we demonstrated in chapter 2, much has changed in American culture and politics since the 1950s. Women are more welcome in party organizations and no longer confined to "lickin' and stickin'" duties. Attitudes toward women in the workplace, particularly the political preparatory professions of law and business, are more accepting. More and more women are in the eligibility pool for political office.

However, we still know little about whether there are differences between men and women in deciding to step beyond the eligibility pool and run for office. In this chapter, we apply Schlesinger's *Ambition and Politics* to explore the political ambitions of women candidates. More specifically, studying congressional widows provides a unique opportunity to explore the differences between "discrete" and "static" ambition. We examine why some congressional widows simply serve out the term of their deceased husbands while others choose to pursue congressional careers and run for office in their own right. Our analysis of the thirty-nine widows who served in the House from 1916 to 2004 shows that they are not a monolithic group. Women who stepped down after completing the terms of their husbands have very different backgrounds than the women who ran for reelection. The widows who sought congressional careers were more likely to be younger when they first ran to succeed their husbands. They were also more likely to have substantial political experience, either working as political partners to their husbands or holding political office themselves. In addition, cultural factors also play a role: widows who were from outside the South and those who were elected after

---

[4] The total number of elections is drawn from Schlesinger, 1966, 61. The number of women winning a House election during these years was calculated from our data.

[5] Donald Matthews, *U.S. Senators and Their World* (Chapel Hill: University of North Carolina Press, 1960).

[6] Matthews, 1960, 14.

[7] Schlesinger, 1966, 172.

1970 were also more likely to run again. These results challenge the stereotype of congressional widows as demure stand-ins. Some were, but many more were not. A substantial proportion of these women, when given the opportunity, were politically ambitious. Moreover, there are identifiable and systematic factors that can predict this ambition.

Deciding to Run for Office

The Citizen Political Ambition Study (CPAS) conducted in 2002 provides some of the best insight available into the initial decision to run for office. This study surveyed approximately 3,000 people in the three fields that tend to produce the most candidates for public office: law, business, and education.[8] In general, only about 12 percent of the people surveyed seriously considered running for office, but men were twice as likely as women to have considered the possibility. Almost two-thirds of the women indicated that they never thought about running for office, while only 46 percent of the men never thought about it. This difference is even more striking, because in other forms of political participation—voting, community involvement, and interest group membership—there were no differences based on gender.[9] Moreover, when asked how they felt about participating in the kinds of activities associated with running for office, such as attending fundraisers, going door-to-door to meet with constituents, and dealing with the press, women were much more likely to feel positive about them. In addition, women had substantially fewer negative feelings about the time-consuming nature of running for office.[10]

The CPAS also revealed substantial differences in how respondents perceived their qualifications. In spite of the fact that there were no gender differences in levels of political participation, the survey found that women were 20 percent less likely than men to rate themselves as qualified or very qualified to run for office. This is quite surprising, especially given that the survey respondents largely had the same professional backgrounds; the resumes of the women and men in the study were virtually the same. But, as Representative Loretta Sanchez (D-CA) explained,

---

[8] See Richard Fox, "Gender, Political Ambition and the Decision Not to Run for Office" (New Brunswick, N.J.: Rutgers University, Center for American Women and Politics, 2003), http://www.rci.rutgers.edu/~cawp/Research/Reports/Fox2003.pdf (accessed July 1, 2005); Richard Fox, Jennifer Lawless, and Courtney Feeley, "Gender and the Decision to Run for Office," *Legislative Studies Quarterly* 26 (2001): 411–35; and Jennifer Lawless and Richard Fox, *It Takes a Candidate: Why Women Don't Run for Office* (New York: Cambridge University Press, 2005). The survey was initially mailed to a total of 5,400 people, 2,700 men and 2,700 women, based on randomly drawn samples of lawyers, businesspeople, professors, university administrators, and public school teachers and principals. The samples of men and women were roughly equal with respect to race, residence (urban, suburban, and rural), region, education level, and income, but women were much more likely to be Democrats, while men were more likely to be Republicans and Independents.

[9] Fox, 2003, 4; but see Conway, Steuernagel, and Ahern, 1997.

[10] Fox, 2003, 5.

> When you ask a man to run, he says, 'Okay, but the party is going to have to do this for me, and the party is going to have to do that for me, and you are going to have to throw a fundraiser for me.' When you ask a woman to run, she says, 'Do you think I'm qualified?'[11]

When a woman thinks about running for office, she considers her qualifications, the impact on her family, and her chances of winning. When a man considers the question, often the only thing that he considers is whether he wants to run.[12] (See figure 3.1.)

The survey also revealed that women were told less often that they should consider running for office. They were half as likely to receive suggestions about running for office from party officials, political activists, or other elected officials, and about 10 percent less likely to receive suggestions from friends or coworkers. Even spouses and family members were less likely to suggest that they run for office.[13] The good news is that if women receive a suggestion to run, they are almost equally as likely as men to consider running.[14] Moreover, the suggestion to run from someone else can be quite powerful. For example, Beverly Moore, former mayor of Kalamazoo, Michigan, said that a neighbor

Fig. 3.1 Karen O'Connor, director of the Women and Politics Institute (second from left); Representative Loretta Sanchez (D-CA; second from right); and Brandi Chastain, World Cup and Olympic soccer player (far right), encourage Julie Foudy, World Cup and Olympic soccer player (far left), to run for Congress. Photo by Barbara Palmer.

---

[11] Personal interview with Barbara Palmer, September 28, 2004.
[12] See for example Virginia Sapiro, *The Political Integration of Women* (Urbana: University of Illinois Press, 1983); and Timothy Bledsoe and Mary Herring, "Victims of Circumstances: Women in Pursuit of Political Office," *American Political Science Review* 84 (1990): 213–23.
[13] Fox, 2003, 9.
[14] Richard Fox and Jennifer Lawless, "The Impact of Sex-Role Socialization on the Decision to Run for Office" (paper presented at the Southern Political Science Association Annual Meeting, January 2002, Atlanta).

who was on the school board talked her into running for a position on the board:

> At that time, I had not even thought of entering into any kind of politics. I had children in the school system. I've always been one that, if it sounds interesting, why not try it?. . . . I decided to be on the side of the table that makes the decisions.[15]

After serving for four years on the school board, she ran for city commission and was elected mayor.

Sometimes telling a woman she "can't" will have the opposite effect. Patty Murray was a suburban mom in Seattle with two children who was very active in her children's preschool; in addition to leading sing-alongs, she taught parent education classes on nutrition and child development. In 1980, the Washington State Legislature proposed cutting funds for parent-child preschool programs. Murray took her children with her as she lobbied legislators to fight the cuts. One male state senator told her, "'You can't do anything. You're just a mom in tennis shoes.'"[16] A friend of Murray's said that this remark, instead of discouraging her, was like "'wav[ing] a red flag in front of a bull.'"[17] She organized 12,000 families and successfully blocked the funding cuts. Three years later, she ran for the school board. In 1992, when she successfully ran for U.S. Senate, she used the "mom in tennis shoes" message as an integral part of her campaign.[18]

One of the most striking findings of the CPAS was the impact of family arrangements on the decision to run for office. Women in the survey were much less likely than the men to be married and have children. In spite of the progress women have made, studies show that tremendous hostility still exists in the workplace toward women who have children, particularly in the fields of law, business, and higher education. Consequently, many women who reach the highest ranks within these professions are unmarried and childless.[19] Moreover, the women in the survey who were married and had children were nine times more likely than their spouses to be responsible for housework and child care. Only 5 percent of the men responded that they did more housework than their wives and were responsible for child care. For men, there was no relationship between the household division of labor and their likelihood to consider running for office. For women, as housework and child care

---

[15] Interview by C. Allen Alexander, in *Social Changes in Western Michigan, 1930 to 1990: Alexander Oral History Project*, vol. 2, ed. Henry Vance Davis (Kalamazoo: Western Michigan University, 1997), 123–32.

[16] Quoted from Bingham, 1997, 33.

[17] Quoted from Bingham, 1997, 33.

[18] Karen Foerstel, *Biographical Dictionary of Congressional Women* (Westport, Conn.: Greenwood Press, 1999), 198.

[19] See for example Joan Williams, *Unbending Gender: Why Family and Work Conflict and What to Do about It* (Oxford: Oxford University Press, 2000).

responsibility increased, the likelihood they would consider running for office declined.

The Citizen Political Ambition Study surveyed women who were accomplished in their fields; they were partners in law firms, business owners, professors, and school principals. Although these women have clearly overcome professional barriers, their family situations still indicate that their attitudes about running for office may be a reflection of more traditional views of women's roles.[20]

Do younger women, who typically do not have the same family time demands, have similar feelings toward running for office? In 2003, the CPAS was replicated on a younger "eligibility pool," college students who participated in the American University Washington Semester Program. Students in the Washington Semester Program come from all over the country to take seminars and intern on Capitol Hill, with political consultants, and with a wide variety of nonprofits. These students chose to come to D.C. and, as a result, were much more interested in politics and government than typical college students. Thus, they offer a unique opportunity to study an emerging "eligibility pool" of twenty to twenty-one year olds.[21] In 2003, two-thirds of the participants in the Washington Semester Program were female, suggesting that they might be more likely than their older counterparts to consider running for office. Unfortunately, these expectations were not borne out. Female students in the college-level eligibility pool were almost 20 percent less likely than their male counterparts to consider running for political office. Like their older counterparts, however, they had equally positive feelings about engaging in campaign activities like fundraising, going door-to-door, meeting with the media, and giving their time.[22]

The study of these eligibility pools leads to a number of conclusions. First, given that they look favorably upon the tasks demanded in a run for office, the women in these samples do not regard campaigning as exclusively a "man's business." Gone are the days, described in chapter 1, when women themselves held to this belief. Second, for a variety of reasons, women are not conscious or appreciative of the fact that their skills and positions in society make them qualified to run for office. Third, women are as responsive as men when it is suggested or recommended that they run for office. The question, then, is not *whether* women are as ambitious as men, but rather why the process of recruitment—formal and informal—does not call upon women in the eligibility pool more regularly.

---

[20] Fox, 2003, table 1.

[21] The average age of the respondents in the CPAS was forty-seven; Fox, 2003, table 1.

[22] Jennifer Drinkard, "The Disparity of Women Running for Congress," American University Washington Semester Program, American University, Washington, D.C., 2003. Drinkard's sample included 127 undergraduates. Her sample was 67 percent female; 62 percent of all Washington Semester Program students were women. Fifty-nine percent of the respondents were political science majors.

Political Ambition Theory

While gender clearly does play a role in whether people consider themselves qualified to run for office, what prompts those who believe in their qualifications to become candidates? Studying what is ultimately a personal decision poses several challenges. For example, it is relatively easy to find people who decided to run and won; there are 535 of them who hold seats in Congress. Those who decided to run and lost at least had to file papers with their state election office and can be tracked down. It is, however, extremely difficult to identify people who may have thought about running and decided not to, or people who may have been viable candidates and simply never thought about it at all. Studying possible candidates can even cause political controversy. Sandy Maisel and Walter Stone, two political scientists who received a National Science Foundation grant in 1997 to conduct a nationwide survey regarding the decision to run for office, found themselves embroiled in a major confrontation with Congress. A few members were convinced that this study would actually encourage qualified challengers to run against them. Labeling the project an "affront," a "travesty," and an "embarrassment," they tried to cut the funding and quash the study.[23]

Given the practical restrictions on identifying would-be candidates for the House, we develop an approach for studying ambition that is more indirect. We revisit Schlesinger's theory of ambition, focusing on female members of the House. The point of departure in Schlesinger's theory is the hierarchy of public offices in American politics, or the "political opportunity structure." His analysis shows that pursing a career in politics is a product of ambition, party competition, and the opportunities to enter and to advance in the hierarchy. There are, according to his analysis, three types of ambition: discrete, static, and progressive. "Discrete ambition" refers to an officeholder who serves only briefly and then steps down. "Static ambition" refers to those who are elected to an office and then strive to retain the position for as long as possible. "Progressive ambition" refers to a politician who, after elected to one office, seeks to advance upward in the hierarchy and run for an office perceived as more attractive and prestigious.[24]

Schlesinger suggested that discrete ambition, stepping down after a short term of service, is most common for many local and some state legislative offices.[25] For example, it is easy to envision civic-minded individuals who agree to serve a single elected term on school boards, town councils, and other locally elected offices. Discrete ambition was not, however, the focus of Schlesinger's analysis. His primary concern was to study the progression of the

---

[23] Sandy Maisel and Walter Stone, "The Politics of Government-Funded Research: Notes from the Experience of the Candidate Emergence Study," *PS: Political Science and Politics* 31 (1998): 811–17, 815.

[24] Schlesinger, 1966, 10.

[25] Schlesinger, 1966, 10.

ambitious through the hierarchy of political offices. In fact, discrete ambition has not been studied in any detail at all. This is especially true for the U.S. House of Representatives, where careerism (i.e., static ambition) and advancement to higher office (i.e., progressive ambition) are the dominant goals of members. Consequently, to examine the distinction between discrete and static ambition, we focus upon a subset of those women elected to the U.S. House, congressional widows.

Ambition Theory and Congressional Widows

Studying the women who were elected to the House as successors to their husbands provides a novel opportunity to investigate discrete ambition. Of the forty women who have succeeded their husbands in the House, all but one were widows.[26] Katherine Langley (R-KY) is the exception. Her election to the House was not because her husband died, but because he was thrown in jail. Katherine was the daughter of Representative James Gudger (D-NC) and the wife of John Langley, a Kentucky Republican first elected in 1906. John and his father-in-law served together as members of the House during the 62nd and 63rd Congresses (1911–1915).[27] In 1924, Congressman Langley was tried and convicted of "conspiring illegally to transport and sell liquor."[28] He attempted to bribe a Prohibition officer. While his case was under appeal in November 1924, he was reelected to his tenth term in the U.S. House. He had to resign his seat on January 11, 1926, and was subsequently jailed at the federal penitentiary in Atlanta.

In 1926, Katherine won the 10th District seat vacated by her husband with 58.4 percent of the vote.[29] She was, however, hardly a political neophyte. As secretary to her husband throughout his career, she was quite familiar with electoral politics and the ways of Washington, D.C. When she ran for reelection in 1928, she was called the "guardian angel of patronage."[30]

---

[26] There has not, as of yet, been a congressional widower. One husband, however, recently tried. Representative Patsy Mink (D-HI) died on September 28, 2002, a week after easily winning her primary, but two days after the deadline to replace her name on the ballot. She actually won the general election in November. An election was held on November 30 for the remaining five weeks of her term and won by Democrat Ed Case. Another special election to fill her two-year term was held in January 2003. John Mink, Patsy's widower, ran in a field of forty-three candidates, but Case held on to the seat; B. J. Reyes, "Case Wins Hawaii's 2nd Congressional District," Associated Press State and Local Wire, January 5, 2003. There has also been one woman who was elected after the death of a female member. Representative Nancy Pelosi (D-CA) was elected in a special election in 1987 following the death of Representative Sala Burton (D-CA), who, ironically enough, had been elected in a special election in 1983 after the death of her husband, Representative Phillip Burton (D-CA).

[27] Foerstel, 1999, 155–56.

[28] Hope Chamberlin, *A Minority of Members: Women in the United States Congress* (New York: Praeger, 1973), 63.

[29] In a letter from prison, John Langley appealed to family values, urging voters to "'send my wife, the mother of our three children, to Washington' because 'she knows better than anyone else my unfinished plans;'" Chamberlin, 1973, 64.

[30] Chamberlin, 1973, 65. The response to Katherine among the capital community elite was less than favorable. Evidently, Washington society regarded the election of a convicted felon's spouse as "gauche"; Chamberlin, 1973, 63.

President Calvin Coolidge, at Katherine's urging, issued a grant of clemency to her husband; his release was subject to the condition that he would not seek election to any public office. In 1929, a less-than-grateful John declared himself a candidate for his former seat. Katherine, however, refused to give up her seat "for John or anyone else."[31] While there is no record of a primary race between husband and wife, historical accounts refer to a "family feud" and "marital spat" that ultimately led to her 1930 defeat by the Democrat, A. J. May, the same candidate she had defeated in 1926 and 1928.[32]

Like Katherine Langley, many of the first women elected to the House succeeded their husbands. Fourteen of the twenty-eight women (50 percent) elected to the House prior to World War II succeeded their spouses. Between 1942 and 1970, one-third (15/42) of the women elected to the House were widows. Since 1972, the "widow route" has become much less prominent. Of the 132 women elected to the House between 1972 and 2004, only ten (8.3 percent) were widows. In the 109th Congress (2005 session), four of the sixty-six female House members were serving in seats held by their deceased husbands: these include Jo Ann Emerson (R-MO), Lois Capps (D-CA), and Mary Bono (R-CA).[33] Doris Matsui (D-CA) was elected in March 2005 in a special election after her husband died from a rare bone marrow disease. She beat eleven other opponents with 71.6 percent of the vote.[34]

---

[31] Chamberlin, 1973, 65.

[32] Little is known about what transpired after Katherine's defeat, but we do know that they were buried in separate cemeteries. John Langley died on January 17, 1932, and was buried in the Langley Cemetery in MiddleCreek, Kentucky. Katherine Langley died on August 15, 1948, and is buried in Johnson Memorial Cemetery in Pikeville, Kentucky; *Biographical Directory of the American Congress* (Washington, D.C.: U.S. Government Printing Office, 1971), 1262.

[33] Jean Carnahan was the most recent widow to serve in the Senate. Aside from gaining a seat from a spouse, ten female members of Congress have gained spouses from Congress: they married male members of Congress. Two women married men while they were both serving in Congress together: Representative Susan Molinari (R-NY) married Representative Bill Paxon (R-NY) in 1994, and Representative Martha Keys (D-KS) married Representative Andrew Jacobs (D-IN) in 1975. Two women married members of Congress after they had served together: Representative Olympia Snowe (R-ME) married former Representative John McKernan Jr. (R-ME) in 1989 after he became governor of Maine, and Senator Nancy Kassebaum (R-KS) married former Senator Howard Baker (R-TN) in 1996 after he retired. Two other women married members with whom they did not serve: Senator Elizabeth Dole (R-NC, 2003–present) served after her husband, former Senator Bob Dole (R-KS, 1969–1996), and Representative Marjorie Margolies-Mezvinsky (D-PA, 1993–1995) also served after her husband, former Representative Ed Mezvinsky (D-IA, 1973–1977). Representative Emily Taft Douglas (D-IL, 1945–1947) preceded her husband, Senator Paul Douglas (D-IL, 1949–1967). And finally, Representative Ruth McCormick (R-IL, 1929–1931) was married to two members of Congress: before her service in the House, she was married to Medill McCormick (R-IL, House, 1917–1919 and Senate 1919–1925). After he died, she ran for House and met Albert Gallatin Simms (R-NM, 1929–1931), and they married after they both left the House; Mildred Amer, "Women in the United States Congress: 1917–2004" (Washington, D.C.: Congressional Research Service, 2004), http://www.senate.gov/reference/resources/pdf/RL30261.pdf, 5–6 (accessed July 3, 2005).

[34] Greg Lucas, "Matsui Wins Election to Late Husband's Seat," *San Francisco Chronicle*, March 9, 2005, B3.

As late as the 1970s, much of the attention devoted to women in Congress focused on the widow connection.[35] This was characterized as the primary route to the House and the Senate for women. The prevailing wisdom, particularly in the press, was that women who served in Congress got there "over their husband's dead bodies."[36] In fact, there emerged a "widow stereotype" that included a common plot or storyline describing the widow's journey to elective office: after a member of Congress died, party leaders and other local elites often recruited the bereaved and politically reluctant widow to run in the special election to fill her departed husband's seat. This served two ends. First, it capitalized on public sympathy to ensure that the party held the seat in the interim. Second, it helped the party avoid internal disputes and provide time to recruit a "real" replacement.[37] In many cases, the understanding, whether explicit or implicit, was that the widow would not try to retain the seat during the next election cycle. For example, Representative Frances Bolton (R-OH) noted that party support for her candidacy to succeed her deceased husband was forthcoming because "they were sure I would get tired of politics in a few months and flit on to something else."[38] Thus, congressional widows were presumed to be the quintessential examples of discrete ambition—dutiful, but temporary, officeholders.

A vivid example of the stereotype was, in fact, the very first congressional widow, Mae Ella Nolan (R-CA). In 1922, Representative John Nolan, chair of the House Labor Committee, died shortly after his fifth reelection to the House. Civic leaders convinced Mae to run in the special election held to fill his seat; she defeated six men in the primary. In addition to securing a spot on the Labor Committee, she became chair of the Committee on Expenditures in the Post Office Department, making her the first woman committee chair. After completing the two-year term, Mae declared that she would not seek reelection, explaining that "[p]olitics is entirely too masculine to have any attraction for feminine responsibilities."[39] Nolan was not alone among the widows to express her distaste for political life. At the beginning of the three months she served to complete her husband's term, Representative Pearl Oldfield (D-AR) announced that she would "gladly retire to where women

---

[35] See for example Emmy Werner, "Women in Congress: 1917–1964," *Western Political Quarterly* 19 (1966): 16–30; Martin Gruberg, *Women in Politics: A Source Book* (New York: Academic Press, 1968); Kirsten Amundson, *The Silenced Majority: Women and American Democracy* (Englewood Cliffs, N.J.: Prentice-Hall, 1971); Charles Bullock and Patricia Lee Findley Heys, "Recruitment of Women for Congress: A Research Note," *Western Political Quarterly* 25 (1972): 416–23; Jeane Kirkpatrick, *Political Woman* (New York: Basic Books, 1974); Susan Tolchin and Martin Tolchin, *Clout: Womanpower and Politics* (New York: Coward, McCann & Geoghegan, 1974); and Irwin Gertzog, "The Matrimonial Connection: The Nomination of Congressmen's Widows for the House of Representatives," *Journal of Politics* 42 (1980): 820–33. See also Irwin Gertzog, *Congressional Women: Their Recruitment, Integration, and Behavior*, 2nd ed. (Westport, Conn.: Praeger Press, 1995).

[36] Kincaid, 1978, 96. See also Gertzog, 1980.

[37] Kincaid, 1978, 97.

[38] Foerstel, 1996, 30.

[39] Foerstel, 1999, 203.

belong—in the home."[40] Similarly, Representative Florence Gibbs (D-GA), whose term was also three months, left the House because the job was not "to her liking."[41]

Such examples notwithstanding, the problem with the "widow stereotype" is that it rests on several tenuous assumptions. First, it tends to apply the stereotype to all women who served prior to the 1980s, whether they were widows or not. Second, it assumes that all of the widows conform to the examples of Nolan, Oldfield, and Gibbs. Third, it creates the impression that the widow-as-successor is the most common method of filling vacancies. But if one looks at the number of incumbents who died in office, very few wives succeeded their husbands. From 1917 to 1976, for example, 487 members died in office, and widows were the successors only thirty-five (7 percent) times.[42] This suggests that the congressional widow is not as common as typically presumed, particularly in light of the number of opportunities for widows to succeed their husbands.[43]

Another assumption of the stereotype is that widows were "given" the seats vacated by their dead husbands. This is simply inaccurate. Although vacant Senate seats can be filled by appointment, vacant House seats must be filled through special elections. Many widows who served in the House faced substantial competition in special primary and general elections; there were several widows who ran for their husbands' seats and were defeated.[44]

More importantly, as table 3.1 illustrates, many widows did not step down after their initial terms expired. Many had lengthy careers. Twelve widows served at least ten years in the House; four of these twelve were elected to ten

---

[40] Foerstel, 1999, 212.

[41] Foerstel, 1999, 98.

[42] Kincaid, 1978, 97. See also Gertzog, 1980, 1995.

[43] Many men have, of course, also benefited from family connections, George W. Bush and Al Gore being two of the most obvious examples. There is evidence that at least 10 percent of the men in Congress have benefited from a family name that was well known in politics; Joan Hulce Thompson, "Career Convergence: Election of Women and Men to the House of Representatives, 1916–1975," Women & Politics 5 (1985): 69–90. In fact, there have been men who even benefited from the political connections of their mothers. Five women in the House and two woman in the Senate had sons serve in Congress. Representative Frances Bolton (R-OH, 1940–1969) served with her son, Representative Oliver Bolton (R-OH, 1953–1957 and 1963–1965). Representative Carrie Meek (D-FL, 1993–2003) was succeeded by her son, Representative Kendrick Meek (2003–present). Representative Katharine Byron (D-MD, 1941–1943) was the mother of Representative Goodloe Byron (D-MD, 1971–1978). Representative Maude Kee (D-WV, 1951–1965) was succeeded by her son, Representative James Kee (D-WV, 1965–1973). Representative Irene Baker (R-TN, 1964–1965) was the stepmother of Senator Howard Baker (R-TN, 1967–1985). Senator Rose McConnell Long (D-LA, 1936–1937) was the mother of Senator Russell Long (D-LA, 1948–1987); Amer, 2004, 7. After Senator Jean Carnahan (D-MO) lost her seat in 2002, her son, Russ (D-MO), was elected to the House in 2004; "New House Member Profile: Russ Carnahan," CQ Weekly, November 6, 2004, 2644. The only sisters to serve are Representatives Loretta (D-CA, 1996–present) and Linda Sanchez (D-CA, 2002–present).

[44] Kincaid, 1978, 101. There is no source that systematically gathers and presents data on these special elections. Additionally, as one goes back in time, information on these elections becomes increasingly sparse. As a result, it would be terribly difficult to determine the number of special elections in which the widow unsuccessfully sought to replace her husband.

Table 3.1 Women Who Succeeded Their Husbands in the House

Name	Service Begins	Service Ends	Ambition (Terms)
Pre–World War II			
Mae Ella Nolan (R-CA)	*1/23/1923*	*3/3/1925*	*Discrete*
Florence Kahn (R-CA)	5/4/1925	1/3/1937	Static (6)
Edith Nourse Rogers (R-MA)	1/30/1925	9/10/1960	Static (18)
Katherine Langley (R-KY)	3/4/1926	3/3/1931	Static (2)
Pearl Oldfield (D-AR)	*1/11/1929*	*3/3/1931*	*Discrete*
Effigene Wingo (D-AR)	*4/4/1930*	*3/3/1933*	*Discrete*
Willa McCord Eslick (D-TN)	*12/5/1932*	*3/3/1933*	*Discrete*
Marian Clarke (R-NY)	*12/28/1933*	*1/3/1935*	*Discrete*
Elizabeth Gasque (D-SC)	*1/13/1938*	*1/3/1939*	*Discrete*
Clara McMillan (D-SC)	*1/3/1940*	*1/3/1941*	*Discrete*
Margaret Chase Smith (R-ME)	1/3/1940	1/3/1949	Static (5)
Frances Bolton (R-OH)	1/27/1940	1/3/1969	Static (15)
Florence Gibbs (D-GA)	*1/3/1940*	*1/3/1941*	*Discrete*
Katharine Byron (D-MD)	*1/11/1941*	*1/3/1943*	*Discrete*
1942–1970			
Veronica Boland (D-PA)	*1/19/1942*	*1/3/1943*	*Discrete*
Willa Fulmer (D-SC)	*1/16/1944*	*1/3/1945*	*Discrete*
Marguerite Church (R-IL)	1/3/1951	1/3/1963	Static (6)
Maude Kee (D-WV)	7/26/1951	1/3/1963	Static (7)
Vera Buchanan (D-PA)	8/1/1951	11/26/1955	Static (3)
Leonor Sullivan (D-MO)	1/3/1953	1/3/1977	Static (12)
Kathryn Granahan (D-PA)	11/6/1956	1/3/1963	Static (3)
Edna Simpson (R-IL)	*1/3/1959*	*1/3/1961*	*Discrete*
Catherine Norrell (D-AR)	*4/18/1961*	*1/3/1963*	*Discrete*
Louise Reese (R-TN)	*5/16/1961*	*1/3/1963*	*Discrete*
Corrine Riley (D-SC)	*4/10/1962*	*1/3/1963*	*Discrete*
Charlotte Reid (R-IL)	1/3/1963	10/7/1971	Static (5)
Irene Baker (R-TN)	*3/10/1964*	*1/3/1965*	*Discrete*
Lera Thomas (D-TX)	*3/26/1966*	*1/3/1967*	*Discrete*
Elizabeth Andrews (D-AL)	*4/4/1971*	*1/3/1973*	*Discrete*
1972–Present			
Corrine (Lindy) Boggs (D-LA)	3/20/1973	1/3/1991	Static (9)
Cardiss Collins (D-IL)	6/7/1973	1/7/1997	Static (12)

(Continued)

Table 3.1 Women Who Succeeded Their Husbands in the House (*Continued*)

Name	Service Begins	Service Ends	Ambition (Terms)
Shirley Pettis (R-CA)	4/29/1975	1/3/1979	Static (2)
Beverly Byron (D-MD)	1/3/1979	1/3/1993	Static (7)
Jean Ashbrook (R-OH)	*7/12/1982*	*1/3/1983*	*Discrete*
Sala Burton (D-CA)	1/21/1983	2/1/1987	Static (3)
Catherine Long (D-LA)	*4/4/1985*	*1/3/1987*	*Discrete*
Jo Ann Emerson (R-MO)	11/5/1997	Present	Static (4)
Lois Capps (D-CA)	3/17/1998	Present	Static (4)
Mary Bono (R-CA)	4/21/1998	Present	Static (4)
Doris Matsui (D-CA)	3/3/2005	Present	???

or more terms. Representative Edith Nourse Rogers (R-MA) won reelection seventeen times, making her the longest serving woman in congressional history (1925–1960). During World War I, she traveled across Europe with her husband, John Jacob Rogers. After he died, she ran for his House seat and made veterans' issues her highest priority. She ultimately became chair of the Veterans Affairs Committee.[45] Cardiss Collins (D-IL) served for nearly twenty-four years (1973–1997) and is the longest serving African American woman in Congress.[46] Representative Leonor Sullivan (D-MO) served for twenty-three years (1952–1975) and became a well-known advocate of consumer protection, chairing the Banking and Currency Subcommittee on the Consumer Affairs Committee and chairing the Merchant Marine and Fisheries Committee.[47] Overall, the average length of service among widows who sought reelection to the House is 13.4 years.

It should also be recognized that, as widows, women do have substantial electoral advantages. These include inherited name recognition, familiarity with potential donors, and a ready-made staff. Many of them worked on their husbands' campaigns and, as a result, knew their districts well. Representative Corrine "Lindy" Boggs (D-LA) is a noteworthy example. She was first elected to the House in 1973 after her husband, Majority Leader Hale Boggs, disappeared in a plane crash in Alaska. After a two-month search for the plane, the House declared the seat vacant, and Lindy won the seat with 81 percent of the vote in the special election. Her political career, however, had begun well before that. Her grandfather was a state legislator, and her cousin was the mayor of New Orleans. For twenty-five years, she served as her husband's campaign manager and worked in his congressional office in Washington. She also chaired the inaugural ball committees for John F. Kennedy and Lyndon

[45] Foerstel, 1999, 233.
[46] Foerstel, 1999, 264.
[47] When she retired at the age of seventy-five, Representative Dick Gephardt won her seat; Foerstel, 1999, 263–64.

Johnson. Boggs served in the House for almost twenty years, retiring in 1991.[48] As her daughter, journalist Cokie Roberts, explained, "Politics is our family business."[49] Her case illustrates that congressional widows can be as politically inclined as their husbands and have access to resources and advantages similar to those enjoyed by incumbents.[50]

It is clear, then, that congressional widows are not a monolithic group. Not all widows conform to the stereotype or its storyline. While some eschew politics, others relish it. While some pursue political careers, others voluntarily forego that opportunity. Congressional widows thus provide us with an ideal "natural experiment" for examining the differences between discrete and static ambition among women in the political arena. The question underlying this analysis is straightforward: why do some congressional widows choose to pursue a career in the House while others simply serve out the term of their deceased husbands?

Understanding Discrete and Static Ambition

Because there is very little systematic analysis of discrete ambition, we draw from a wider body of research associated with the recruitment and political ambitions of women. To explore the differences between the widows who exhibit discrete and static ambition, we will examine four factors commonly deemed important to understanding the entry and success of women in the electoral arena: (1) their age, (2) whether they worked outside the home, (3) whether they lived in the South, and (4) whether they were elected in 1972 or later.

Age. Women do tend to be older than men when they first run for office.[51] The primary reason, confirmed by the Citizen Political Ambition Study results regarding housework and child care, is that women usually wait until their children are grown before they run for office. Women who do run for Congress while they have small children often have to deal with criticism that their male

---

[48] Foerstel, 1999, 28.

[49] "Women's History Month: A New Reason to Celebrate Louisiana Women's History Every Day," http://www.senate.gov/~landrieu/whm/boggs.html (accessed March 30, 2005).

[50] R. Darcy, Susan Welch, and Janet Clark, *Women, Elections, and Representation*, 2nd ed. (Lincoln: University of Nebraska Press, 1994), 91–92.

[51] See Kirkpatrick, 1974; Irene Diamond, *Sex Roles in the State House* (New Haven, Conn.: Yale University Press, 1977); Gertzog, 1980; Ruth Mandel, *In the Running: The New Woman Candidate* (New Haven, Conn.: Ticknor and Fields, 1981); Virginia Sapiro, "Private Costs of Public Commitments or Public Costs of Private Commitments? Family Roles versus Political Ambition," *American Journal of Political Science* 26 (1982): 265–79; Susan Carroll, "Political Elites and Sex Differences in Political Ambition: A Reconsideration," *Journal of Politics* 47 (1985): 1231–43; Robert Bernstein, "Why Are There So Few Women in the House?" *Western Political Quarterly* 39 (1986): 155–64; Barbara Burrell, "The Political Opportunity of Women Candidates for the U.S. House of Representatives in 1984," *Women and Politics* 8 (1988): 51–68; and Barbara Burrell, *A Woman's Place Is in the House: Campaigning for Congress in the Feminist Era* (Ann Arbor: University of Michigan Press, 1994); but see Kathleen Dolan and Lynne Ford, "Change and Continuity among Women State Legislators: Evidence from Three Decades," *Political Research Quarterly* 50 (1997): 137–51.

colleagues with small children do not have to face. For example, in her 1964 House campaign, Patsy Mink was accused of "abandoning her children."[52] In 1971, when Barbara Boxer ran in her first race for county supervisor at the age of thirty-two, she sought the advice of her next-door neighbor, who said, "I don't think you should do this. Your kids are young and it doesn't seem right."[53] During her first campaign in 1972, Pat Schroeder was constantly asked how she could run for Congress with two small children. Frustrated at the press for ignoring her position on the Vietnam War and instead focusing on her parenting skills, she finally told one reporter, "Jim and I get up very early—about 6 A.M. We bathe and dress the children and give them a wonderful breakfast. Then we put them in the freezer, leave for work and when we come home we defrost them. And we all have a wonderful dinner together."[54] In the spring of 1998, Mary Bono, who had two children, ages seven and nine, ran for her husband's seat in a special election against Ralph Waite, the actor who played "Pa" on *The Waltons*. Representative Sonny Bono (R-CA), former mayor of Palm Springs and costar of *The Sonny and Cher Show*, had been killed in a ski accident. A week before the election, Mary's mother-in-law, Jean Bono, wrote a letter to the editor of the *Riverside Press Enterprise*, stating, "Sonny Bono cannot rest in peace. . . . It would disturb him greatly that, if you hired her for the job, his children would essentially become orphans open to abuse by strangers." In an interview, she said, "I want her to stay home."[55] Mary's thirty-nine-year-old stepdaughter, Christy, responded that Mary would probably be a better representative than her father.[56]

There is, however, evidence that these attitudes about the compatibility of motherhood and public office are changing.[57] For example, Representative Shelley Berkley (D-NV) was thirty when she was deciding between running for the state assembly and taking time off to have children. She assumed that she would have to choose between one or the other. Her mother told her to "do both."[58] Representative Debbie Wasserman Schultz (D-FL) first ran for the Florida State Legislature at the age of twenty-six in 1992. While in office, she had twins. When she learned that Representative Peter Deutsch's seat was going to be open in 2004, she decided to run for Congress. In August 2003, she

[52] Foerstel and Foerstel, *Climbing the Hill: Gender Conflict in Congress* (Westport, Conn.: Praeger Press, 1996), 113.

[53] Barbara Boxer, *Strangers in the Senate: Politics and the New Revolution of Women in America* (Washington, D.C.: National Press Books, 1993), 83.

[54] Foerstel and Foerstel, 1996, 114.

[55] Mark Henry, "Bono's Mother Doesn't Want His Widow Elected," *Riverside Press Enterprise*, March 28,1998, A1.

[56] Mark Henry, "Phone Call Discouraged Election Run," *Riverside Press Enterprise*, March 31, 1998, B1.

[57] Linda Witt, Karen Paget, and Glenna Matthews, *Running as a Woman: Gender and Power in American Politics* (New York: Free Press, 1995). The first woman to have a baby while serving in Congress was Representative Yvonne Brathwaite Burke (D-CA), elected in 1972, who gave birth during her first term. The next woman to give birth while serving in Congress was Representative Enid Waldholtz (R-UT) in 1995; Foerstal, 1999, 41.

[58] Interview with Barbara Palmer, March 20, 2002.

had a baby girl, Shelby, whom she took on the campaign trail with her. At one point in her campaign, she brought Shelby with her to a lunch meeting with Susannah Shakow, president of Women Under Forty Political Action Committee. As Shakow explained:

> We met at this really nice restaurant in downtown Washington to talk about how our PAC could help her. She came with her finance director, her campaign manager, and her three-month-old baby. I told a lot of people about that meeting.
>
> Some people were shocked that she would bring her baby along to meetings where she was trying to present herself as a serious candidate. But most people I talked to thought it was great that she brought her child. Young women who have children too often feel pressure to hide that fact when they are doing business. Debbie is a role model for proving that a woman can be professional and a mother at the same time.[59]

Many women no longer feel that a political career and raising a family are mutually exclusive. Senator Mary Landrieu (D-LA) said:

> It breaks my heart when I meet older women who once made a choice between career and a family. There was a time, not long ago, when many women *had* to make that choice. Now these women are retired, and they have no children, no grandchildren. In some cases, not all, they were forced to sacrifice one great joy for another. It just doesn't seem right. I want to make sure that picture is changed for good. If I can do it, other women can.[60]

While attitudes about mothers and children on the campaign trail are changing, the election of young women to congressional offices is still quite uncommon. As table 3.2 shows, only thirty-six women under forty years old have served in the House. All but nine of these have been elected since 1972. Only one woman under the age of forty has been elected to the Senate; Blanche Lambert Lincoln (D-AR) ran in 1998 at the age of thirty-eight. She ran for the House in 1992 at the age of thirty-two. The first woman to serve in Congress, Representative Jeannette Rankin (R-MT), ran at the relatively young age of thirty-six. The youngest woman to serve in the House was Representative Elizabeth Holtzman (D-NY), elected at the age of thirty-one.[61] In 1972,

---

[59] Interview with the authors, November 14, 2004.

[60] Barbara Mikulski et al., *Nine and Counting: The Women of the Senate* (New York: William Morrow, 2000), 25.

[61] There have been two other women who were elected at age thirty-one, Susan Molinari (R-NY) and Olympia Snowe (R-ME), but they are both a couple of months older. Molinari served as the youngest member of the New York City Council at the age of twenty-six and ran for the House seat vacated by her father in 1990. Snowe, who first ran for the state legislature in 1973 at the age of twenty-six, now serves in the U.S. Senate.

Table 3.2 Women under Forty Years Old Who Have Served in the House

Name	Age When First Elected to the House	Dates of Service
	Pre–World War II	
Jeannette Rankin (R-MT)	36	1917–1919, 1941–1943
Mae Ella Nolan (R-CA)	36	1923–1925
Katherine Langley (R-KY)	38	1926–1931
Kathryn O'Laughlin McCarthy (D-KS)	38	1929–1931
	1942–1970	
Katharine Byron (D-MD)	37	1941–1943
Clare Boothe Luce (R-CT)	39	1943–1947
Winnifred Stanley (R-NY)	33	1943–1945
Patsy Mink (D-HI)	36	1965–1977, 1990–2002
Margaret Heckler (R-MA)	35	1967–1983
	1972–Present	
Elizabeth Holtzman (D-NY)	31	1973–1981
Barbara Jordan (D-TX)	36	1973–1979
Patricia Schroeder (D-CO)	32	1973–1997
Mary Rose Oakar (D-OH)	36	1977–1993
Olympia Snowe (R-ME)	31	1979–1995
Claudine Schneider (R-RI)	33	1981–1991
Marcy Kaptur (D-OH)	36	1983–present
Jill Long (D-IN)	37	1989–1995
Ileana Ros-Lehtinen (R-FL)	37	1989–present
Susan Molinari (R-NY)	31	1990–1997
Blanche Lincoln (D-AR)	32	1993–1997
Cynthia McKinney (D-GA)	37	1993–2003, 2005–present
Nydia Velazquez (D-NY)	39	1993–2005
Maria Cantwell (D-WA)	34	1993–1995
Enid Greene Waldholtz (R-UT)	36	1995–1997
Lynn Rivers (D-MI)	37	1995–2005
Linda Smith (R-WA)	34	1995–1999
Loretta Sanchez (D-CA)	36	1997–present
Diana Degette (D-CO)	39	1997–present
Mary Bono (R-CA)	36	1999–present
Heather Wilson (R-NM)	37	1999–present

(Continued)

Table 3.2 Women under Forty Years Old Who Have Served in the House (*Continued*)

Name	Age When First Elected to the House	Dates of Service
Tammy Baldwin (D-WI)	36	1999–present
Melissa Hart (R-PA)	38	2001–present
Linda Sanchez (D-CA)	34	2003–present
Stephanie Herseth (D-SD)	33	2004–present
Cathy McMorris (R-WA)	33	2005–present
Debbie Wasserman Schultz (D-FL)	37	2005–present

Holtzman, who never held political office before, defeated a twenty-five-term Democratic incumbent, Representative Emanuel Celler, by six hundred votes in the primary. Celler was chair of the House Judiciary Committee and had blocked the Equal Rights Amendment in his committee for twenty years. Holtzman got his seat on the committee and participated in the impeachment hearings against President Richard Nixon. In 1977, she cofounded the Congressional Caucus for Women's Issues. [62]

In the 109th Congress (2005 session), the youngest woman was Representative Stephanie Herseth (D-SD), age thirty-three. Herseth's first attempt at running for Congress was in 2002, when she ran for South Dakota's open at-large seat. Her opponent was Republican Bill Janklow, the state's "larger than life" former governor. [63] Janklow won with 53 percent of the vote, but a few months later, he ran a stop sign at over seventy miles per hour and hit and killed a motorcyclist. [64] After Janklow's manslaughter conviction, Herseth ran again in the special election held in June 2004, defeating Larry Diedrich, a state legislator. Five months later, she defended her seat and defeated Diedrich again with 53 percent of the vote. [65] The youngest man in the 109th Congress

---

[62] Foerstel, 1999, 123. See also Elizabeth Holtzman with Cynthia Cooper, *Who Said It Would Be Easy? One Woman's Life in the Political Arena* (New York: Arcade Press, 1996).

[63] Janklow was a fixture in South Dakota politics for over thirty years. As attorney general in 1975, he charged into the capitol with an automatic rifle during a hostage situation. After Jerry Brown, governor of California, refused to extradite Dennis Banks, a prominent member of the American Indian Movement, Janklow said he would pardon criminals in South Dakota if they agreed to move to California; Conrad deFiebre, "Janklow Case: He Did Politics His Way; Roughshod Style Made Him SD Icon," *Minneapolis Star Tribune*, December 14, 2003, 1B.

[64] Janklow had a reputation for speeding. He was stopped by police at least sixteen other times since 1994; "Janklow Trial Begins, Could Shake Up State's Political Scene," *The Bulletin's Frontrunner*, McClean, Virginia, December 2, 2003.

[65] Herseth has noted how a recent change in FEC rules might actually help young women: candidates can now draw a salary from their campaign. She explained that running for office is a full-time job and, as a result, quit her lucrative job as an attorney. She saved money to cushion the loss of income, but being allowed to draw a salary from her campaign meant that she did not have to accumulate more debt on top of her student loans. Diedrich actually tried to make this an issue in the campaign. Herseth hopes, however, that her successful precedent will make the practice a nonissue and that people with modest means—more young people, particularly women—will be able to run. Speech at WUFPAC event, Washington, D.C., July 20, 2004.

(2005 session) was newly elected Representative Patrick McHenry (R-NC), age twenty-nine. Prior to running for Congress, he served one term in the North Carolina General Assembly and was active in Republican politics.[66]

There are political consequences to running later in life. Entry into the leadership structure of Congress depends upon longevity and seniority. This is especially true within the committee system where the key positions, chairs and ranking members, are based upon continuous service on committees and subcommittees. As Shakow explained, "Women need to get in early, and stay in, so that more leadership positions are open to them. In Washington, political tenure equal[s] political power."[67] To date, women have not been well represented in the leadership hierarchy. Only two women have held top party leadership positions in Congress: Representative Nancy Pelosi (D-CA) has served as the House Democratic whip (2001–2002) and as minority leader (2002–present), and Senator Margaret Chase Smith (R-ME) was chair of the Senate Republican Conference (1967–1972). As table 3.3 shows, in the history of Congress, eleven women have chaired standing committees. In the 109th Congress (2005 session), only two women were committee chairs, Senators Olympia Snowe and Susan Collins of Maine.[68]

If the younger members of Congress today are the leadership of Congress in the future, women will be substantially underrepresented. It was not until the 108th Congress (2004 session) that there was at least one woman on every committee.[69] In the 109th Congress (2005 session), four women were under forty years old: Representatives Stephanie Herseth (D-SD), Cathy McMorris (R-WA), Linda Sanchez (D-CA), and Debbie Wasserman Schultz (D-FL). There were twenty-two men under forty. The importance of starting young becomes particularly apparent given that twelve of the last nineteen presidents first ran for elective office before they reached the age of thiry-five; for example,

---

[66] http://www.mchenryforcongress.com/assets/NewsLetters/CQarticle.htm (accessed March 30, 2005). In the 2004 election, there were 2 twenty-six-year-old women who ran for Congress. Capri Cafaro (D) lost her race against incumbent Steve LaTourette in Ohio's 14th district, and Samara Barend (D) lost her race for the open seat in New York's 29th district. If either woman won, she would have become the youngest woman to be elected and the youngest person in the current Congress.

[67] Interview with the authors, July 19, 2004. Women Under Forty Political Action Committee (WUFPAC) is a nonpartisan political action committee that provides financial support to women under forty years old who are running for Congress; see http://www.wufpac.org (accessed July 10, 2005).

[68] In the House, there were no female committee chairs in the 109th Congress (2005 session), but three women were ranking members. Chapter 4 will explore this in more depth. Women who have chaired other nonstanding committees include Representative Pat Schroeder (D-CO), who was chair of the Select Committee on Children, Youth and Families, and Yvonne Brathwaite Burke, who chaired the House Select Committee on the Beauty Shop.

[69] Michael Hardy and Karen McCurdy, "Representational Threshold: Women in Congressional Committees" (paper presented at the Southern Political Science Association, January 2005, New Orleans).

Table 3.1 Women Who Have Been Chairs of Standing Committees

House

Name	Committee	Dates of Service
Mae Ella Nolan (R-CA)	Expenditures (Post Office Department)	1923–1924
Edith Nourse Rogers (R-MA)	World War Veterans	1947–1948, 1953–1954
Mary Norton (D-NJ)	District of Columbia	1931–1937
Mary Norton (D-NJ)	Labor	1937–1946
Mary Norton (D-NJ)	Administration	1949–1950
Caroline O'Day (D-NY)	Elections	1937–1942
Leonor Sullivan (D-MO)	Merchant Marine and Fisheries	1973–1976
Nancy Johnson (R-CT)	Standards of Official Conduct	1995–1996
Jan Meyers (R-KS)	Small Business	1995–1996

Senate

Name	Committee	Dates of Service
Hattie Caraway (D-AR)	Enrolled Bills	1933–1944
Nancy Kassebaum (R-KS)	Labor and Human Resources	1995–1996
Susan Collins (R-ME)	Governmental Affairs	2003–present
Olympia Snowe (R-ME)	Small Business and Entrepreneurship	2003–present

Sources: Karen McCurdy, "The Institutional Role of Women Serving in Congress: 1960–2000," in *Representation of Minority Groups in the U.S.*, ed. Charles Menifield (Lanham, Md.: Austin and Winfield, 2001); and Mildred Amer, 2004; *Biographical Directory of the United States Congress*, http://bioguide.congress.gov/biosearch/biosearch.asp (accessed July 3, 2005).

Teddy Roosevelt was twenty-four when he first ran for state assembly in New York and Lyndon Johnson was twenty-nine when he first ran for the U.S. House.[70]

The 109th Congress (2005 session) is also the oldest in the history of both the Senate and the House; the average age in the Senate is sixty, and the average age in the House is fifty-five.[71] Senator Strom Thurmond (R-SC) holds the record as the oldest person to serve. He retired at the age of one hundred in January 2003, after forty-eight years in Congress.[72] Among all women to serve in the House between 1916 and 2004, the average age when they first ran for office was forty-nine. The average age of widows was fifty-three; for nonwidows, the average was forty-seven. In the 109th Congress

---

[70] Ruth Mandel and Katherine Kleeman, *Political Generation Next: America's Young Elected Leaders* (New Brunswick, N.J.: Rutgers University, 2004). See also Marie Wilson, *Closing the Leadership Gap: Why Women Can and Must Help Run the World* (New York: Viking, 2004).

[71] Amer, 2005.

[72] He died a few months later on June 26, 2003; http://www.strom.clemson.edu/strom/bio.html (accessed July 3, 2005).

(2005 session), the average age of male House members when they first ran was forty-four; female House members were forty-nine. Given the importance of age in both the hierarchy of offices and in acquiring internal influence, we expect that the likelihood of a widow seeking a career will vary inversely with her age.[73]

Working outside the Home. One of the most consistent predictors of political ambition among women is whether they worked outside the home and whether their jobs helped them to acquire useful political skills.[74] With regard to working outside of the home, two aspects are most relevant to our analysis of congressional widows and political ambition. The first involves whether the woman worked closely, in either a paid or unpaid capacity, with her husband when he served as a member of the House. This kind of experience provides a familiarity with the concerns and interests of constituents, how to organize an effective campaign, and the responsibilities and routines of running a congressional office. A second aspect of working outside the home pertains to whether a woman was active in politics independent of her husband's political career. The nature of this independent experience may include holding elective office or appointive office, or serving in the organization of a local, state, or national party.

One example of a widow who had a great deal of political experience was Sala Burton (D-CA). Her husband, Representative Phillip Burton, was a powerful House member and leader of the liberal wing of the Democratic Party in the 1970s and early 1980s. Although Sala was never formally on his congressional staff, Phillip called her his "political partner," and she was an integral part of his thirty-year political career.[75] Pansy Ponzio, a member of the local Democratic Party, explained that "she knew just about as much about the office and the constituents and the people who live in San Francisco as he did."[76] Phillip and Sala met at a Young Democrats convention in 1950. When her husband was a member of the California State Legislature, she organized the California Democratic Council and then served as vice president. She also served on the San Francisco Fair Housing Committee, served as a member of the state Democratic Party Steering

---

[73] In the analysis, we use the age of sixty as a cutoff point to create a dummy variable.

[74] Gertzog, 1980, 1995; Janet Clark, Charles Hadley, and Robert Darcy, "Political Ambition among Men and Women State Party Leaders," *American Politics Quarterly* 17 (1989): 194–207; Edmond Constantini, "Political Women and Political Ambition," *American Journal of Politics* 34 (1990): 741–70; Barbara Norrander and Clyde Wilcox, "The Geography of Gender Power," in *Women and Elective Office: Past, Present and Future*, ed. Sue Thomas and Clyde Wilcox (New York: Oxford University Press, 1998), 103–17; and Kathryn Pearson and Eric McGhee, "Strategic Differences: The Gender Dynamics of Congressional Candidacies, 1982–2002" (paper presented at the American Political Science Association Annual Meeting, September 2004, Chicago).

[75] James Dickenson and Paul Taylor, "Widow of Burton Will Seek Election to His House Seat," *Washington Post*, April 19, 1983, A7.

[76] Wallace Turner, "Burton's Widow among 4 Considering Race for Congress Seat," *New York Times*, April 18, 1983, A12.

Committee, and chaired the Democratic Women's Forum. After Phillip became a member of Congress, she served on the boards of the National Security Committee, the National Council on Soviet Jewry, and the Women's National Democratic Club.[77] She was also the president of the Democratic Wives of the House and Senate and a delegate to four Democratic presidential conventions.[78] While serving in his tenth term, Phillip died of an embolism in April 1983. Sala announced she would run for his seat eight days after his death and defeated ten other candidates in the special election with 56.9 percent of the vote.[79] Within days of her victory, she announced that she would run for reelection in 1984.[80] She ran again in 1986 and won, but unfortunately was diagnosed with cancer and died shortly after being sworn in for her third term.[81] Because of the independent political experience gained while her husband was alive, she easily won the support of party leaders, knew how to campaign, and became a successful member of Congress in her own right.

With respect to independent experience, there are marked differences between widows and nonwidows. Nonwidows entered their first campaign for a House seat with an average of 9.8 years of experience; almost half served in other political offices for over ten years. Widows, on the other hand, averaged 3.7 years of experience, with only 15.4 percent (6/39) holding offices for ten years or more. Thus, we expect those widows with more political experience, whether it was from working with their husbands or their own independent activities, to run for reelection.[82]

The South. We have noted that, prior to the 1970s, American culture treated politics as primarily a man's game. In a variety of ways, women were discouraged from entering the electoral arena. The barriers faced by women, however, were even more restrictive in the American South.[83] This is attributed to a

---

[77] Barbara Gamarekian, "'The Popular Burton' and Her Mission," *New York Times*, July 29, 1983, A10.

[78] Foerstel, 1999, 43.

[79] Barbara Gamerekian, "'The Popular Burton' and Her Mission," *New York Times*, July 29, 1983, A10.

[80] "Widow of Rep. Burton Is Elected in California Congressional Race," *New York Times*, June 23, 1983, A16.

[81] Foerstel, 1999, 43.

[82] In this analysis, we use dummy variables to represent these aspects of working outside the home. The first assumes a value of one if the widow worked in partnership with her husband. The second takes on a value of one if the widow had independent political experience of her own. The biographies written by Foerstel (1999) are excellent for making this determination. She reports whether the wife worked with or for her husband and provides a great deal of specificity about the kind of work she did (e.g., organized and ran the Washington office). We also recorded the total numbers of years that the woman served in elective or appointive offices in her own right. We do not "double count" those years in which a woman served in more than one capacity (e.g., state legislature and member of state party central committee), and we apply a strict rule of independence in making these calculations. Thus, service in the party organization (state, local, or national) is counted while service as an officer in the Congressional Wives Club does not. It should be noted that these two aspects of "working outside the home" are not mutually exclusive.

[83] Deanne Stephens Nuwer, "Southern Women Legislators and Patriarchy in the South," *Southeastern Political Review* 28 (2000): 449–68.

uniquely traditionalist culture that "function[ed] to confine real political power to a small and self-perpetuating elite who often inherit their right to govern through family title or social position."[84] This traditionalism also includes "a clear predisposition with regard to social conservatism and particularly women's rights."[85] As one historian explained, in the antebellum South, "even though the master's wife and daughters were white and members of the planter class, 'they were . . . in this rigidly hierarchical society, subjected to male rule.' . . . In fact, an educated and well-bred woman . . . was not even allowed to initiate a political conversation."[86] In spite of the dramatic social and economic changes in the South, these regional distinctions "have shown remarkable resilience."[87] Of the eleven states in the Confederacy, only Texas ratified the Equal Rights Amendment.[88]

The impact of southern traditionalism is particularly noteworthy in the early years of our study. Between 1916 and 1970, only three of the nineteen southern women to serve in the House won their seats in regularly scheduled House elections.[89] The political careers of these three women are particularly illustrative of southern political culture. Representative Alice Robertson (see figure 3.2), a Republican from Oklahoma and a teacher, farmer, and restaurateur, was the first woman elected from the South and the second woman to serve in Congress. In the campaign of 1920, she defeated incumbent Democrat William Hastings by the narrow margin of 48.8 to 48.4 percent. Robertson was an ardent antisuffragist who "incurred the wrath of such groups as the League of Women Voters, the National Women's Party, and the Daughters of the American Revolution."[90] These groups took umbrage at Robertson's opposition to an appropriation for the Children's Bureau in the Department of Labor designed to "promote maternity and infant care."[91] In a floor speech, Robertson dismissed as "absurd" the "'sob stuff' claim that 680 babies die

---

[84] Daniel Elazar, *American Federalism: A View from the States* (New York: Crowell, 1966), 93.

[85] Christina Wolbrecht, *The Politics of Women's Rights: Parties, Positions, and Change* (Princeton, N.J.: Princeton University Press, 2000), 187.

[86] Nuwer, 2000, 450.

[87] John Shelton Reed, *The Enduring South: Subcultural Persistence in Mass Society* (Chapel Hill: University of North Carolina Press, 1986).

[88] Wolbrecht, 2000, 187.

[89] Thirteen were widows elected to succeed their deceased husbands. Two women also won special elections to fill a vacancy. In February 1946, Helen Mankin (D-GA) won the seat left open by the resignation of Representative Robert Ramspeck. She served in the House from February 12, 1946, until the end of the term on January 3, 1947. Under the Georgia county unit system, Mankin lost her bid for renomination in 1946 despite a popular vote victory; Foerstel, 1996, 170–71. For over twenty years, Eliza Pratt (D-NC) worked as a "top assistant to a parade of representatives from North Carolina's 8th Congressional District"; Foerstel, 1999, 219. She won a special election in June 1946 to succeed her boss, Representative William Burgin; she did not run in 1948, citing the difficulties of fundraising; Foerstel, 1999, 220.

[90] Foerstel, 1999, 231.

[91] "An Undeleted History of Women," http://www.undelete.org/woa/woa01-02.html (accessed May 15, 2005).

Fig. 3.2 Representative Alice Robertson was the first woman elected from the South and the second woman to serve in Congress. Photo courtesy of the Library of Congress.

every day from the failure to enact this bill."[92] In addition, Robertson opposed bills creating a Department of Education, U.S. entry into the League of Nations, and bonuses for veterans of World War I.[93] It was this last transgression that led to her 1922 defeat.[94] William Hastings easily reclaimed his seat by a margin of 57.7 to 41.7 percent.

The second woman from the South, Representative Ruth Bryan Owen (D-FL), was the daughter of three-time presidential nominee and former Secretary of State William Jennings Bryan.[95] At twenty-three, she served as secretary to her father during his unsuccessful 1908 presidential campaign

---

[92] Quoted in Foerstel, 1999, 232.
[93] Foerstel, 1999, 232.
[94] Foerstel, 1999, 232.
[95] Owen was the first woman elected from a state in the Confederacy.

against Republican William Howard Taft. Following the divorce from her first husband, she became a "single mom" and supported her family as a lecturer and newspaper writer. She later married Reginald Owen, a former British military officer. Because of Reginald's illness, they moved to Florida and lived with her parents. Following her father's death in 1925, Owen began her own political career and ran for the House. She narrowly lost the Democratic primary to incumbent William Sears in 1926. After her husband's death in 1927, Ruth again announced her candidacy, defeated Sears to win the primary in 1928, and then went on to an easy victory in the general election, defeating Republican William Lawson by a wide margin, 65 to 35 percent. Lawson, however, challenged the election, arguing that she had forfeited her citizenship and eligibility to run for the House when she married a British citizen. The House upheld her election. Owen was reelected in 1930 and, during her time in the House, served on the Foreign Relations Committee and was an advocate of mothers' pensions, a program later included in the legislation creating the Social Security System. Owen was defeated in the 1932 Democratic primary where her opponent, J. Mark Wilcox, attacked her support for Prohibition.[96]

Twenty-six years would pass until the next southern woman was elected in her own right. In the 1940s, Democrat Iris Blitch became known as the "Queen of the Legislature" during her service as one of the lone women in the Georgia House and Senate.[97] While in the Georgia legislature, Blitch supported expanding the "county unit system," an indirect method of determining election results that disproportionately favored sparsely populated rural counties. She argued that this system was "another weapon in opposing the Communistic trend" of determining election results by direct popular vote.[98] In 1954, Blitch defeated four-term incumbent William Wheeler, charging him with disloyalty to the Democratic Party,[99] and ran unopposed in the general election. During her tenure, Blitch was clearly a member of the southern "segregationist" bloc. In 1956, she signed the Southern Manifesto decrying the 1954 U.S. Supreme Court decision in *Brown v. Board of Board of Education* and voted against the Civil Rights Act of 1957. Three years later, she was on the record as opposed to

---

[96] Foerstel, 1999, 213–14; and Steven Gillon, *That's Not What We Meant to Do: Reform and Its Unintended Consequences in Twentieth-Century America* (New York: W.W. Norton, 2000), 43–46.

[97] Foerstel, 1999, 27.

[98] Albert Saye, "Georgia's County Unit System of Election," *Journal of Politics* 12 (1950): 93–106, 100. In Georgia during this time, the winner of a primary election was not based upon the popular vote. Rather, each county was assigned a specific number of unit votes (three, two, or one), and the popular vote in that county would determine the winner of the county's unit votes. The system was discriminatory because it diluted the influence of urban counties. For example, by winning four rural counties and getting their four unit votes, a candidate could offset an opponent's victory in an urban county worth three unit votes.

[99] The charge of party disloyalty rendered against her opponent is somewhat baffling. As it turns out, Blitch's and Wheeler's voting records were almost identical.

the Civil Rights Act of 1960.[100] In 1961, she opposed the effort led by Democratic Speaker of the House Sam Rayburn to expand the membership of the
House Rules Committee, which would have ended the conservative southern
lock on the committee and allowed civil rights legislation to progress.[101] A year
after her retirement from the House in 1963, she switched parties and
announced her support for Republican Barry Goldwater in the presidential
election of 1964.

We define the South as the eleven states of the Confederacy plus Oklahoma
and Kentucky. Numerous state and regional studies have shown that southern
traditionalism produces proportionally fewer female candidates and officeholders than the rest of the country.[102] And as the examples of Robertson and
Blitch show, conservative social attitudes in the South were not limited to men.
In fact, many southern women still "maintain a cult-of-domesticity mind
frame."[103] Between 1956 and 2004, there were 6,326 nomination opportunities
for southern House seats, and women won the nomination only 273 times, a
rate of 4.3 percent. The comparable rate outside of the South is nearly double,
8.3 percent (1,285/15,406). Similarly, of the 3,163 general elections for the
House in the South, women won 3.6 percent (113/3,021), compared to a rate
of 7.5 percent (577/7,703), more than double, outside the South. As a result,
we would expect widows from the South to be less likely to pursue congressional careers.[104]

Running after 1970. We use 1972 as the "critical moment"[105] to mark the point
at which the Women's Movement began to influence attitudes toward women
and their entry into the electoral arena. While dating the rise of any social
movement is somewhat arbitrary, the period from 1970 to 1972 is appropriate
for several reasons. As we noted in chapter 2, a series of events occurred that
fostered the beginning of a fundamental shift in American political culture.

---

[100] Officially, Blitch was "paired against" this civil rights bill. Members of Congress are "paired"
when there is an "agreement between two lawmakers on opposite sides to withhold their votes
on roll calls so their absence from Congress will not affect the outcome of record voting";
Congress and the Nation, 1948–1964 (Washington, D.C.: CQ Press, 1965), 171a.

[101] The Rules Committee plays a powerful role in the House of Representatives because it controls
whether a bill passed by an authorizing committee is sent to the floor. In addition, it establishes
the rules (e.g., length of debate, amendment procedures) under which the bill is debated.
During the 1950s, the Rules Committee was dominated by a conservative alliance of Republicans and southern Democrats. The successful effort to increase the size of this committee was
designed to add three more liberals to the panel and thus break this conservative alliance;
Milton Cummings and Robert Peabody, "The Decision to Enlarge the Committee on Rules: An
Analysis of the 1961 Vote," in *New Perspectives on the House of Representatives*, 2nd ed., ed.
Robert Peabody and Nelson Polsby (Chicago: Rand McNally, 1969).

[102] See for example Constantini, 1990; Clark, Hadley, and Darcy, 1989; Burrell, 1994; Darcy,
Welch, and Clark, 1994; Gertzog, 1995; Susan Welch and Donley Studlar, "The Opportunity
Structure for Women's Candidacies and Electability in Britain and the United States," *Political
Research Quarterly* 49 (1996): 861–74; Norrander and Wilcox, 1998, and Nuwer, 2000.

[103] Nuwer, 2000, 451.

[104] Gertzog, 1980.

[105] Edward Carmines and James Stimson, *Issue Evolution: Race and the Transformation of American Politics* (Princeton, N.J.: Princeton University Press, 1989).

The number of women's groups skyrocketed, along with media coverage of women's issues and activism. The Supreme Court handed down two landmark women's rights cases: for the first time in history, the Supreme Court voided a sex-based classification as a violation of the Equal Protection Clause and struck down a state law banning abortion. The Democratic Party changed its rules and dramatically increased the number of female delegates attending the national convention. Congress passed the Equal Rights Amendment and sent it to the states for ratification, and passed other landmark women's rights legislation. Organizations such as the National Women's Political Caucus and the Women's Campaign Fund were created to provide financial support for women candidates.

The unfolding of these events corresponded with an increase in the number of women obtaining public office. Beginning in 1972, more women were running in primaries, winning primaries, and winning congressional seats. Attitudes about women's roles were changing; gradually, the perception that politics was a "man's game" was dissolving. As Senator Barbara Boxer (D-CA) explained, "[I]n 1972 you never mentioned being a woman. You never brought it up, and you hoped nobody noticed."[106] Today, as Gilda Morales at the Center for American Women in Politics explained, the presumption that female candidates are "inherently vulnerable 'has disappeared.'"[107] As noted earlier, it was largely assumed that the only way women could obtain elective office was by following a dead husband, whether they actually did or not. The Women's Movement and the events of the early 1970s fostered a shift in attitudes about the capabilities of women running for office in their own right.

As table 3.1 shows, from 1916 to 1940, a twenty-four-year period, fourteen widows were elected to the House. From 1942 to 1970, a twenty-eight-year period, fifteen widows were elected. From 1972 to 2005, a twenty-three-year period, only eleven widows served after the death of their husbands. Moreover, widows as a proportion of the number of women elected dropped considerably; prior to 1970, widows were 41.2 percent of all women elected. After 1972, widows were only 8.2 percent of all women elected. More women were running without the benefit of a dead husband. Consequently, we expect that these cultural shifts about the appropriateness of women running for office will also affect widows themselves and that more of them who were elected after 1970 would pursue careers.

Explaining Discrete and Static Ambition

We expect that the decision of widows to seek a second term in the House will be influenced by these four factors. Widows who are under the age of sixty

---

[106] Boxer, 1993, 82.

[107] Allison Stevens, "The Strength of These Women Shows in Their Numbers," *CQ Weekly,* October 25, 2003, 2625.

when they first obtain office will be more likely to run for reelection. Widows who worked outside the home, whether they worked directly for their husbands or had independent political experience of their own, would also be more likely to run for reelection. In addition, women from districts outside the South and those who ran after the rise of the Women's Movement in the early 1970s would also be more likely to run for reelection and exhibit static ambition. There were thirty-nine congressional widows who served in the House between 1916 and 2004.[108] Nineteen (48.7 percent) sought reelection after their initial term. It is our expectation that these four factors will explain the choices made by these widows.

As table 3.4 shows, each of our expectations is met.[109] The table reveals that age is strongly related to the decision of whether to seek a career in the House. Only two of eleven widows (18.2 percent) age sixty or older sought reelection compared to 60.7 percent (17/28) of those widows younger than sixty years of age. The probability of a widow seeking a second term is strongly related to whether she worked outside the home. First, the likelihood that she will pursue a congressional career increases when she has worked with her husband. Almost half of the widows worked with or for their husbands. And thirteen of the eighteen widows (72.2 percent) who worked with their husbands sought a second term compared to only six of the twenty-one widows (28.6 percent) not actively engaged in their husband's career. In addition, there is a clear

Table 3.2 When Congressional Widows Seek Reelection to the House

Characteristics Predicting Discrete versus Static Ambition among Widows	Percentage of All Widows Who Possess the Characteristic	Percentage of Widows with Characteristic Who Seek Reelection
First elected under the age of sixty	71.8% (28/39)	60.7% (17/28)
Worked with or for husband when he served in the House	46.2 (18/39)	72.2 (13/18)
Had political experience independent of husband	28.2 (11/39)	79.3 (9/11)
Elected from district outside of the South	60.0 (23/39)	79.3 (17/23)
Elected to first term in 1972 or later	28.2 (11/39)	79.3 (17/23)

---

[108] Our analysis excludes Doris Matsui, who was elected in March 2005. Her situation will be discussed in the conclusion of this chapter.

[109] The full results of our statistical model are presented in Barbara Palmer and Dennis Simon, "Political Ambition and Women in the U.S. House of Representatives, 1916–2000," *Political Research Quarterly* 56 (2003): 127–38. Our results and discussion here largely reflect the results of this analysis. Additional evidence is presented in Lisa Solowiej and Thomas Brunell, "The Entrance of Women to the U.S. Congress: The Widow Effect," *Political Research Quarterly* 56 (2003): 283–92.

relationship between independent political experience and seeking reelection. While only about a quarter of the widows had independent political experience, nine of the eleven (81.8 percent) sought reelection to the House; only 35.7 percent (10/28) of those without this experience sought reelection.

The prevailing political and social culture also has an influence on whether a widow will run again. The probability of seeking a second term decreases if the widow is from the South. In our data, sixteen of the thirty-nine women are from the South. Only two of them pursued a House career: Katherine Langley (R-KY), after her husband's unfortunate incarceration, and Lindy Boggs (D-LA). Among those widows representing districts outside the South, 79.3 percent (17/23) sought election to a second term. The probability of pursuing a career has also increased since 1972, in the wake of the Women's Movement. Most widows (71.8 percent) were elected before 1972. Of the twenty-eight widows who were first elected to the House before 1972, only eleven (39.3 percent) sought a second term. Of the eleven elected since 1972, eight (79.3 percent) pursued a career in the House. Overall, table 3.4 demonstrates that there are differences between careerist and noncareerist widows. As such, the results reveal that there is a systematic and measurable distinction between discrete and static ambition.

Our analysis correctly predicts the decision of widows to seek a second term in thirty-four of thirty-nine cases.[110] Table 3.5 reports the probability that a widow will seek reelection and pursue a career given combinations of the five measures we use.[111] Probabilities equal to or greater than .50 lead to a prediction of static ambition and the widow seeking a second term; entries below .50 lead to a prediction of discrete ambition and retirement. Several important relationships are clear. The first pertains to the historical time period and region. The first row presents the scenarios associated with women elected from the South prior to 1972. The probabilities of seeking a House career are uniformly low. In fact, the only situation that leads to a probability greater than .50 that the widow will run for reelection is the instance where

---

[110] Palmer and Simon, 2003, 133.

[111] For a complete explanation of this analysis, see Palmer and Simon, 2003. In our statistical model, political experience is measured as a continuous variable, the total number of years that a woman served in political office. We performed the simulation by first combining the variables to form a set of officeholder profiles (e.g., elected before 1972, from the South, did not work with her husband, and held no office independent of her husband). The set of profiles includes all possible combinations of the binary independent variables in tandem with three values of the experience variable (zero, five, ten). This produced a set of forty-eight officeholder profiles. The estimated coefficients of the model were then used to simulate the probability of seeking reelection for each profile. To obtain these probabilities, we used the Clarify suite of programs (a STATA module) developed in Michael Tomz, Jason Wittenberg, and Gary King, *Clarify: Software for Interpreting and Presenting Statistical Results* (Cambridge, Mass.: Harvard University Press, 2001). See also Gary King, Michael Tomz, and Jason Wittenberg, "Making the Most of Statistical Analyses: Improving Interpretation and Presentation," *American Journal of Political Science* 44 (2000): 341–55. The program was set to perform 1,000 simulations for each profile. The probabilities reported in table 3.5 are the average probabilities over the 1,000 simulations.

Table 3.3 The Probability That Congressional Widows Will Seek Reelection to the House

Time Period and Region	Age and Independent Experience	Did Not Work with or for Husband	Worked with or for Husband
1916–1970 South	60 or Older		
	No independent experience	.00	.01
	Five years of experience	.00	.04
	Ten years of experience	.01	.10
	Less Than 60		
	No independent experience	.02	.26
	Five years of experience	.07	.44
	Ten years of experience	.17	**.62**
1916–1970 Non-South	60 or Older		
	No independent experience	.04	.27
	Five years of experience	.08	.44
	Ten years of experience	.17	**.62**
	Less Than 60		
	No independent experience	.30	**.83**
	Five years of experience	**.51**	**.93**
	Ten years of experience	**.71**	**.98**
1972–2004 South	60 or Older		
	No independent experience	.02	.14
	Five years of experience	.04	.27
	Ten years of experience	.11	.44
	Less Than 60		
	No independent experience	.21	**.63**
	Five years of experience	.35	**.77**
	Ten years of experience	**.51**	**.86**
1972–2004 Non-South	60 or Older		
	No independent experience	.18	**.66**
	Five years of experience	.32	**.82**
	Ten years of experience	**.51**	**.92**

(Continued)

Table 3.3 The Probability That Congressional Widows Will Seek Reelection to the House (*Continued*)

Time Period and Region	Age and Independent Experience	Did Not Work with or for Husband	Worked with or for Husband
	Less Than 60		
	No independent experience	*.74*	*.97*
	Five years of experience	*.87*	*.99*
	Ten years of experience	*.94*	*.99*

Note: The cell entries represent the probability of seeking reelection to the House and were generated using the Clarify program module; Michael Tomz, Jason Wittenberg, and Gary King, *Clarify: Software for Interpreting and Presenting Statistical Results* (Cambridge, Mass.: Harvard University, 2001). The highlighted and italicized probabilities represent values that would generate a prediction that the widow will run for reelection.

the woman is under sixty years of age, has worked with her husband, and also has accumulated ten years of independent political experience. Outside of the South, the probabilities also remain low, with six of twelve profiles less than .50. In these instances, running for reelection depends upon either substantial experience or working for or with the husband. In fact, table 3.5 highlights the importance of this wife-husband political partnership, which can be seen by comparing the third and fourth columns of the table. There are seven instances in which, all other factors being equal, a political partnership with the husband moves the probability that the widow will run for reelection over the .50 threshold.

The table also highlights the change that has occurred since 1972. In the South, there are four profiles, compared to one in the years before 1972, associated with a probability greater than .50 (less than sixty years old, with either ten years of experience or working with the husband, regardless of experience). Outside the South, the change is even more pronounced. Of the twelve profiles shown in the fourth row of the table, only two have associated probabilities less than .50 (sixty years or older, with less than ten years of experience and no association with the husband's career). Regardless of age or experience, a partnership with the husband produces probabilities ranging from .66 to virtual certainty. The probability that a nonsouthern widow less than sixty years old who had worked with her husband would run for reelection is .97. In other words, these women will run again and seek a congressional career.

Conclusion

For much of the twentieth century, it was largely assumed that the typical congressional widow was Veronica Boland (D-PA). After the death of her husband in 1942, she ran unopposed in the special election to fill his seat. She held the office for only forty-five days, did not serve on any committees, and did not make any floor speeches.[112] Our analysis shows, however, that she was hardly the quintessential congressional widow; her story is not the norm at all. The more typical congressional widow is Jo Ann Emerson (R-MO), who ran for Congress for the first time at age forty-six. When her husband, Representative Bill Emerson (R-MO), died of lung cancer in 1996, local and national Republican Party leaders asked her to run in the special election to fill his seat. Given the timing of her husband's death, she technically had to run in two races: as a Republican in the special election to fill the remainder of the current term, and as an Independent in the general election because the filing deadline for running in the Republican primary had passed. Although she never held public office, she had extensive political experience, working as a lobbyist on Capitol Hill and as the deputy communications director for the National Republican Congressional Committee. She actually grew up living next door to House Majority Leader Hale Boggs and his family. Cokie Roberts was her babysitter. Her father was executive director for the Republican National Committee. In 2004, she was elected to her 5th term with 72 percent of the vote.[113]

Representative Doris Matsui (D-CA) is the most recent widow to serve in Congress. She provides an opportunity for us to use our analysis to predict whether she will seek reelection. Matsui was elected in March 2005 to succeed her husband, who served for twenty-six years in the House. She was sixty years old when she ran in the special election and won the seat with 69 percent of the vote. Her closest opponent received 8.5 percent of the vote.[114] Although she never held elective office, she was a member of the Clinton administration from 1992 to 1998, serving as the deputy assistant to the president and as deputy director of public liaison in the White House. From 1998 to her election in 2005, she was a lobbyist for a Washington firm that represented medical technology, telecommunications, and financial organizations.[115] Shortly after her swearing in, Ted Gaebler, city manager of Rancho Cordova, emphasized her experience by stating that "nothing about her is a rookie. I am amazed at her comfort and her ease."[116] Her constituency, the 5th District of California, is considered solidly Democratic and covers the state's capital city of Sacramento and a few of its first-tier suburbs.[117] In the three months before

---

[112] Foerstel, 1999, 30.

[113] National Journal Almanac, http://nationaljournal.com/pubs/almanac/2004/people/mo/rep_mo08.htm (accessed May 20, 2005).

[114] Kevin Yamamura, "Matsui Set to Be Sworn in Today and Cast First Vote as a Congressman's Widow and Washington Veteran," *Sacramento Bee*, March 10, 2005, A3.

[115] *Biographical Directory of the United States Congress*, http://bioguide/congress.gov/scripts/bio-dispaly.pl?index=M0011163 (accessed May 20, 2005).

[116] David Whitney, "Freshman Matsui Learns Life in Congress Is Hectic," *Sacramento Bee*, March 20, 2005, A3.

[117] Michael Barone, *The Almanac of American Politics 2002* (Washington, D.C.: National Journal Group, 2003), 178.

the special election, she raised over $1.1 million. After the campaign, she had $172,000 left, a sizable war chest compared to other area House incumbents.[118]

Matsui is a sixty-year-old, nonsouthern widow elected after 1970, with thirteen years of independent experience, although none of it was working with her husband. According to table 3.5, the probability that she will run for reelection is .51. Although it is a "close call," our analysis predicts that she will seek reelection. However, she is exactly sixty years of age. Were she below that cutoff, the probability that she will run for reelection jumps to .94, near certainty. In either case, our model suggests that she will exhibit static ambition and pursue a career in the House. In September of 2005, Matsui's press secretary, Adriana Surfas, confirmed that she would seek reelection in 2006.[119]

Studying the decision to run for office poses several challenges. Identifying the eligibility pool and those in the pool who considered but decided not to run are quite difficult; there is also the danger of incurring the wrath of Congress. Studying the decisions of congressional widows, however, provides a unique opportunity to assess how women might make the decision to pursue a congressional career. Rather than being a monolithic group, there are clear differences between those who resigned after completing their husband's terms and those who went on to serve multiple terms in the House. Women who are younger when they first obtain their husband's seat are more likely to run for reelection. Prior political experience, especially if they worked in a political partnership with their husband, has a substantial effect on whether they will seek their own congressional careers. Finally, cultural factors play a role. Women from outside the South and those who ran since the advent of the Women's Movement in 1970 are also more likely to be careerists. In fact, widows who share all four of these characteristics are almost certain to run again. Over time, congressional widows have come to look more and more like women who run without the benefit of a dead husband—careerists whose objective is long-term service in the House. In this sense, our analysis challenges the conventional stereotype of the congressional widow as a placeholder or demure stand-in.

---

[118] David Whitney, "Matsui Has Money in Bank for '06 Race," *Sacramento Bee*, April 27, 2005, A3.
[119] Interview with Barbara Palmer, September 20, 2005.

4

When Women Run for Higher Office
Static versus Progressive Ambition

While the distinction between discrete and static ambition was the focus of our last chapter, here we broaden our analysis to examine the distinction between static and progressive ambition. Why do some women pursue a career in the House while others leave the security of their seat and run for higher office? When faced with the opportunity to run for the Senate, do women respond to the same strategic considerations as men?

The objective of those with static ambition is to retain their seats and acquire the influence that comes with long service. Representative Nancy Pelosi (D-CA) is an example of a House careerist who has met this goal.[1] Pelosi first came to Congress in June 1987 after winning a special election to fill the vacancy created by the death of Representative Sala Burton (D-CA). During her second term, she served on the Appropriations Committee, one of the most influential committees in the House. In 1992, Pelosi had the opportunity to run for the Senate in California; both Senate seats were available. Senator Alan Cranston had announced his retirement, and Senator Pete Wilson had resigned in January 1991 after he was elected governor. His appointed successor, Republican John Seymour, had to stand for election again in 1992. Pelosi, however, chose not to enter either of the campaigns that ultimately resulted in the election of Democrats Barbara Boxer and Dianne Feinstein. Instead, Pelosi continued to accumulate seniority in the House. She eventually became ranking member of the Appropriations Subcommittee on Foreign Operations.[2] She was then elected minority whip by the Democratic

---

[1] Pelosi was born into a political family. Her father, Thomas D'Alesandro, was a member of the House from 1939 to 1947. He also served as mayor of Baltimore, as did her brother; Karen Foerstel, *Biographical Dictionary of Congressional Women* (Westport, Conn.: Greenwood Press 1999), 216.

[2] Foerstel, 1999, 217.

Caucus during the 107th Congress (2001 session) and rose to the position of minority leader in the 108th Congress (2002 session).[3] In 2004, she was elected to her tenth term in the House. Pelosi's career reflects the payoff for those with static ambition: as she gained seniority, she moved into more powerful leadership positions.

Politicians with progressive ambition attempt to climb the career ladder by running for more desirable and prestigious offices. Progressive ambition is well illustrated by the career of Margaret Chase Smith (R-ME). Smith was a congressional widow who defied the conventional wisdom. Not only did she seek reelection to the House, but she also ran successfully for the Senate and then pursued the very top rung of the American political career ladder, the presidency. After winning her husband's House seat in a special election in 1940, Smith successfully retained her seat in the regular election that fall and was reelected to the House three more times. When Senator Wallace White, the incumbent Republican, retired in 1948, she decided to run for the Senate. She faced three men in the primary. Despite the fact that she met Clyde Smith three years after his divorce, her opponents were not above accusing her of causing the divorce.[4] She won the primary with more votes than the combined total of all her competitors, and then won the general election. Smith became the first woman elected to the House and then to the Senate.[5] In 1964, during an event at the Women's National Press Club, she announced her candidacy for president. On the campaign trail, she handed out muffins, which generated so much publicity that one of her opponents, Nelson Rockefeller, tried to capitalize on her success by giving out his fudge recipe.[6] Smith became the first woman to have a major party place her name in nomination for president; she won twenty-seven delegates at the Republican National Convention.[7] Her congressional career ended in 1972 at the age of seventy-four, when she lost a close election for her fifth Senate term to William Hathaway, a Democratic member of the House. Smith returned to Maine, having served in Congress for more than thirty-two years.

Our analysis in this chapter is designed to explain the different career paths followed by Pelosi and Smith. It is important to keep in mind that congressional careerism—the product of static ambition—is a twentieth-century phenomenon. In fact, the movement of women into the electoral arena began when the desire to pursue long careers in the House reached historic highs.

---

[3] *Biographical Directory of the United States Congress*, http://bioguide.congress.gov/scripts/biodisplay.pl?index=P000197 (accessed June 24, 2005).

[4] Marcy Kaptur, *Women of Congress: A Twentieth-Century Odyssey* (Washington, D.C.: CQ Press, 1996), 89.

[5] As a senator, Smith achieved national attention and acclaim for her "Declaration of Conscience" speech on June 1, 1950. From the Senate floor, she castigated Senator Joseph McCarthy for his reckless accusations and the way his committee conducted its investigations of communist influence. In the wake of this speech, stories in the media suggested her as a possible vice president for Dwight Eisenhower; Foerstel, 1999, 253–56.

[6] Kaptur, 1996, 95.

[7] Kaptur, 1996, 95.

As we pointed out in chapter 2, women were first running for Congress just as the political glass ceiling was being set. In this chapter, we show that the women who overcame this barrier to win a seat in the House are as careerist as their male counterparts. In addition, our analysis of progressive ambition demonstrates that, like men, women are strategic when deciding whether to run for the Senate. This decision systematically varies with the cost of running, the probability of winning, the value of a House seat, and whether the woman is a "risk taker." We then use our analysis of progressive ambition to identify those women currently serving in the House who are most likely to run for the Senate in 2006, 2008, and 2010, and speculate about the presidential prospects of those women currently serving in the Senate.

The Decision to Seek Reelection

We showed in chapter 3 that a substantial proportion of congressional widows exhibited static ambition and sought reelection. Is this true of most women who have served in Congress? How often have the women in Congress exhibited discrete, static, and progressive ambition? Table 4.1 summarizes the service of those women elected to the House between 1916 and 2000.[8] Of the 169 women included in table 4.1, only eight, less than 5 percent, fall into the noncareerist category of discrete ambition. The two best examples of discrete ambition are Isabella Greenway (D-AZ), who retired in 1937 after two terms to spend more time with her family,[9] and Shirley Pettis (D-CA), who also retired after two terms in 1979. The remaining six women are, in one sense or another, special cases. Jeannette Rankin (R-MT) had two very short House careers. After her first election in 1916, she voted against American entry into World War I and then ran unsuccessfully for the Senate in 1918. Rankin again won a House seat in 1940 and, after voting against American entry into World War II, chose not to run for reelection in 1942.[10] Winnifred Stanley (R-NY) was recruited to run for a new, at-large seat in 1942. At the time she agreed to run, it was known that the state legislature would enact a redistricting plan for 1944 that would eliminate this at-large seat.[11] Clare Boothe Luce (R-CT) was elected to the House in 1942 and served two terms. During her second term, she battled the emotional trauma caused by the death of her daughter in an automobile accident. In 1946, Luce announced that she would not seek a third

---

[8] Specifically, this group includes all nonwidows elected to the House between 1916 and 2000. Because they have yet to face the decision to run for a third term, women elected in 2002 and 2004 are not included in the count. The tally also includes the nineteen widows who, as we showed in chapter 3, exhibited static ambition by seeking an additional term after their initial election to succeed their husbands.

[9] Foerstel, 1999, 108.

[10] In January 1968, Rankin, at the age of eighty-seven, returned to Capitol Hill. True to her pacifist roots, she led over 5,000 women, organized as the "Jeannette Rankin Brigade," in a demonstration against the war in Vietnam; see http://www.theglassceiling.com/biographies/bio27.htm (accessed June 16, 2005).

[11] Foerstel, 1999, 261.

Table 4.1 The Political Ambitions of Female Members of the House

Type of Ambition	Number of Women	Percentage
Discrete		
Retired after one or two terms	8	4.7
Static		
Retired after three or more terms	37	27.4
Died after three or more terms	4	2.4
Defeated in primary or general election	44	26.0
Current members who served three or more terms	50	29.6
Total	135	79.8
Progressive		
Ran for Senate	19	11.2
Ran for or appointed to other office	7	4.1
Total	26	15.4

term in the House, converted to Catholicism, and returned to her former career as a writer.[12] Jessica Weis (R-NY) withdrew from her third campaign in 1962 because of illness and died of cancer shortly after completing her second term.[13] Blanche Lincoln (D-AR) was elected to the House in 1992 and reelected in 1994. In January 1996, Lincoln announced that she was pregnant with twins and would not run for reelection in November.[14] Lincoln, however, returned to the political arena in November 1998 when she won the open Senate seat vacated by Democrat Dale Bumpers.

The last woman in this category is Representative Enid Greene (R-UT), who announced her retirement approximately two months after Blanche Lincoln, making her the most recent woman to leave office after a short period of service. In 1992, Greene ran for Congress for the first time and narrowly lost in an open-seat race against Democrat Karen Shepherd. During the campaign, given the conservative constituency, Shepherd ran as a moderate, reform-oriented Democrat and emphasized that "she was a wife and mother while Greene was single."[15] Shepherd outspent Greene $617,000 to $446,000.[16]

---

[12] *Women in History: Living Vignettes of Notable Women in U.S. History,* http://www.lkwdpl.org/wihohio/luce-cla.htm (accessed June 16, 2005).

[13] Foerstel, 1999, 277–78.

[14] Alan Greenblatt and Jonathan D. Salant, "Retirement: Out with the Old and the New: Myers, Lincoln Will Retire," *CQ Weekly,* January 13, 1996, 102.

[15] Michael Barone and Grant Ujifusa, *Almanac of American Politics, 1994* (Washington, D.C.: National Journal, 1993), 1289.

[16] Barone and Ujifusa, 1993, 1290.

The campaign of 1994 featured a rematch with Greene, now wed to Joseph Waldholtz, running under her married name. Waldholtz exploited the vulnerabilities of Shepherd as a first-term incumbent, particularly her vote for the Clinton tax increase of 1993.[17] This time, Waldholtz won.[18] But the spending in the 1994 campaign far surpassed that of the previous race. Shepherd spent $1 million. Waldholtz spent almost twice that, with an estimated $1.6 million coming from her "own resources." Shortly after her swearing in, she appeared to be a rising Republican star and was awarded a seat on the prestigious House Rules Committee. In March 1995, she announced that she was pregnant. Later that year, her political career collapsed. Her husband, who served as her campaign manager, had embezzled $4 million from her father through a phony real estate assets scheme.[19] A large portion of this money had been funneled into Waldholtz's campaign. In March 1996, at the behest of Republican leaders in Washington, D.C., and Utah, Waldholtz announced that she would not seek a second term in the House.[20] On June 6, 1996, Joseph Waldholtz pleaded guilty in federal district court to numerous tax, campaign, and banking violations.[21] Enid divorced him the same day. Subsequent investigations cleared her of any legal wrongdoing.[22] "She trusted her husband," noted her attorney. "A lot of people trust their spouses."[23]

As table 4.1 shows, these examples of discrete ambition are the exception, not the rule. Three times as many women can be classified as exhibiting progressive ambition. Nineteen of these women ran for the Senate and will be discussed later in this chapter. Four women left the House to run for governor. Representative Ella Grasso (D-CT) was elected governor of Connecticut in 1974 and reelected to a second term in 1978. Representative Barbara Kennelly (D-CT) was the Democratic nominee for governor in 1998 but lost her race to Republican John Rowland. Both Representatives Helen Delich Bentley (R-MD) and Jane Harman (D-CA) lost their nomination races for governor, in 1994 and 1998 respectively. In 2000, Harman regained her seat in the House by defeating the incumbent Republican, Steve Kuykendall, who had succeeded her in 1998. In addition, two women left their House seats to run for other offices. In 1978, Representative Yvonne Brathwaite Burke (D-CA) lost her nomination race for California attorney general. Representative Geraldine Ferraro (D-NY) left her house seat to become the first female vice presidential nominee in 1984. This category also includes one appointee:

[17] Michael Barone and Grant Ujifusa, *Almanac of American Politics, 1996* (Washington, D.C.: National Journal, 1995), 1350.

[18] This campaign was actually a three-way race and included Merrill Cook, the president of a mining and explosives company.

[19] Barone and Ujifusa, 1997, 1422; and Foerstel, 1999, 106–7.

[20] Michael Barone and Grant Ujifusa, *Almanac of American Politics, 1998* (Washington, D.C.: National Journal, 1997), 1422.

[21] Dennis Roddy, "Admission of Guilt: Waldholtz Admits Financial Violations, Apologizes to All but Ex-Wife," *Pittsburgh Post Gazette*, June 6, 1996, A6.

[22] Foerstel, 1999, 107.

[23] Roddy, 1996, A6.

Representative Charlotte Reid (R-IL) resigned her House seat after Richard Nixon selected her to serve on the Federal Communications Commission.

Finally, table 4.1 shows that the largest category is static ambition. Nearly 80 percent of the women elected to the House sought long-term careers. This includes forty-one women who retired or died after serving three or more terms, and fifty women in the 109th Congress (2005 session) who have already been elected to three or more terms. An additional forty-four women attempted to pursue careers but suffered electoral defeat. The desire for long careers among women in the House is now the norm.

Examining those who have served "super careers," twenty years or more in the House, is also instructive. Representative John Dingell (D-MI) currently holds the record for longest consecutive service, forty-nine years.[24] Ranking second is former Speaker of the House Sam Rayburn (D-TX), who served continuously from 1913 until his death in 1961. The longest serving woman was Edith Nourse Rogers (R-MA), who was a House member for thirty-six years after being elected in 1925. As expected, among men, "super careers" have increased over the past one hundred years. In 1917, corresponding with our earlier measures of careerism, there were only twenty-six men, 6.0 percent, who had served for ten or more terms in the House. In 1971, just before the number of women in Congress began to rise, there were eighty-seven men, 20.0 percent, who had served for ten or more terms in the House.[25] During the 109th Congress (2005 session), there were seventy-two men, but only four women, who have served for ten or more terms. As table 4.2 shows, few women have enjoyed the opportunity for the "super career." In fact, there have been only fourteen women who served ten or more terms in the House. In the 109th Congress (2005 session), Nancy Johnson (R-CT) and Marcy Kaptur (D-OH) share the title of most senior woman. Both were first elected in 1982 and are currently serving their twelfth terms in the House. The paucity of "super careers" among women is, however, not all that surprising given that 45 percent of the careerist women to serve in the House were elected in 1992 or later. Among the women serving in the 109th Congress (2005 session), almost 90 percent (58/66) were elected between 1992 and 2005.

The House committee leadership in the 109th Congress (2005 session) illustrates the value of lengthy careers most dramatically. Among the twenty-one Republican chairs of the standing House committees, the average number of terms served was ten. Among the Democrats who were ranking members on full committees, the average length of service was thirteen terms. No Republican woman chaired a full committee in the House, but there were nine

[24] Amer, 2004, 4.
[25] Charles Bullock, "House Careerists: Changing Patterns of Longevity and Attrition," *American Political Science Review* 66 (1972): 1295–300.

Table 4.2 Women Who Have Served Ten or More Terms in the House

Name	Year First Elected	Terms
Mary Teresa Norton (D-NJ)	1924	13 terms
Edith Nourse Rogers (R-MA)	1925	18 terms
Frances Bolton (R-OH)	1940	15 terms
Leonor Sullivan (D-MO)	1952	12 terms
Edith Green (D-OR)	1954	10 terms
Martha Griffiths (D-MI)	1954	10 terms
Patricia Schroeder (D-CO)	1972	12 terms
Cardiss Collins (D-IL)	1972	12 terms
Marilyn Lloyd (D-MD)	1974	10 terms
Margaret Roukema (R-NJ)	1980	11 terms
Nancy Johnson (R-CT)	1982	12 terms*
Marcy Kaptur (D-OH)	1982	12 terms*
Louise Slaughter (D-NY)	1986	10 terms*
Nancy Pelosi (D-CA)	1987	10 terms*

*Currently serving in the 109th Congress (2005–2007).

Republican women who chaired subcommittees.[26] Among the nine, the average length of service was 5.6 terms. Four female Democrats served as ranking members of full committees. Their average length of service was seven terms.[27] Examination of seniority and the committee system suggests, then, that the "threshold" for moving into the leadership structure is roughly five terms of service.

What all this suggests is that women in the House are as careerist as their male counterparts. Moreover, almost one-sixth of the women in the House have exhibited progressive ambition and ran for the Senate or another office. Women now have the opportunity to be as careerist as men.

The Decision to Run for Higher Office: The Lure of the Senate

What makes a seat in the Senate attractive to a House member? Why is the Senate considered a "higher step" on the political career ladder? As a smaller chamber whose members are accountable to a statewide electorate, a seat in the Senate is perceived as more prestigious. As an institution, the Senate is less hierarchical. Given the tradition of the filibuster, individual senators have a great deal of power. Not only is there an ethic of "one among equals,"

---

[26] Judy Biggert (IL), Jo Ann Davis (VA), Nancy Johnson (CT), Sue Kelly (NY), Candice Miller (MI), Marilyn Musgrave (CO), Deborah Pryce (OH), Ileana Ros-Lehtinen (FL), and Heather Wilson (NM).

[27] Jane Harman (CA), Juanita Millender-McDonald (CA), Louise Slaughter (NY), and Nydia Velazquez (NY).

but authority within the committee system is more dispersed.[28] Unlike House members, senators need not wait eight or ten years to acquire a position of influence on a committee. For example, all of the new Republicans elected to the Senate in 2004 served as subcommittee chairs in the 109th Congress (2005 session).[29] This dispersion of authority provides senators with greater opportunities for position taking and credit claiming. In addition, the Senate is less rule-bound than the House. The Senate frequently operates on the basis of unanimous consent agreements so that individual members, regardless of seniority, are given influence in structuring the agenda. Fewer restrictions on amendments and the absence of a germaneness rule in floor proceedings also provide greater opportunities for creative legislating.[30]

While the Senate may be more attractive to ambitious politicians, campaigning and winning a seat are more difficult. Running for the Senate is quite different than running for the House. Campaigns for the Senate have to reach a much broader constituency and, consequently, require a shift from "retail politics," cultivating a constituency through personal, one-on-one contact, to "wholesale politics," attracting media attention, continuous and substantial fundraising, and running a media campaign.[31] In fact, many House members who ran for the Senate have lamented how they missed the intimacy and familiarity of their House district campaigns.[32] As Representative James Abourezk (D-SD), who served in both the House and Senate, explained, "House members have a good sense of what their district is. Senators have a harder time getting a handle on a state."[33]

Moreover, fundraising for a Senate race can be daunting. The average cost of running for the Senate in 2004 was almost $2.6 million.[34] The most expensive race in 2004 was the successful effort by Republican John Thune to unseat incumbent Democrat Tom Daschle, the Senate minority leader. The combined cost of the campaign was over $36 million in a state with only 750,000 people. The candidates spent $92.04 per vote. In 2002, women were candidates in the most expensive Senate races. Senator Elizabeth Dole (R-NC) spent almost $14 million and won her open-seat Senate campaign against Erskine Bowles, who spent $13 million. In second place, Senator Jean Carnahan (D-MO) spent

[28] Lewis Froman, *The Congressional Process* (Boston: Little Brown, 1967); and Walter Oleszek, *Congressional Procedures and the Policy Process*, 6th ed. (Washington, D.C.: CQ Press, 2004).

[29] "CQ's Guide to Committees." *CQ Weekly*, April 11, 2005, 898.

[30] "Germaneness" requires that amendments be related to the legislation. For example, a school prayer amendment to the ERA is not germane. See for example Oleszek, 2004; and Barbara Sinclair, *Unorthodox Lawmaking* (Washington, D.C.: CQ Press, 1997).

[31] See for example Ross Baker, *House and Senate*, 2nd ed. (New York: W.W. Norton, 1995), 49–50; and Richard Fenno, *Senators on the Campaign Trail* (Norman: University of Oklahoma Press, 1996).

[32] Baker, 1995, 105–6.

[33] Baker, 1995, 115.

[34] Open Secrets, "2004 Election Overview: Stats at a Glance," http://www.opensecrets.org/overview/stats.asp?cycle=2004&type=A&display=A (accessed June 17, 2005).

over $12 million and lost her bid to retain the seat to which she was appointed just two years earlier after her husband died in a plane crash. Her opponent, Jim Talent, spent $8.3 million.[35] Running in large, populous states, such as California, New Jersey, and New York, can cost tens of millions of dollars. The most expensive Senate race in history was the 2000 campaign of Democrat Jon Corzine in New Jersey. He raised and spent over $63 million, the vast majority of which came from his personal fortune, and defeated his Republican opponent, Bob Franks, who raised and spent $6.5 million.[36] As these examples suggest, the path to the Senate requires the ability to raise substantial campaign funds.

In chapter 2, we showed that, for many years, the political career path to the Senate for women was almost exclusively through appointment after a death or unscheduled vacancy. Overall, of the thirty-three women who served in the Senate, fifteen were interim appointees; only two of the fifteen senators, Hattie Caraway (D-AR) and Maurine Neuberger (D-OR), were subsequently elected. Table 4.3 lists the eighteen women who won election to the Senate, their prior political experience, and the length of their service.

As noted earlier, the first nonwidow elected to the Senate was Margaret Chase Smith in 1948. The next woman, Nancy Landon Kassebaum (R-KS), would not be elected until 1978, thirty years after Smith's initial Senate campaign. Kassebaum is among the least experienced of the women elected to the Senate. She had only two years of nonelective experience on the Kansas governmental ethics commission and had only two years of elective experience on a local school board.[37] Kassebaum did have the advantage of name recognition and the tinge of political celebrity. She was the daughter of Alfred Landon, former governor of Kansas and Republican nominee for president in 1936. This family connection proved useful in the crowded 1978 Senate primary field that included eight men and another woman, future Representative Jan Meyers. Kassebaum won the Republican primary with 31 percent of the vote and easily defeated her Democratic opponent.[38]

Very few women came to the Senate without prior political experience. The Senate was the first elective office for only three women. Although she never held elective office, Susan Collins (R-ME) gained twenty years of nonelective experience as a congressional staffer. She worked on the staff of Senator William Cohen (R-ME) from 1975 to 1987 and rose to the position of staff director of the Senate Governmental Affairs Subcommittee on the Oversight

---

[35] Open Secrets, "The Big Picture: 2002 Cycle, Most Expensive Races," http://www.opensecrets.org/bigpicture/topraces.asp?cycle=2002 (accessed June 27, 2005).

[36] Open Secrets, "New Jersey Senate Race: 2000 Campaign Money Profile," http://www.opensecrets.org/races/summary.asp?ID=NJS1&Cycle=2000 (accessed June 17, 2005).

[37] Foerstel, 1999, 143.

[38] Michael Barone, Grant Ujifusa, and Douglas Matthews, *Almanac of American Politics, 1980* (New York: E. P. Dutton, 1979), 318.

Table 4.3 Women Elected to the Senate

Name	Prior Experience: Nonelective	Prior Experience: Elective	Terms in the House	Dates of Senate Service
Margaret Chase Smith (R-ME)	4 years	9 years	4	1949–1973
Nancy Landon Kassebaum (R-KS)	2 years	2 years	0	1979–1997
Paula Hawkins (R-FL)	2 years	8 years	0	1981–1987
Barbara Mikulski (D-MD)	None	16 years	5	1987–present
Dianne Feinstein (D-CA)	6 years	18 years	0	1993–present
Barbara Boxer (D-CA)	2 years	16 years	5	1993–present
Carol Moseley Braun (D-IL)	9 years	11 years[a]	0	1993–1999
Kay Bailey Hutchison (R-TX)	3 years	8 years[a, b]	0	1993–present
Patty Murray (D-WA)	6 years	8 years[a]	0	1993–present
Olympia Snowe (R-ME)	4 years	22 years[a]	8	1995–present
Mary Landrieu (D-LA)	None	16 years[a, b]	0	1997–present
Susan Collins (R-ME)	20 years	None	0	1997–present
Blanche Lincoln (D-AR)	3 years	4 years	2	1999–present
Debbie Stabenow (D-MI)	None	24 years[a]	2	2001–present
Hillary Rodham Clinton (D-NY)	18 years	None	0	2001–present
Maria Cantwell (D-WA)	None	9 years[a]	1	2001–present
Lisa Murkowski (R-AK)	5 years	4 years[a]	0	2002–present
Elizabeth Dole (R-NC)	7 years	None	0	2003–present

[a]Service includes election to state legislature.
[b]Service includes election to statewide office.

of Government Management.[39] In addition to holding several administrative positions in Maine, Collins also won the Republican nomination for governor in 1994 but was defeated in the general election. Hillary Clinton and Elizabeth Dole are both part of contemporary "power couples" and were far from inexperienced. Hillary Clinton served as legal counsel to the House Judiciary Committee during the impeachment proceedings against President Richard Nixon in 1974. She served as first lady of Arkansas for ten years and the first lady of the United States for eight years. As first lady, she headed the administration's task force on health care reform and played a prominent role in shaping the domestic policy agenda of the administration.[40] Elizabeth Dole served as a cabinet member in two presidential administrations. From 1983 to 1987, she was secretary of transportation in the Reagan administration and served in the Bush administration as secretary of labor from 1989 to 1990. In 1999, she campaigned for the Republican presidential nomination but withdrew before the start of the primary season in 2000.[41] Both Clinton and Dole entered their Senate races with widespread name recognition. Clinton defeated four-term House incumbent Rick Lazio (R-NY) and Dole defeated Erskine Bowles, a former chief of staff in the Clinton administration.

Table 4.3 reveals that the sixteen women elected to the Senate since 1980 had substantial prior experience. Collectively, these women accumulated 249 years of political experience before entering the Senate, with an average of 15.6 years. Thirteen of the sixteen served in elective office. The average time in elective office among the thirteen was 12.6 years. Three senators, Olympia Snowe (R-ME), Debbie Stabenow (D-MI), and Maria Cantwell (D-WA), followed the classic pattern of ambition, moving from the state legislature to the U.S. House and then to the Senate.[42] Overall, seven women senators previously served in the U.S. House. What prompted these women to run? Can we predict which female House members will run for the Senate and exhibit progressive ambition?

Understanding Progressive Ambition

In chapter 3, we focused upon the widows of the House to show that there were systematic differences between those who retired and those who sought a career, and thereby illustrated the distinction between discrete and static ambition. Having shown in this chapter that the women of the House are as careerist as their male counterparts, we now come to the question of progressive

---

[39] *Biographical Directory of Congress,* http://bioguide.congress.gov/scripts/biodisplay.pl?index=C001035 (accessed June 13, 2005).

[40] Bob Woodward, *The Agenda: Inside the Clinton White House* (New York: Simon and & Schuster, 1994).

[41] Harold Stanley and Richard Niemi, *Vital Statistics on American Politics 2003–2004* (Washington, D.C.: CQ Press, 2003), 67.

[42] Cantwell's path was not continuous, however. She was elected to the House in 1992 but defeated for reelection in the 2nd District of Washington in 1994 by Rick White. In 2000, she defeated incumbent Slade Gorton to win her Senate seat.

ambition, the decision to forsake one office to run for a higher and more prestigious position. Here, we build upon the work of political scientist David Rohde. Refining Schlesinger's distinction between static and progressive ambition, Rohde assumes that almost all members of the House possess progressive ambition in the following sense: if a member of the House, "on his first day of service, were offered a Senate seat . . . without cost or risk, he would take it."[43] In other words, all things being equal, most politicians would prefer advancing to a higher office. There are, however, costs and risks. In a given election cycle, House members exhibit static ambition not only because they value their current office, but also because they perceive the costs of running and the risks to their political career as too high. The question then becomes: under what conditions will members forsake a career in the House and run for the Senate?

The Opportunity to Run

First and foremost, the decision to run for the Senate is not an arbitrary choice made by members of the House. Rather, the strategic calculations that underlie this choice depend on whether there is an *opportunity to run*. The concept of opportunity is critical to understanding the movement of politicians through the hierarchy of offices. Opportunities are a function of the party of the incumbent and the electoral calendar: a House member has an opportunity to run for the Senate when there is a scheduled election that involves an incumbent of the opposition party seeking reelection or an open seat vacated by an incumbent of either party. We assume that no opportunity exists when an incumbent of the House member's own party stands for reelection to the Senate. In this situation, the member must challenge the incumbent senator in a primary, must risk alienating party members by instigating an intraparty dispute, and, as we pointed out in chapter 2, would most likely lose. In addition, in order to run for the Senate, House members must surrender their seats.[44] This requires that members consider the costs of giving up their seats as well as the probability of winning the Senate election.

---

[43] David Rohde, "Risk-Bearing and Progressive Ambition: The Case of Members of the United States House of Representatives," *American Journal of Political Science* 23 (1979): 1–26. Rohde also explores House members who consider running for governor. Our analysis focuses solely on the Senate. As noted earlier, there have only been only four women who left the House to run for governor. See also Paul Hain, Philip Roeder, and Manuel Avalos, "Risk and Progressive Candidacies: An Extension of Rohde's Model," *American Journal of Political Science* 25 (1981): 188–92; Paul Brace, "Progressive Ambition in the House: A Probabilistic Approach," *Journal of Politics* 46 (1984): 556–71; and Gary Copeland, "Choosing to Run: Why House Members Seek Election to the Senate," *Legislative Studies Quarterly* 14 (1989): 549–65.

[44] There is one qualification in our definition of "opportunity." If a woman is elected to the House in a special election at any time before a regularly scheduled election (e.g., in March of an election year), the subsequent general election in November, regardless of conditions, is not counted as an opportunity. As Rohde notes, "[B]ecause of the necessity of planning ahead for a statewide race, such congressmen are almost precluded from running and, in fact, no such member did run"; Rohde, 1979, 14.

Based on these criteria, we calculated the number of opportunities for the 171 careerist women who were elected to the House between 1916 and 2002. During this period, the opportunities to run for a Senate seat varied widely. Sixty of the women who served in the House, over one-third, had no opportunity to run for the Senate. In fact, among these sixty, there were fifteen women who served in the House for ten years or more without an opportunity. Among the remaining women, the number of opportunities ranged from one to nine. Fifteen female House members had four or more opportunities to run over the course of their careers. The opportunity "leaders" were Mary Teresa Norton (D-NJ), with nine opportunities over her thirteen-term career; Edith Nourse Rogers (R-MA), with eight opportunities in eighteen terms; and Marge Roukema (R-NJ), with seven opportunities over the course of her eleven-term career.

According to Rohde, when faced with an opportunity to run, a member of the House will make a strategic calculation about whether to give up the House seat and seek election to the Senate. This decision will be a function of four factors: (1) the costs of running, (2) the probability of winning, (3) the value of the member's current office, and (4) whether the member is a risk taker.[45]

Costs of Running

As a general indicator of the costs of running, we use the size of the state, which captures several challenges that House members face when running for the Senate. The size of the state reflects the coincidence of House and Senate constituencies; the smaller the state, the more a House district overlaps with the target electorate in a Senate race. The more overlap there is, the more the character and strategy of the campaigns will be similar and the jump from the House to the Senate is easier. In fact, when House members run for the Senate in states with only one or two congressional districts, they use a virtually duplicate campaign strategy.[46] But for House members from large, populous states, running for the Senate requires a "monumental change" in campaign style and tactics in order to reach a larger audience.[47] Rather than using population to measure the cost of running, we follow Rohde's logic and use the number of congressional districts in a state as a measure of size. Small states are those with three or fewer congressional districts; large states are those with twenty-two or more congressional districts.

Our data show that the opportunities to run are distributed in roughly the same proportion as the women elected from states of different size. Almost 13 percent of the careerist women elected to the House hailed from states with

---

[45] Rohde, 1979, 5–12.
[46] Baker, 1995, 106.
[47] Baker, 1995, 105.

three or fewer congressional districts; 12.6 percent of all opportunities to run occurred in these small states. Similarly, 36.3 percent of the careerist women were elected from large states; large states accounted for 34.3 percent of the opportunities. Our expectation is that the probability of running for a Senate seat, given the opportunity, will vary inversely with the size of the state. The smaller the state, the more likely the female House member will run for the Senate.

Probability of Winning

The probability of winning is influenced by incumbency as well as party. Because incumbents are virtually assured reelection, the opportunity to run in an open seat is the most desirable because this presents the highest chance of winning. The next best scenario would be to run against a marginal incumbent of the opposition party. Typically, marginal incumbents are perceived to be vulnerable and often make fundraising by the opposition party easier. Running against a safe incumbent is the least desirable. In our data, 39.7 percent of the opportunities occurred in open-seat elections; 32.6 percent were in situations where a marginal incumbent, defined as an incumbent who won the previous election with less than 55 percent of the vote, was seeking reelection; and 27.6 percent involved races in which the opponent was a safe incumbent. Given an opportunity, we expect that female House members will be more likely to run for the Senate in open-seat elections and least likely to run in elections with a safe incumbent.

Value of the Member's Current Office

The value of a House seat to its current occupant is largely determined by seniority. In general, this value grows as the member serves more terms and as both knowledge of the policy process and the internal influence of the member increase. As noted earlier, House members typically rise to a position of influence in the committee system after five terms. Once this point is reached, the House seat substantially increases in value as the member moves upward in the leadership hierarchy. As this occurs, there are greater costs in giving up the House seat that make the Senate seat less attractive. Therefore, House members who have served five or more terms are going to value their seats more than House members who are midcareer. We define "midcareer" members as those who have served between two and five terms during the year in which the opportunity to run occurs. Of the 239 opportunities to run in our data, 56.9 percent (136) fell to those at midcareer. We expect, then, that the women most likely to run for the Senate are House members at midcareer.

Risk Takers

Finally, the decision to run for the Senate depends on the House member's willingness to take risks. As one House member who ran for the Senate put it, "The senate seat is by definition more precarious politically than the average House seat. . . . [T]here is more uncertainty."[48] We recognize that any campaign for office requires candidates to put a great deal at risk. However, the degree of risk is relative. As Rohde explains, "[I]f two House members are presented with similar opportunities to seek higher office, and one is a 'risk taker' and the other is not, then the 'risk taker' will have a greater probability of running for higher office than the other."[49]

Risk taking focuses upon the circumstances in which a member *first* runs, successfully or unsuccessfully, for a seat in the House. Risk takers are defined as those who first run for the House in a campaign where the probability of winning was low. These are races when a House member ran (1) against an incumbent of her own party for the nomination in a primary, (2) against an incumbent of the opposition party in the general election, or (3) in an open district where the opposition party had a secure hold on the district.[50] Of the 171 female careerists in the House, sixty-six, 38.6 percent, are classified as risk takers. Thirty-six defeated incumbents in the general election, ten defeated incumbents of their own party in the primary, and twenty won open seats that previously were secure for the opposition party. Of the sixty-six risk takers, however, twenty-three, 34.8 percent, had no opportunity to run for the Senate during their House careers. Among those with opportunities, we expect that risk takers will run for the Senate in proportionally greater numbers than non–risk takers.

Explaining Progressive Ambition

There has been little attention devoted to studying the decisions made by female members of the House to run for the Senate.[51] Our core proposition is that women behave in a strategic manner and, therefore, the decisions of women serving in the House to seek a seat in the Senate will be subject to the same systematic influences identified by Rohde. The likelihood that a female member of the House will run for the Senate when she has the opportunity increases when she comes from a small state, the probability of winning is high, she is midcareer, and she is a risk taker. Of the 238 opportunities in our data set, there were nineteen cases, 8.0 percent, when a female House member

---

[48] Baker, 1995, 114.
[49] Rohde, 1979, 12.
[50] This is the definition employed by Rohde, 1979. In open districts where the opposition party held the seat, a secure hold is determined by averaging the proportion of the two-party vote won in the three previous elections. By Rohde's definition, those districts where the opposition party averaged 57 percent of the vote or more are labeled "secure."
[51] Rohde's analysis covers the years from 1954 to 1974. Of the 1,463 opportunities examined, only 43 involved an opportunity for a female member to run for the Senate.

actually ran for the Senate. Clearly, this is a "rare event."[52] The rarity of running for the Senate, however, is not confined to women. Rohde's analysis covered the years of 1954 to 1974. Of the 1,463 opportunities for House members to run for a Senate seat, only eighty-five members, about 6 percent, chose to run.[53] Thus, it appears that overall, women are about as likely as men to pursue the Senate.

As table 4.4 shows, the size of the state is related to the likelihood that a woman will run for the Senate. The proportion of opportunities resulting in a bid for the Senate are 23.3 percent (7/30) in small states and 5.8 percent (12/208) in medium and large states. Two of the candidacies come from the state of Maine. Margaret Chase Smith (R-ME) served in the House when the state had three congressional districts, and Olympia Snowe later served as one of the state's two representatives when she ran for the Senate. The other small state candidates include Representatives Jeannette Rankin, a Republican from Montana; Claudine Schneider, a Republican from Rhode Island; Gracie Pfost, a Democrat from Idaho; and Patsy Mink, a Democrat, and Patricia Saiki, a Republican, both from Hawaii.

The overlap among constituencies in small states is well illustrated by the case of Jeannette Rankin (R-MT). In 1916, Montana elected its two representatives using an at-large, statewide arrangement. Thus, Rankin campaigned for her House seat in what was a de facto Senate constituency. In that election, there were six candidates running for two House seats: two Democrats, two Republicans, and two Socialists. One Democrat, John Evans, was an incumbent. In the election, Rankin was elected to the House by finishing in second place, with 76,932 votes to 84,499 for Evans. In 1918, the Montana legislature replaced the at-large arrangement with two single-member districts. Rankin, now a controversial figure because of her vote against entry into World War I, was placed in the same district as Evans, the incumbent Democrat.[54] Instead of challenging Evans, Rankin opted to run statewide for the Republican nomination for Senate. She lost the primary and unsuccessfully ran in the general election as an independent candidate.

The decision to run for the Senate is also clearly based on the probability of winning. The proportion of women pursuing an opportunity is the highest when the odds of winning are the highest, 10.5 percent (10/95) in open-seat contests and 9.0 percent (7/78) in races with a marginal incumbent.

---

[52] In addition to its substantive meaning, the term has statistical consequences. The methodological requirements for working with rare events are fully addressed in Palmer and Simon, 2003, 133–35. We use three alternative techniques to estimate the statistical model: a probit, a logit, and a logit model adjusted for rare events. See Gary King and Langche Zeng, "Logistic Regression in Rare Events Data," *Political Analysis* 9 (2001): 1–27; and Michael Tomz, Gary King, and Langche Zeng, *RELOGIT: Rare Events Logistical Regression, Version 1.1* (Cambridge, Mass.: Harvard University Press, 1999). The results of estimating these models are consistent with the descriptive statistics reported here.

[53] Rohde, 1979, 18.

[54] Foerstal and Foerstal, 1996, 4.

Table 4.4 Progressive Ambition among Female Incumbents in the House

	Percentage of Opportunities in Which Female House Members Ran for the Senate
Cost of Running	
Small state	23.3%
	(7/30)
Medium or large state	5.8%
	(12/208)
Probability of Winning	
Open seat	10.5%
	(10/95)
Marginal incumbent of opposition party	9.0%
	(7/78)
Safe incumbent of opposition party	3.1%
	(2/65)
Value of House Seat	
Midcareer (2–5 terms)	10.3%
	(14/136)
Early or late career	4.9%
	(5/102)
Risk Taking	
Member is a risk taker	12.2%
	(12/98)
Member is not a risk taker	5.0%
	(7/149)

Only 3.1 percent of female House members ran for the Senate in states with a safe incumbent; two women out of sixty-five chose to exercise their opportunity when a safe incumbent of the opposition party stood for reelection, Representatives Bobbi Fiedler (R-CA) and Claudine Schneider (R-RI). In 1986, with Democrat incumbent Senator Alan Cranston standing for reelection, Fiedler gave up her House seat to enter the Republican primary. Fiedler was a single-issue candidate who rose in politics as an opponent of busing. She was first elected to the House in 1980, defeating a Democrat incumbent, James Corman.[55] In 1986, she was the only woman among the thirteen candidates

---

[55] Barone and Ujifusa, 1985, 147–48.

seeking the Republican nomination. Fiedler finished in fourth place in a field of candidates that included Arthur Laffer, the advocate of supply-side economics, and Eldridge Cleaver, a former Black Panther and author of *Soul on Ice*.[56] Schneider, serving her fifth term in the House, ran unopposed for the Republican nomination for the Senate in 1990. In November, she faced Senator Claiborne Pell, the incumbent Democrat seeking his sixth term. In what was described as an "exquisitely polite race," Pell defeated Schneider, 62 to 38 percent.[57]

Table 4.4 also shows that the value of the House seat influences the decision to run for the Senate. Twice as many women who were midcareer, 10.3 percent, acted on the opportunity to run for the Senate compared to those in their first terms or serving six or more terms, only 4.9 percent. For example, in 1980, Representative Elizabeth Holtzman (D-NY), after serving in the House for four terms, ran for the Senate with the intention of challenging incumbent Republican Jacob Javits, who was seeking his fifth term. The field of Democratic candidates included John Lindsay, a former Republican mayor of New York who switched parties, and Bess Meyerson, a former Miss America and longtime panelist on the television quiz show, *I've Got a Secret*.[58] While Holtzman handily won the Democratic primary, Javits—among the most liberal Republicans in the U.S. Senate—was defeated in the Republican primary by Alfonse D'Amato, a township supervisor and functionary in the Nassau County Republican Party.[59] Javits, however, won the nomination of the New York Liberal Party. As a result, voters in New York could choose among three candidates: the Democrat Holtzman, the Republican D'Amato, and Javits, now listed on the ballot as the candidate for the Liberal Party. In November, D'Amato narrowly defeated Holtzman, 45 to 44 percent. The difference in the contest was Javits; he won over 660,000 votes. Many of these Javits voters probably would have supported Holtzman over D'Amato in a two-candidate race.[60]

It is easy to understand why more senior women did not give up their seats in the House to run for the Senate. For example, when faced with the opportunity to run in 1972, Representative Martha Griffiths (D-MI) was the fourth ranking member of the House Ways and Means Committee. Despite several opportunities during her career, Representative Patricia Schroeder (D-CO) chose to maintain her position as chair of the Armed Services Subcommittee on Military Installations and Facilities.[61] Republican women made similar

---

[56] Jay Matthews, "California's GOP Primary a Free-for-All," *Washington Post*, June 1, 1986, A8; and Eldridge Cleaver, *Soul on Ice* (New York: McGraw-Hill, 1968).

[57] Michael Barone and Grant Ujifusa, *Almanac of American Politics 1992* (Washington, D.C.: National Journal, 1991), 1103.

[58] See http://bess-myerson.biography.ms (accessed June 20, 2005).

[59] This county organization is described as "one of the last of the old-fashioned political organizations"; Alan Ehrenhart, ed., *Politics in America 1982* (Washington, D.C.: CQ Press, 1981), 803.

[60] Ehrenhart, 1981, 803.

[61] Michael Barone and Grant Ujifusa, *Almanac of American Politics 1990* (Washington, D.C.: National Journal, 1989), 196.

decisions after their party captured control of the House in 1994, including Representative Marge Roukema (R-NJ), who chaired the Subcommittee on Financial Institutions and Consumer Credit of the House Banking and Financial Services Committee,[62] and Representative Nancy Johnson (R-CT), a high-ranking member of the Ways and Means Committee who chaired its Subcommittee on Health.[63]

Finally, risk taking exerts a noticeable impact on the decision to run. Among those classified as risk takers, 12.2 percent (12/98) of the opportunities resulted in a run for the Senate. The percentage for non–risk takers was less than half, 5.0 percent (7/149). The behavior of risk takers is well illustrated by the career of Debbie Stabenow (D-MI). After a long career in the Michigan state legislature, Stabenow ran for the House for the first time in 1996 by challenging and defeating a Republican incumbent, Representative Dick Chrysler. After two terms in the House, she decided to run for Senate, once again taking on a Republican incumbent. In 2000, Stabenow won an uncontested Democratic primary and challenged Senator Spencer Abraham. Despite being outspent $13 million to $7.9 million, Stabenow defeated Abraham, winning 50.5 percent of the two-party vote.[64]

Denise Majette (D-GA) is another example of a risk taker. In 2002, Majette challenged the Democratic incumbent, Representative Cynthia McKinney (D-GA), in the primary. McKinney became known as one of the more outspoken members of the House, for example, faxing a memo to news organizations in 2000 that Al Gore, the Democratic presidential nominee, had a low "Negro tolerance level,"[65] and claiming that members of the Bush administration had prior knowledge of the September 11 attacks.[66] Georgia has an open primary system, and Republican leaders encouraged party members to cross over and vote for Majette. Evidently, the strategy worked: Majette beat McKinney with 58 percent of the vote and thus unseated a sitting Democratic incumbent. A group of McKinney supporters filed a lawsuit, calling the "malicious" crossover voting a violation of the Voting Rights Act and asking that the results be thrown out.[67] Two years later, McKinney announced that she would run against Majette and reclaim her House seat. The next day, Majette, who qualified as a risk taker under our definition because she challenged McKinney in her first campaign for the

---

[62] Barone and Ujifusa, 1995, 860.

[63] Michael Barone and Richard Cohen, *Almanac of American Politics, 2004* (Washington, D.C.: National Journal, 2003), 353.

[64] Barone and Cohen, 2003, 815–17.

[65] "McKinney, Cynthia A.," in *CQ's Politics in America 2002: The 107th Congress*, CQ Electronic Library, CQ Voting and Elections Collection (Washington, D.C.: CQ Press, 2001), http://library.cqpress.com/elections/pia107-0453055035, document ID pia107-0453055035.

[66] J. L. Moore, "Majority-Minority District," in *Elections A to Z*, CQ Electronic Library, CQ Voting and Elections Collection (Washington, D.C.: CQ Press, 2003), http://library.cqpress.com/elections/elaz2d-156-7490-402760, document ID elaz2d-156-7490-402760.

[67] "Federal Court Asked to Throw Out McKinney Defeat," Associated Press State and Local Wire, October 4, 2002.

House, announced she would give up her House seat and run to replace retiring Democratic Senator Zell Miller. While Majette won the Democratic nomination, she lost the general election to Republican Johnny Isakson with only 40 percent of the vote. McKinney, however, reclaimed her seat in the House.

Overall, table 4.4 shows that each of our four expectations is met. The decision to run for the Senate is a strategic calculation based on the costs of running, the probability of winning, the value of the member's House seat, and whether the member is a risk taker. Thus, the difference between static and progressive ambition among the women in the House is systematic and predictable. Table 4.5 summarizes the electoral fate of those sitting female House members who gave up their seats to run for the Senate.[68] Four women were defeated in their party's primary, ten won their party's nomination but lost in the general election, and five were elected to the Senate. The list includes several campaigns that illustrate the intensity and, at times, nasty character of Senate elections.

For example, the 1950 contest for the open Senate seat in California ranks as one of the most unusual and bitter campaigns in modern history. The contest featured two members of California's delegation to the House, Democrat Helen Gahagan Douglas, first elected in 1944, and Republican Richard Nixon, first elected in 1946. Nixon had become a national figure through his service on the House Un-American Activities Committee and the celebrated conspiracy and perjury investigation of former State Department official Alger Hiss.[69] The campaign themes emerged during the primary season, when Manchester Boddy, the publisher of the *Los Angeles Daily News* and Douglas's opponent in the Democratic primary, charged her with being "part of a small subversive clique of red-hots" and giving "comfort to the Soviet tyranny."[70] In spite of these attacks, Douglas defeated Boddy, but the divisive Democratic contest provided Nixon with a clear strategy. Using rhetoric that previously appeared in the California newspapers, Nixon commonly referred to Douglas as the "Pink Lady."[71] His campaign organization distributed "the pink sheet," fliers critical of Douglas's voting record that were printed on pink paper.[72] In stump speeches, Nixon regularly criticized Douglas by asserting that she was "pink right down to her underwear."[73] For her part, Douglas

---

[68] There are two other women who have served in both the House and Senate, but they were not sitting House members when they ran for the Senate. Blanche Lincoln (D-AR) served in the House from 1992 to 1996; she opted not to run for the House to retain her seat in 1996 because she was pregnant with twins. She ran for the Senate in 1998. Maria Cantwell (D-WA) was elected to the House in 1992 and was defeated in her 1994 reelection bid. She ran for Senate in 2000.

[69] Stephen Ambrose, *Nixon: The Education of a Politician, 1913–1962* (New York: Simon & Schuster, 1987), 166–96.

[70] Ambrose, 1987, 210.

[71] Greg Mitchell, *Tricky Dick and the Pink Lady: Richard Nixon vs. Helen Gahagan Douglas—Sexual Politics and the Red Scare, 1950* (New York: Random House, 1998).

[72] Ambrose, 1987, 216.

[73] Ambrose, 1987, 218.

Table 4.5 Sitting Female House Members Who Ran for the Senate

Name	State	Party	Year	Outcome
Jeannette Rankin	Montana	R	1918	Lost primary to Oscar Lanstrum
Ruth Hanna McCormick	Illinois	R	1930	Lost general to James Lewis
Margaret Chase Smith	Maine	R	1948	**Elected to the Senate**
Helen Gahagan Douglas	California	D	1950	Lost general to Richard Nixon
Gracie Pfost	Idaho	D	1962	Lost general to Len Jordan
Patsy Mink	Hawaii	D	1976	Lost primary to Spark Matsunaga
Bella Abzug	New York	D	1976	Lost primary to Patrick Moynihan
Elizabeth Holtzman	New York	D	1980	Lost general to Alfonse D'Amato
Millicent Fenwick	New Jersey	R	1982	Lost general to Frank Lautenberg
Barbara Mikulski	Maryland	D	1986	**Elected to the Senate**
Bobbi Fiedler	California	R	1986	Lost primary to Ed Zschau
Lynn Martin	Illinois	R	1990	Lost general to Paul Simon
Claudine Schneider	Rhode Island	R	1990	Lost general to Claiborne Pell
Patricia Saiki	Hawaii	R	1990	Lost general to Daniel Akaka
Barbara Boxer	California	D	1992	**Elected to the Senate**
Olympia Snowe	Maine	R	1994	**Elected to the Senate**
Linda Smith	Washington	R	1998	Lost general to Patty Murray
Debbie Stabenow	Michigan	D	2000	**Elected to the Senate**
Denise Majette	Georgia	D	2004	Lost general to Johnny Isakson

popularized the term "Tricky Dick" and referred to Nixon as a "pipsqueak" and a "pee wee."[74] Ironically, Douglas's candidacy received the support of Ronald Reagan, who was then serving as president of the Screen Actors Guild, while John F. Kennedy, a member of the House, delivered a $1,000 donation to the Nixon campaign from his father, Joseph P. Kennedy.[75] Capitalizing upon the unpopular Truman administration and the growing fear of communism, Nixon soundly defeated Douglas with 59.2 percent of the two-party vote.

In 1976, Representative Bella Abzug (D-NY), a three-term House incumbent and widely recognized leader of the Women's Movement, announced her candidacy for the seat held by the Conservative Party incumbent, James Buckley. Abzug was one of five Democratic candidates who included former Attorney General Ramsey Clark and Daniel Patrick Moynihan, a professor who had served in the administrations of Kennedy, Johnson, Nixon, and Ford. Abzug and Moynihan emerged as the front-runners. Moynihan criticized

---

[74] Mitchell, 1998, ch. 1.
[75] Ambrose quotes Kennedy as telling Nixon that "I obviously can't endorse you but it isn't going to break my heart if you can turn the Senate's loss into Hollywood's gain;" Ambrose, 1987, 211.

Abzug as too liberal and too pacifist. Abzug stressed Moynihan's link to the Nixon administration. At one point in the campaign, Abzug ran a radio ad featuring a recording of Nixon introducing Moynihan as his advisor on domestic policy. The ad began with the announcement "[T]he following tape comes to you from the Nixon White House." When it was pointed out that Nixon made the introduction a month before he took office, the ad was taken off the air.[76] Moynihan narrowly defeated Abzug in the primary, 36.4 to 35.3 percent, and went on to defeat Buckley, 54.7 to 45.3 percent, in the general election.

In 1982, an open Senate seat was created in New Jersey when Democratic Senator Harrison Williams resigned from his seat in the wake of expulsion proceedings stemming from his indictment in the ABSCAM scandal.[77] Representative Millicent Fenwick, a Republican first elected to the House with the "Watergate Class" of 1974, entered the race to succeed Williams. With a reputation as a likeable pipe-smoking eccentric,[78] Fenwick gained notoriety for her resemblance to Congresswoman Lacey Davenport, a character in the *Doonesbury* comic strip by Garry Trudeau.[79] Despite attacks on her voting record as too "liberal," Fenwick defeated Republican Jeffrey Bell in the Republican primary. Frank Lautenberg, the multimillionaire CEO of Automatic Data Processing, surprisingly emerged from the field of ten candidates to win the Democratic nomination. In the fall campaign, Lautenberg questioned Fenwick's fitness for the job, accused her of supporting "voting-rights opponent Strom Thurmond," and outspent her $6.4 million to $2.6 million.[80] During one of their televised debates, Fenwick said, "If my opponent had spent these floods of money on explaining his position, I would have nothing to say. But too much, in my opinion, has been spent attacking falsely my record and my position and my character. I call it outrageous."[81] Despite trailing Fenwick by

---

[76] Tom Wicker, *New York Times*, September 12, 1976, sec. 4, 17; James Reston, *New York Times*, September 5, 1976, sec. 4, 13; and Ronald Smothers, *New York Times*, September 4, 1976, 11. These sources were obtained from the Information Bank Abstracts made available by Lexis-Nexis. The original titles of the stories are not reported in these abstracts.

[77] Ehrenhart, 1981, 745–46. In 1980, the FBI conducted an elaborate sting operation and caught several House members on videotape taking thousands of dollars from a fake sheik, Kambir Abdul Rahman (actually an ex-convict in disguise), in exchange for promises of influence on the Hill. One of the more infamous images was of Representative Richard Kelly (R-FL), who was taped stuffing $25,000 into his coat and pants as he asked, "Does it show?" Six members of Congress were ultimately sentenced to jail; Shelly Ross, *Fall from Grace: Sex, Scandal, and Corruption in American Politics from 1702 to the Present* (New York: Ballantine Books, 1988), 257–61.

[78] Fenwick began smoking a pipe when her doctor advised her to stop chain-smoking cigarettes. Although there were always two pipes in her purse, she stopped being photographed with them because she believed "it would be a bad influence on the young"; Joseph Sullivan, "U.S. Senate Race Tops Jersey Elections," *New York Times*, October 31, 1982, 40.

[79] Barone and Ujifusa, 1985, 832. One Doonesbury website noted that "Lacy [*sic*] arrived in Congress two years before Mrs. Fenwick did, but the similarities seemed too distinctive to be coincidental. Indeed, so many people assumed Lacey was Millicent, it seemed ungallant to deny it"; see http://www.doonesbury.com/strip/faqs/faq_ch.html (accessed June 20, 2005).

[80] Michael Norman, "Mrs. Fenwick and Lautenberg Meet in Final Debate," *New York Times*, November 1, 1982, B13.

[81] Norman, 1982, "Mrs. Fenwick," B13.

eighteen points in voter surveys at the start of the campaign, Lautenberg won the general election with 51.5 percent of the two-party vote.[82]

All of these female representatives ran when the value of their seats was relatively low; all were midcareer members of the House. Table 4.6 shows how the value of a seat interacts with the other factors that influence the decision to run for the Senate.[83] As we did in chapter 3 to predict which congressional widows would seek House careers, we can calculate the probability that a female member of the House will act on the opportunity to run for the Senate.[84] Probabilities equal to or greater than .50 lead to a prediction of progressive ambition.

The top row of table 4.6 reports the probability of running for those female House members who are not at midcareer. The probabilities are typically small; there are only two situations where the probability of running exceeds .25, risk takers in small states with either an open seat or a marginal incumbent. The bottom row shows that the probability of running increases substantially for those members in midcareer; seven of the profiles equal or exceed .25. Aside from the stage of career, the most noteworthy differences occur between risk takers and non–risk takers. For each situation, the probability of running is substantially greater for risk takers compared to their non-risk-taking counterparts. Risk-taking, midcareer female representatives facing an open seat in a small state have a .70 probability of running.

Looking to the Future: Running for the Senate

We can use our analysis of progressive ambition to speculate about those women serving in the 109th Congress (2005 session) who are well situated to run for the Senate in 2006, 2008, and 2010. We first identified those women

---

[82] Fenwick was actually quite surprised about her defeat and admitted, "I never thought I would lose. . . . The fascination of that job is that I couldn't wait to get there"; Michael Norman, "Rep. Fenwick Tries to Figure Out Why She Lost," *New York Times*, November 4, 1982, B15. When asked what she would do after leaving Congress, Fenwick replied that she planned on "sleeping late, take up gardening and 'get fat on truffles and veal piccata'"; Norman, 1982, "Rep. Fenwick," B15. Lautenberg retired in 2000 after three terms in the Senate. In 2002, he reentered electoral politics in circumstances similar to those of 1982. Amidst growing charges of corruption, incumbent Democrat Robert Torricelli withdrew from his reelection campaign in September 2002. The New Jersey Democratic Party won a court victory that allowed the party to substitute Frank Lautenberg for Torricelli on the ballot. Lautenberg went on to defeat his Republican opponent; Barone and Cohen, 2003, 1029–30.

[83] The cell entries represent the probability that a member will run for the Senate (given the opportunity) and were generated using the Clarify program module; Tomz, Wittenberg, and King, 2001.

[84] This model is presented in Palmer and Simon, 2003, 135, table 3. We update the original simulation by adding the opportunities from the 2004 election cycle. Because running for the Senate is a rare event, the simulated probabilities are low. Nonetheless, they are meaningful, especially in comparing the prospects of one officeholder to another. For example, the average probability of those who ran for the Senate (.24) is three times larger than the probability of those who did not run (.08).

Table 4.6 The Probability That Female House Incumbents Will Run for Senate

Career in the House	Incumbency and State Size	Non–Risk Taker	Risk Taker
Served One Term or More Than 5 Terms	Incumbent is safe, medium state	.00	.01
	Incumbent is safe, large state	.01	.03
	Incumbent is safe, small state	.03	.10
	Incumbent is marginal, medium state	.01	.05
	Incumbent is marginal, large state	.02	.10
	Incumbent is marginal, small state	.09	.33
	Open seat, medium state	.02	.08
	Open seat, large state	.04	.17
	Open seat, small state	.14	.44
Midcareer: Served 2–5 Terms	Incumbent is safe, medium state	.01	.04
	Incumbent is safe, large state	.02	.07
	Incumbent is safe, small state	.07	.26
	Incumbent is marginal, medium state	.03	.13
	Incumbent is marginal, large state	.07	.25
	Incumbent is marginal, small state	.23	.57
	Open seat, medium state	.05	.20
	Open seat, large state	.11	.35
	Open seat, small state	.35	.70

who will be at midcareer in each of these election cycles. Of the sixty-six women now serving, thirty-five will find themselves in midcareer in 2006, thirty will be at that stage in 2008, and twenty-four in 2010. Next, we determined which of those women at midcareer will face an opportunity to run in each cycle. In this part of our analysis, "definite" opportunities occur when an incumbent senator of the opposition party is scheduled to face reelection. In addition, we identified, for 2008 and 2010, a set of "speculative" opportunities based upon the age of the current Senate incumbent. Finally, we used the factors considered in our analysis of progressive ambition and calculated the probability of running for each midcareer female House member who will have an opportunity to run.

Table 4.7 shows that eleven women will face an opportunity to run for the Senate in 2006.[85] Three are from small states. Democratic Representative Shelley Berkley represents Nevada's 1st District, which includes Las Vegas. It is

---

[85] In its February 14, 2005, edition, on page 410, *CQ Weekly* listed two retirements: Senator Mark Dayton (D-MN) and Senate Majority Leader Bill Frist (R-TN). Both of their states, Minnesota and Tennessee, have women in their congressional delegation.

Table 4.7 Women and Progressive Ambition: The 2006, 2008, and 2010 Election Cycle

Women in Midcareer in Year of Opportunity	Risk Taker	State Size	Incumbent Status	Probability of Running
2006 Definite Opportunity				
Mary Bono (R-CA)	No	Large	Safe	0.02
Ginny Brown-Waite (R-FL)	Yes	Large	Marginal	0.25
Katherine Harris (R-FL)	No	Large	Marginal	0.07
Julia Carson (D-IN)	No	Medium	Safe	0.01
Candice Miller (R-MI)	Yes	Medium	Marginal	0.13
Betty McCollum (D-MN)	No	Medium	Open	0.06
Shelley Berkley (D-NV)	No	Small	Safe	0.07
Heather Wilson (R-NM)	No	Small	Safe	0.07
Stephanie Tubbs-Jones (D-OH)	No	Medium	Safe	0.01
Marsha Blackburn (R-TN)	Yes	Medium	Open	0.20
Shelley Moore Capito (R-WV)	Yes	Small	Safe	0.26
2008 Definite Opportunity				
Cynthia McKinney (D-GA)	Yes	Medium	Marginal	0.13
Judy Biggert (R-IL)	No	Medium	Safe	0.01
Betty McCollum (D-MN)	No	Medium	Marginal	0.04
Candice Miller (R-MI)[a]	Yes	Medium	Marginal	0.13
2008 Speculative Opportunity				
Heather Wilson (R-NM)[b]	No	Small	Open	0.35
Jo Ann Davis (R-VA)[c]	No	Medium	Open	0.06
Thelma Drake (R-VA)[c]	No	Medium	Open	0.06
Shelley Moore Capito (R-WV)[d]	Yes	Small	**Open**	**0.70**
2010 Definite Opportunity				
Marilyn Musgrave (R-CO)	No	Medium	Marginal	0.04
Deb Wasserman Schultz (D-FL)	No	Large	Marginal	0.07
Cynthia McKinney (D-GA)	Yes	Medium	Safe	0.04
Stephanie Herseth (D-SD)	Yes	Small	**Marginal**	**0.57**
Cathy McMorris (R-WA)	No	Medium	Safe	0.01
Allyson Schwartz (D-PA)	No	Medium	Marginal	0.04

(Continued)

Table 4.7 Women and Progressive Ambition: The 2006, 2008, and 2010 Election Cycle *(Continued)*

Women in Midcareer in Year of Opportunity	Risk Taker	State Size	Incumbent Status	Probability of Running
2010 Speculative Opportunity				
Melissa Hart (R-PA)[e]	Yes	Medium	Open	0.20

[a]Senator Carl Levin (D-MI) will be seventy-four years old in 2008 (completing five terms).
[b]Senator Pete Domenici (R-NM) will be seventy-six years old in 2008 (completing six terms).
[c]Senator John Warner (R-VA) will be eighty-one years old in 2006 (completing five terms).
[d]Senator John D. Rockefeller (D-WV) will be seventy-one years old (completing four terms).
[e]Senator Arlen Specter (R-PA) will be eighty years old (completing five terms).

geographically the smallest of the state's three districts. In 2006, Berkley will face the decision of running for a fifth term or challenging Republican Senator John Ensign. Berkley is not classified as a risk taker, and Ensign was elected in 2000 with 57.9 percent of the two-party vote. Thus, her probability of running is low (.07).[86] Republican Representative Heather Wilson (R-NM) faces a situation identical to that of Berkley. Wilson is not a risk taker and would have to run against the Democratic incumbent, Senator Jeff Bingaman, who won his last election with 62 percent of the two-party vote.

Republican Representative Shelley Moore Capito (R-WV), a risk taker, was first elected in 2000 and represents a district that reaches all the way across West Virginia's midsection.[87] This would make her transition to a Senate campaign easier than what Berkley would face. In addition, she is the daughter of former House Member and Governor Arch Moore and thus has name recognition beyond her congressional district. Democratic Senator Robert Byrd's term expires in 2006; he will be ninety years old.[88] In 2000, Byrd was reelected with 80 percent of the two-party vote. If he runs for a ninth term, the probability that Capito would run is .26, the highest

[86] In 2004, Nevada's other districts went solidly Republican. In the 1st District, James Gibbons won with 71.3 percent of the two-party vote and Jon Porter won in the 2nd District with 57.9 percent of the two-party vote.
[87] Capito won the House seat vacated by Democratic incumbent Robert Wise. Wise held the seat for nine terms and chose to run for governor in 2000; Barone and Cohen, 2001, 1640–42.
[88] Of the current senators, he holds the record for serving the longest: eight consecutive terms. In one of the papers from Capito's district, an editorial ran in May 2005 pleading with Byrd to run again and encouraging Capito to wait until he retired, stating that "this is not Capito's time. . . . Her time will come;" "Will Byrd Run?" *The Journal*, Martinsburg, W.Va., May 1, 2005, A6. Insiders in Congress, however, have been encouraging her to run against him if he does not retire, and in June 2005, Capito met with Elizabeth Dole (R-NC), chair of the National Republican Senatorial Committee, and did several public appearances in West Virginia locales outside of her district; Peter Savodnik, "Capito, Dole Discuss Senate Bid," *The Hill*, Washington, D.C., June 27, 2005, http://www.hillnews.com/thehill/export/TheHill/News/Campaign/062705 (accessed June 27, 2005).

probability among the eleven women. Should Byrd retire, Capito would face an open seat. According to our simulation, her probability of running would increase to .70.

There are three risk takers in addition to Capito with opportunities in 2006. The projected retirement of Senator Majority Leader Bill Frist (R-TN) creates a potential opening for Representative Marsha Blackburn (R-TN).[89] Blackburn first ran for the House unsuccessfully in 1992 in Tennesee's 6th District against the safe Democratic incumbent, Bart Gordon.[90] After serving a term in the Tennessee Senate, Blackburn defeated six primary opponents in 2002 to win the Republican nomination for the 7th District seat vacated by Republican Ed Bryant; she cruised to an easy general election victory with 73.2 percent of the two-party vote.[91] If Frist does retire, Blackburn is projected to have a .20 probability of running for the Senate. Representative Candice Miller (R-MI) is another risk taker with an opportunity to run in 2006. Miller first ran for the House in 1986 when she challenged Democratic incumbent David Bonior (D-MI) and lost with 34 percent of the two-party vote.[92] Miller later won two statewide elections for Michigan secretary of state in 1994 and 1998. In 2002, she won the seat vacated by Bonior.[93] In 2006, Miller would face Senator Debbie Stabenow, another risk taker, who was elected in 2000 with only 50.5 percent of the two-party vote. The likelihood that Miller would run is .13. In Florida, Democratic Senator Bill Nelson will stand for reelection in 2006. He was first elected in 2000 with only 51 percent of the vote. Republican Representative Ginny Brown-Waite comes from one of the larger geographic districts in Florida that lies north of the Tampa Bay area. As a member of the Florida Senate, Brown-Waite ran for the House in 2002, beating incumbent Democrat Karen Thurman by less than 2 percent of the vote.[94] According to table 4.7, the probability that Brown-Waite would run in 2006 is .25.[95]

Four women will have definite opportunities during 2008. Two of the women, Representatives Judy Biggert (R-IL) and Betty McCollum (D-MN), are not risk takers and, as a result, their probability of running is low. In Minnesota, McCollum would face marginal incumbent Republican Norm

---

[89] When Frist ran for his first term in 1994, he term-limited himself to two terms during his campaign. There is a great deal of speculation that he will run for president in 2008; http://national-journal.com/pubs/almanac/2004/people/tn/tns1.htm (accessed June 28, 2005).

[90] Barone and Ujifusa, 1993, 1191–92.

[91] Barone and Cohen, 2003, 1497–98.

[92] Barone and Cohen, 2003, 840–41.

[93] Bonior decided to run for governor and lost in the primary to Jennifer Granholm.

[94] Ironically, Thurman also served on the redistricting committee in the Florida Senate in 1992 and drew herself this congressional district; http://nationaljournal.com/pubs/almanac/2004/people_fl/rep_fl05.htm (accessed June 20, 2005).

[95] Katherine Harris will also be midcareer in 2006, but is not considered a risk taker. Harris was elected in 2002 in an open seat vacated by a Republican. She served as Florida's secretary of state from 1998 to 2002; in that capacity, she gained national attention during the highly charged dispute over Florida's electoral votes in the 2000 election; Barone and Cohen, 2003, 419.

Coleman.[96] Representative Cynthia McKinney (D-GA) is considered a risk taker by virtue of her challenging Denise Majette in 2004. McKinney would also face a marginal incumbent, Republican Senator Saxby Chambliss, who defeated incumbent Max Cleland in perhaps the nastiest race of 2002.[97] McKinney, however, faces the disadvantage of southern electoral history: since the end of Reconstruction, no African American from the South has won election to the Senate. Thus, if she were to challenge Chambliss, her chances of winning would be low. Representative Candice Miller (R-MI) faces another interesting opportunity in 2008. If Democratic incumbent Carl Levin decides to seek reelection, Miller's situation is identical to her opportunity in 2006—running against a marginal incumbent. However, Levin will be seventy-four years old in 2008, and if he retires, the probability of Miller making a run for the Senate would increase to .20.

In addition, four women may face the "speculative opportunity" of an open seat in 2008. Senator John Warner (R-VA) will be seventy-one and completing his fifth term of service. If Warner retires, two Republican women, midway in their House careers, will have an opportunity to run: Representatives Jo Ann Davis and Thelma Drake. Neither is a risk taker and, as a result, both have a low probability of running (.06). Prospects are brighter, however, for the other speculative opportunities in 2008. In New Mexico, Republican Senator Pete Domenici will be seventy-six years old and completing his sixth term. Should Domenici retire, Representative Heather Wilson would be presented with another opportunity. Her probability of running in 2008 would increase from .07 in 2006 (against safe Democrat Jeff Bingaman) to .35. Representative Shelley Moore Capito may face an additional opportunity in 2008 as well. Democratic incumbent John Rockefeller will be seventy-one years old. Should Rockefeller retire, the probability that Capito will seek the open seat is .70.

Six women will have definite opportunities and one woman has a speculative opportunity in 2010. As table 4.7 shows, four of the six definite opportunities fall to non–risk takers. There are two instances in which the prospective opponent is a safe incumbent. Representative Cynthia McKinney (D-GA) would face Republican Johnny Isakson, who won his 2004 contest with 59.2 percent of the two-party vote. The opponent of Representative Cathy McMorris (R-WA) would be Democrat Patty Murray, who won 56.1 percent of the two-party vote in her reelection bid of 2004.

---

[96] Coleman narrowly defeated former Senator and Vice President Walter Mondale in 2002. Mondale was drafted by the Democratic-Farmer-Labor Party (the Democratic Party in Minnesota) after the incumbent, Paul Wellstone, was killed in an airplane accident one week before the election; Barone and Cohen, 2003, 867–69. McCollum did think briefly about running in 2006 after Democratic incumbent Senator Mark Dayton announced he was retiring, but decided against it; Rob Hotakainen, "McCollum Passes on Senate Bid, Will Seek 4th Term to U.S. House," *Minneapolis Star Tribune*, March 8, 2005, 7B.

[97] Cleland lost both his legs and one arm in Vietnam. In October 2002, Chambliss began running a television ad critical of Cleland's position on the Homeland Security bill. The ad featured photos of Osama bin Laden; http://nationaljournal.com/members/adspotlight/2002/10/1015scga1.htm (accessed June 20, 2005).

Fig. 4.1 Representative Stephanie Herseth, the youngest woman in the 109th Congress (2005 session), will have the opportunity to run for the Senate in South Dakota in 2010. Photo by Barbara Palmer.

The best prospect is Representative Stephanie Herseth (D-SD; see figure 4.1). South Dakota has one congressional district and, as a result, she currently represents a statewide constituency. She first ran for the House in 2002, attempting to win an open seat that was secure for the Republicans.[98] Herseth is thus a risk taker. She won her seat in a special election held in June 2004 to fill the vacancy caused by the resignation of incumbent Bill Janklow, her 2002 opponent. Five months later, Herseth successfully defended the seat, winning 53.5 percent of the two-party vote. In addition, she comes from a political family. Her grandfather was governor, her grandmother was secretary of state, and her father was a state legislator for twenty years.[99] Herseth has publicly announced that she will seek a second term in the House in 2006, but beyond that, "Let's just say that while I haven't mapped out any long-term strategy, I'm not ruling anything out."[100] In 2010, Herseth would face Senator John Thune, who won his 2004 race over Democrat Tom Daschle with only 51 percent of the two-party vote. The probability that Herseth will challenge Thune, as shown in table 4.7, is .57.

---

[98] The seat was vacated by three-term incumbent Republican John Thune, who successfully ran for the U.S. Senate. In his three House races, Thune averaged 68.7 percent of the two-party vote.

[99] http://www.house.gov/herseth/about_stephanie_herseth.html (accessed June 20, 2005).

[100] Joe Kafka, "Herseth Feeling More Settled in Washington," Associated Press State and Local Wire, January 30, 2005.

Another opportunity for 2010 may arise in Pennsylvania. In 2004, Republican Senator Arlen Specter won reelection with just over 55 percent of the two-party vote. Specter will be eighty years old and completing his fifth term in the Senate in 2010.[101] If Specter decides to seek reelection, the probability that Democratic Representative Allyson Schwartz will act on her opportunity is only .01; should Specter retire, her probability of running would increase to .06. A Specter retirement, however, would also present an opportunity to Republican Representative Melissa Hart. Unlike Schwartz, Hart is a risk taker, winning her first election for an open seat in a district that had not elected a Republican in nine election cycles.[102] Should Specter retire, the probability that Hart would seek the open Senate seat is .20.

Overall, twenty-one women serving in the 109th Congress will be faced with either a definite or speculative opportunity to run for the Senate in the next three election cycles. Five of these women will have two opportunities: Representatives Shelley Moore Capito (R-WV), Betty McCollum (D-MN), Cynthia McKinney (D-GA), Candice Miller (R-MI), and Heather Wilson (R-NM). Among those with an opportunity, the most probable Senate candidates include Democrat Stephanie Herseth and Republicans Capito, Miller, Wilson, and Ginny Brown-Waite. That only five women in the House will have reasonable opportunities over the six years reinforces our analyses in chapters 1 and 2. The Senate projections in table 4.7 illustrate how the schedule of Senate elections, the electoral advantages of incumbency, and the longevity of incumbents make advancing through the pipeline quite difficult.[103] This suggests that increases in the number of women in the Senate will depend on lateral entry and capitalizing upon name recognition gained elsewhere, much like the paths taken by Nancy Kassebaum, Hillary Clinton, and Elizabeth Dole.

The Ultimate in Progressive Ambition: Running for President

At the apex of the political career ladder in the United States is the presidency. While the paths to the presidency are numerous, the Senate has been called "little more than a halfway house for more or less ambitious presidential contenders."[104] Many senators have, in fact, run for president. Of our forty-three presidents, more than one-third (15) have been senators.[105] In the 2004 Democratic presidential primary race, five of the ten major Democratic

---

[101] In 2005, Specter was diagnosed with advanced Hodgkin's disease and began chemotherapy. He noted, "I have beaten a brain tumor, bypass heart surgery and many tough political opponents; and I'm going to beat this, too"; Keith Perine, "Specter Diagnosed with Hodgkin's, Vows to Stick to Judiciary Agenda," *CQ Weekly*, February 21, 2005, 463.

[102] Barone and Cohen, 2003, 1371.

[103] Another route to the Senate is from the governorship of a state. While there are a number of men who were elected to the Senate after serving as governor (e.g., Republican Lamar Alexander of Tennessee), there are no women, to date, who followed this path to the Senate.

[104] Robert Peabody, Norman Ornstein, and David Rohde, "The United States Senate as Presidential Incubator: Many Are Called but Few Are Chosen," *Political Science Quarterly* 9 (1976): 237–58, 237.

[105] Peabody, Ornstein, and Rohde, 238, and updated by the authors.

contenders were senators or former senators. In 1972, ten Democratic senators, almost one-fifth of the Democrats in the Senate, announced that they
were considering running against President Richard Nixon.[106]

In light of its reputation as an "incubator for presidential candidates,"[107] we
can speculate about those women currently serving in the Senate and their
prospects for running for president. We have adapted the model created by
political scientists Abramson, Aldrich, and Rohde to calculate the probability
that each woman currently serving in the Senate will enter the race for the
presidential nomination in 2008.[108] Two of the same factors that predict
whether a House member will run for the Senate also predict whether a senator will run for president: risk taking and low opportunity costs, that is, the
senator is not up for reelection during a presidential election cycle. Unlike all
House members, most senators, because their reelections are not synchro-
nized with presidential elections, need not give up their seats to run for president. Beyond these two factors, the new concept of "candidate liabilities" is
adopted here.[109] These liabilities include age, the first term of service in the
Senate, racial and religious minorities, and an unsuccessful prior campaign for
the presidency.[110]

Table 4.8 reveals that four senators in the 109th Congress (2005–2006)
share the highest probability of running for president: Kay Bailey Hutchison
(R-TX), Blanche Lincoln (D-AR), Debbie Stabenow (D-MI), and Maria

---

[106] Peabody, Ornstein, and Rohde, 238.

[107] Peabody, Ornstein, and Rohde, 237.

[108] Paul Abramson, John Aldrich, and David Rohde, "Progressive Ambition among United States
Senators: 1972–1988," *Journal of Politics* 49 (1987): 3–35. Since the 1970s, governors enjoyed
more success at winning the presidency. Four of the last five presidents have been governors. In
the 108th Congress, several constitutional amendments were proposed to change the citizenship requirements for being president. The main proponents were supporters of California
Governor Arnold Schwarzenegger. Senator Orrin Hatch, former chair of the Senate Judiciary
Committee, emerged as a leading advocate of the change. However, some women's groups have
silently supported this because it would also allow Michigan Governor Jennifer Granholm, who
was born in Canada, to run. Representative John Conyers, a Democrat from Michigan, actually
introduced an amendment in the House; Joe Matthews, "Maybe Anyone Can Be President,"
Los Angeles Times, February 2, 2005, A1. See also http://amendforarnold.com (accessed June
21, 2005). In the 109th Congress, at least three proposed amendments were referred to subcommittee (HJ RES 2; HJ RES 15, and HJ RES 42); http://www.thomas.loc.gov (accessed June
21, 2005).

[109] Abramson, Aldrich, and Rohde, 1987, 9–11. Age is considered a liability if a senator is younger
than forty-two or older than seventy.

[110] The Abramson, Aldrich, and Rohde study covers 1972 to 1988. They assign a liability if the senator is African American, Asian, Hispanic, female, or Jewish. In performing this exercise, we
did not treat being female as a liability in order to examine the probability of running under
the assumption of no gender bias. Were gender to be included as a liability, the probabilities
reported in table 4.8 would be lower. With respect to religious denomination, six of the fourteen female senators are Catholic (Mikulski, Murray, Landrieu, Collins, Cantwell, and
Murkowski), three are Methodist (Stabenow, Clinton, and Dole), two are Episcopalian (Hutchison and Lincoln), two are Jewish (Feinstein and Boxer), and one is Greek Orthodox (Snowe).
Because of flaws in the estimates for Republicans, we relied upon the Democratic equation
reported in Abramson, Aldrich, and Rohde, 1987, 17, to generate the probabilities for all the
senators. In addition, we assigned risk-taker status to Blanche Lincoln based upon her initial
run for the House when she defeated a sitting incumbent of her own party in the primary.

Table 4.8 Progressive Ambition: From the Senate to the Presidential Arena

Name	Year Elected to Senate	Senate Reelection in 2008	Liabilities	Risk Taker	Probability of Running
Barbara Mikulski (D-MD)	1986	No	1	Yes	0.08
Dianne Feinstein (D-CA)	1992	No	2	No	0.01
Barbara Boxer (D-CA)	1992	No	1	No	0.01
Kay Bailey Hutchison (R-TX)	1993	No	0	Yes	0.23
Patty Murray (D-WA)	1992	No	0	No	0.06
Olympia Snowe (R-ME)	1994	No	0	No	0.06
Mary Landrieu (D-LA)	1996	Yes	0	No	0.03
Susan Collins (R-ME)	1996	Yes	0	No	0.03
Blanche Lincoln (D-AR)	1998	No	0	Yes	0.23
Debbie Stabenow (D-MI)	2000	No	0	Yes	0.23
Hillary Clinton (D-NY)	2000	No	0	No	0.06
Maria Cantwell (D-WA)	2000	No	0	Yes	0.23
Lisa Murkowski (R-AK)	2004	No	1	No	0.01
Elizabeth Dole (R-NC)	2002	Yes	3	No	0.00

Cantwell (D-WA). The comparatively high probability is a result of all being risk takers, not facing a reelection race in 2008, and having no liabilities. Stabenow and Cantwell will run for reelection in 2006 and their prospects for president will depend, in part, on their performance in those contests. The youngest of the four are Lincoln, age forty-four, and Cantwell, age forty-six. Senator Kay Bailey Hutchison (R-TX) is currently the most senior Republican woman in the Senate. Throughout the spring of 2005, there were numerous rumors that she would leave her Senate seat in 2006 to challenge the incumbent governor of Texas, Rick Perry, in the Republican primary; she would then launch her campaign, like George W. Bush, as governor. On June 17, 2005, Hutchison put the rumors to rest and announced that she would run for reelection to the Senate. Four days later, she announced her candidacy to chair the Senate Republican Policy Committee.[111] While Hutchison has yet to formally express her presidential aspirations, she "is frequently on lists as a possible vice-presidential candidate."[112]

Among those with the lowest probability of running are Senators Dianne Feinstein (D-CA) and Elizabeth Dole (R-NC). Neither are risk takers. Feinstein will be seventy-five years old in 2008, and although she has been considered a possible contender, she has expressed her disinterest: "People have talked to me

---

[111] R. G. Ratcliffe, "Hutchison to Run for Senate, Not Governor," *Houston Chronicle*, June 18, 2005, 1.
[112] Ratcliffe, 2005, 1.

about running for president . . . and I sort of laughed at it."[113] Elizabeth Dole has the most liabilities of all the women in the Senate. She will be seventy-two years old in 2008, she is serving her first term, and she has already taken a shot at running for president. In fact, Dole did it "backwards" and ran for the Senate in 2002 after she dropped out of the presidential race in October 1999.[114]

Most speculation about 2008 involves Senator Hillary Clinton (D-NY). While our analysis suggests that her probability of running for president is low, her prospects go far beyond her status as a first-term senator. Clinton is sui generis, the only one of her kind. In effect, she does not fit into our model. She is the first spouse of a president to enter electoral politics after her service as first lady. Since the 1992 campaign when Bill Clinton remarked, "Buy one, get one free," it has not been hard to imagine Hillary running in her own right.[115] The assumption, at least among pundits and Hill watchers in Washington, D.C., is that she would win the Democratic nomination in 2008 if she wanted it. On NBC's *Meet the Press*, in February 2005, Senator Joe Biden (D-DE) said that she "is likely to be the nominee. . . . I think she'd be incredibly difficult to beat. . . . I think Hillary Clinton is able to be elected president of the United States."[116] According to a Gallup Poll taken a few months after Biden's statement, Clinton had a name recognition rate of 94 percent; 55 percent viewed her favorably, while 39 percent viewed her unfavorably. She was also the front-runner for the Democratic nomination with support among 40 percent of registered Democrats, compared to 18 percent for John Kerry and 16 percent for John Edwards.[117]

There are three other women who deserve mention. Carol Moseley Braun, the first African American woman to serve in the Senate, ran for president in 2004. Moseley Braun served in the Senate for one term and narrowly lost her reelection campaign in 1998, after being plagued by fundraising and sexual harassment scandals.[118] Following her defeat, she vowed "never to run for public office" again.[119] She was then appointed ambassador to New Zealand and Samoa by President Bill Clinton. Some speculated that she decided to run for president, at least in part, to clear her name.[120] While she was a regular participant in Democratic presidential debates, she only raised $628,000.[121] If we apply our model to her, Moseley Braun would be classified as a risk taker, having taken on and defeated Democratic incumbent Senator

---

[113] Eleanor Clift and Tom Brazaitis, *Madam President* (New York: Scribner, 2000), 168.

[114] Stanley and Niemi, 2003, 67.

[115] Eleanor Clift and Tom Brazaitis, *Madam President*, 2nd ed. (New York: Routlege Press, 2003), 149.

[116] Quoted from Craig Crawford, "Ultimate Glass Ceiling Could Be Tested in 2008," *CQ Weekly*, March 7, 2005, 556.

[117] Frank Newport, "Update: Hillary Rodham Clinton and the 2008 Election," *Gallup Poll News Service*, June 7, 2005. See also Clift and Brazaitis, 2003, ch. 6.

[118] Foerstel, 1999, 197.

[119] Foerstal, 1999, 197.

[120] Darryl Fears, "On a Mission in a Political Second Act; Bush's Record Forced Her to Run, Braun Says," *Washington Post*, July 13, 2003.

Alan Dixon in the primary the very first time she ran for Senate in 1992. She would have, however, at least one liability: being an African American. Moseley Braun felt the sting of racism early in her Senate career, after she single-handedly defeated an amendment proposed by Senator Jesse Helms (R-NC) extending a trademark to the Daughters of the Confederacy on their use of the Confederate flag in their logo. Shortly after the amendment was defeated on the Senate floor, Moseley Braun encountered Helms in the Senate elevator. As she recounted, "He saw me standing there, and he started to sing, 'I wish I was in the land of cotton . . .' And he looked at Senator [Orrin] Hatch and said, 'I'm going to sing Dixie until she cries.' And I looked at him and said, 'Senator Helms, your singing would make me cry if you sang Rock of Ages.'"[122]

Two female members of the House have also run for president. Representative Patricia Schroeder (D-CO) announced her candidacy in 1987. She had been co-chair of Senator Gary Hart's presidential campaign that year, until Hart dared the press to "go ahead and follow me." They did follow him, "staked out" his residence, and reported that he spent the night with Donna Rice, a model who was not his wife.[123] Shortly thereafter, a photograph was published showing Rice sitting on Hart's lap while they cruised on a yacht called *Monkey Business*. After Hart withdrew from the race, Schroeder decided to run "only if I had a good chance of winning."[124] A poll in August 1987 had her running third among the Democratic nominees, but she was not raising enough money to be competitive, so Schroeder withdrew from the race before the start of the formal primary season.[125] During her final press conference, her tears as she announced the end of her candidacy became infamous enough to be parodied on *Saturday Night Live*.[126] The first African American woman to run for president was Representative Shirley Chisholm (D-NY). Chisholm was first elected to the House in 1968. In 1972, she announced her candidacy for the Democratic nomination for president. Her name appeared on the primary ballot in twelve states. When the other Democratic candidates tried to exclude her from the televised debates because she was not "a real candidate," she went to the Federal Communications Commission and got a federal court order allowing her to participate.[127] On the first roll call at the Democratic National Convention, Chisholm won 151 votes.[128] She said, "I knew I wouldn't

---

[121] Federal Election Commission, http://herndon1.sdrdc.com/cgi-bin/cancomsrs/?_04+P40002552 (accessed June 28, 2005).
[122] Quoted from Foerstel, 1999, 196.
[123] Larry Sabato, *Feeding Frenzy: How Attack Journalism Has Transformed American Politics* (New York: Free Press, 1991), 13–14.
[124] Schroeder, 1999, 180.
[125] Foerstel, 1999, 247.
[126] Schroeder, 1999, 187.
[127] Clift and Brazaitis, 2003, xxii.
[128] Foerstel, 1999, 56. In 2004, a documentary of Chisholm's campaign was released, *Chisholm '72: Unbought and Unbossed*, shortly before her death at the age of eighty on January 1, 2005.

be president, but somebody had to break the ice, somebody with the nerve and bravado to do it."[129]

Conclusion

Rohde assumes that all members of the House have progressive ambition and that given the opportunity, they would run for the Senate. But running for this office, especially in a large state, is much riskier and more difficult than running for the House. Not all House members make that transition successfully. For example, in 1980, when Representative John Anderson (R-IL) resigned from the House to launch his third-party presidential campaign, Lynn Martin, a former state senator from his Rockville-based district, decided to run for the open seat, defeating four other candidates in the primary.[130] Considered a rising star in the Republican Party, she was given a seat on the powerful House Budget Committee. In 1984, Vice President George Bush personally asked her to coach him in a series of practices to prepare him for his televised debate against the Democratic vice presidential nominee, Geraldine Ferraro.[131] In 1986, Martin was elected vice chair of the Republican Conference, making her the first Republican woman to serve in a leadership position.[132] In her reelection campaigns, Martin received on average well over 60 percent of the two-party vote. She rose rapidly in the House Republican hierarchy. After her fifth term, she decided to run for the Senate against the popular incumbent Democrat, Paul Simon, well known for his bow ties and unsuccessful presidential bid in 1988. Martin's campaign got off to a rocky start when she referred to southern Illinois voters, Simon's base, as "rednecks" and called him a "twerp."[133] At the time of her announcement as a Senate candidate, she had raised less that $100,000 while Simon had almost $2 million.[134] Her fundraising was disappointing, and she admitted to running "a terrible campaign."[135] When Martin was asked for advice by Barbara Kennelly (D-CT), a House member

---

[129] Clift and Brazaitis, 2003, xxiii.

[130] Martin's very first race for office was actually in the eighth grade for class president. She lost by one vote—her own. She voted for her boyfriend, who had voted for himself. After the election, they broke up; Clift and Brazaitis, 2003, 70. In 1980, in addition to Martin, three other Republican women were elected to the House. This was considered enough of a novelty that they were all asked to appear on Phil Donahue's daytime talk show; Clift and Brazaitis, 2003, 41.

[131] Martin knew Ferraro from serving in the House together, and they had worked as allies on women's issues. In 2000, they started a business, G & L Strategies, that advised companies how to develop women-friendly workplaces; Clift and Brazaitis, 2000, 81.

[132] Known for her quick and sarcastic wit, she was once called the "political version of Joan Rivers"; Foerstal, 1999, 174.

[133] Paul Merrion, "Martin Campaign Lags; Gaffes Raise GOP Doubts, May Imperil Fund-Raising," *Crain's Chicago Business*, October 2, 1989, 4.

[134] "Simon, Martin File Campaign Funding Data," *Crain's Chicago Business*, August 7, 1989, 46. When Bush became president, he asked her to be secretary of labor. In 1995, she ran an exploratory campaign for president, made trips to New Hampshire and Iowa, but after a month decided not to run; Clift and Brazaitis, 2003, 70.

[135] Clift and Brazaitis, 2003, 42.

who decided to run for governor in Connecticut in 1998, she warned, "[D]on't think the whole state knows who you are."[136]

Very few of the female representatives who have run for the Senate were successful; only five of the eighteen, less than one-third, were able to move up the political hierarchy from the House to the Senate. Indeed, very few sitting female House members have made a run for the Senate in the first place: only 19 out of 266, or 7.1 percent. Our analysis shows that this is largely a function of opportunity: the power of incumbency, the longevity of incumbents, and the electoral calendar largely block the career ladder. Consider the situation in California since 1992, when Democrats Barbara Boxer and Dianne Feinstein were elected to the Senate. Feinstein was reelected in 1994 and 2000; Boxer was reelected in 1998 and 2004. Between 1992 and 2002, California elected thirteen female Democrats to the House. None of these women have had an opportunity, as we have defined it, to consider a run for the Senate.

Although it does not happen very often, we can predict which female House members will make a run for the Senate. Women from small states are more likely to take advantage of an opportunity to run for the Senate, given the congruence between their House district and potential Senate constituency. Moreover, women are more likely to run for the Senate when there is an open seat, when they have the highest probability of winning. Rather than sacrifice seniority, women are more likely to take a shot at the Senate in midcareer. Finally, risk taking is an essential feature of progressive ambition. Those women who ran under politically adverse conditions in their first attempt at a House seat are more likely to take the risk and run for the Senate.

Representative Sue Myrick once observed, "Men are raised to play football, to bash their heads and come back for more. Women are raised to stand back. We aren't raised to be risk takers."[137] Our analysis suggests that this is not necessarily true. A substantial proportion of those women elected to the House are classified as risk takers; their first run for the office occurred under conditions that were politically perilous. Some women—like some men—are taught or acquire the ability to take electoral risks when entering congressional politics. This attitude helps explain the differences between static and progressive ambition. Studying the decision to run for the Senate thus suggests that, in moving through the hierarchy of offices, women respond to the same systematic factors as their male counterparts. The primary conclusion to be drawn from this chapter is that women are adept players in the game of electoral politics. Women share the same goals as their male counterparts: electoral survival, spending a career in Congress, reaping the payoffs that accompany political longevity, and the pursuit of higher office when the right opportunity arises. Some of them even run for president.

---

[136] Clift and Brazaitis, 2000, 198.
[137] Foerstal, 1999, 11.

5

Where Women Run
Women and the Competitive Environment

Chapters 3 and 4 suggest that women make strategic calculations that are basically the same as men's when deciding whether to pursue a congressional career or run for higher office. In this chapter, we focus upon the competitive environment faced by careerists, that is, incumbents seeking reelection to the House. Is the electoral environment the same for men and women, or do gender and incumbency interact to create a different competitive playing field for male and female incumbents? Does the presence of female incumbents draw more women into the electoral arena?

There are examples that suggest that the road to reelection may be more perilous for women. Consider the Democratic women first elected in 1992, the Year of the Woman. In this election, fifty-two new Democrats won seats in the House, twenty women and thirty-two men. These first-term Democrats were quickly put into a precarious position when the final version of President Bill Clinton's deficit reduction plan came before the House on August 5, 1993.[1] The plan was especially controversial since deficit reduction was achieved, in part, by $250 billion in new taxes.[2] Voting for the plan among the first-term Democrats were twenty-five, or 78 percent, of the new men, and eighteen, or 90 percent, of the new women. The vote to increase taxes made many of these members vulnerable and the target of Republican efforts in the midterm elections of 1994. In fact, Republican primaries were far more competitive in those districts held by female incumbents. There were contested Republican primaries in only eight of the twenty-five districts, 32 percent, held by the first-term male Democrats who voted for the bill; there were contested

---

[1] "Deficit-Reduction Bill Narrowly Passes," *Congressional Quarterly Almanac, 1993* (Washington, D.C.: CQ Press, 1994), 107.
[2] "Deficit-Reduction Bill Narrowly Passes," 1994, 108.

Republican primaries in ten of the seventeen districts, 59 percent, held by the first-term female Democrats who supported the bill.[3] For example, the Republican primary in the 6th District of Arizona featured four Republican candidates, including one woman, competing to challenge incumbent Karen English, who had won a newly created district in 1992 with over 56 percent of the two-party vote. The winner of the Republican primary was J. D. Hayworth, a sports reporter from Phoenix with no prior political experience.[4] In the 49th District of California, Brain Bilbray defeated three opponents in the Republican primary for the opportunity to challenge Democrat Lynn Schenck, who had won her seat in 1992 with 54 percent of the vote.[5] Jon Fox defeated two male and two female competitors in the 13th District of Pennsylvania and won a rematch with Marjorie Margolies-Mezvinsky.[6]

In the general election of 1994, four of the twenty-five first-term male Democrats who supported Clinton's plan were defeated, giving them a reelection rate of 84 percent.[7] Among the first-term female Democrats who supported Clinton's plan, six of the eighteen were defeated, giving them a reelection rate of only 67 percent. The female incumbents who lost their seats were Representatives Leslie Byrne (VA), Maria Cantwell (WA), Karen English (AZ), Marjorie Margolies-Mezvinsky (PA), Lynn Schenck (CA), and Karen Shepherd (UT). Ironically, the disproportionate support women gave to Clinton's deficit plan resulted in a disproportionate number of defeats among the first-year class elected in the "Year of the Woman."

The example of 1994 suggests that the playing field for men and women may not be level. In this chapter, we explore the impact of incumbency and the competitive environment on the electoral fortunes of women. For the most part, because of the near invincibility of incumbents and the fact that most incumbents are male, it has been assumed that open seats were the primary avenue of entry for women into the House.[8] As a result, there has been very little analysis of female incumbents and their success rates.[9] But the

---

[3] This count excludes the 11th District of Virginia, where the Republican nominee was chosen by party convention.

[4] Michael Barone and Grant Ujifusa, *Almanac of American Politics, 1998* (Washington, D.C.: National Journal, 1997), 58.

[5] Barone and Ujifusa, 1997, 220.

[6] Barone and Ujifusa, 1997, 1162. As we noted in chapter 2, Margolies-Mezvinsky had won the open-seat race against Fox in 1992 by a very narrow margin. He soundly defeated her in 1994.

[7] They were Representatives Don Johnson (GA), Tom Barlow (KY), Ted Strickland (OH), and Eric Fingerhut (OH).

[8] For a discussion of the success of women in open seats, see for example Barbara Burrell, "Women Candidates in Open-Seat Primaries for the U.S. House: 1968–1990." *Legislative Studies Quarterly* 17 (1992): 493–508; Kim Hoffman, Carrie Palmer, and Ronald Keith Gaddie, "Candidate Sex and Congressional Elections: Open Seats before, during, and after the Year of the Woman," in *Women and Congress: Running, Winning and Ruling,* ed. Karen O'Connor (New York: Haworth Press, 2001); and Robert Bernstein, "Might Women Have the Edge in Open-Seat House Primaries?" *Women & Politics* 17 (1997): 1–26.

[9] But see Neil Berch, "Women Incumbents, Elite Bias, and Voter Response in the 1996 and 1998 U.S. House Elections," *Women & Politics* 26 (2004): 21–33. Berch found that female incumbents faced better funded challengers than male incumbents.

conventional wisdom is that a "candidate's sex does not affect his or her chances of winning an election."[10] And there is some evidence that this is, in fact, the case. Female incumbents actually have slightly higher reelection rates than male incumbents. Our analysis, however, goes beyond the reelection rates for incumbents and examines several additional measures of the electoral environment in a district. Although there are variations between the parties, we find that female incumbents are more likely to be challenged than male incumbents in their own primary. In addition, more candidates run in the opposition party primary. Female incumbents are less likely than male incumbents to run unopposed in both their own primary and the general election; in other words, they are less likely to get a "free pass." Moreover, female incumbents are more likely to face female competition. Ultimately, we show that female incumbents have a "hidden influence": while on the surface, women win reelection at rates comparable to those of men, they have to work harder to retain their seats. Their presence also encourages other women to run.

When Women Run against Women

The first time two women faced each other as opponents in a general election was a House race in 1934, when Democrat Caroline O'Day ran against Republican Natalie Couch for New York's at-large open seat. O'Day was active in Democratic Party politics and was selected as a delegate to each Democratic National Convention between 1924 and 1936. She also worked with Jeannette Rankin, lobbying to give women the right to vote in New York in 1917. Her electoral success in 1934 is attributed to her friendship with Eleanor Roosevelt, who campaigned for her—the first time a first lady campaigned for anyone. In each of her three reelection bids, the Republicans nominated a woman to oppose her.[11] The first time two women ran against each other in a general election for the Senate was in 1960, when incumbent Senator Margaret Chase Smith (R-ME) defeated Lucia Cormier. Cormier served six terms in the Maine House of Representatives and was the Democratic floor leader. During the campaign, Cormier and Smith participated in one of the first televised political debates, the same year as the Kennedy-Nixon debate. Cormier spent $20,000 in the effort to oust Smith, who only spent $5,000. Smith won with 62 percent of the vote, the highest vote total of any Republican Senate candidate that year. The race made the cover of *Time Magazine*.[12]

It has only been very recently that women found themselves running against other women candidates with any kind of frequency in primary or

---

[10] Richard Seltzer, Jody Newman, and Melissa Voorhees Leighton, *Sex as a Political Variable* (Boulder, Colo.: Lynne Rienner Publishers, 1997), 79.

[11] Karen Foerstel, *Biographical Dictionary of Congressional Women* (Westport, Conn.: Greenwood Press, 1999), 210–11.

[12] Paul Mills, "Mr. Vacationland and Why We Can't Forget the Lady from Rumford," *Lewiston (Maine) Sun Journal*, September 3, 2000, http://members.aol.com/FAWIDIR/cormier.html (accessed June 15, 2005).

general elections, and as a result, there is very little analysis of this phenome-non.[13] Since 1916, only about 3 percent of all primary and general House and Senate races have featured multiple women candidates.[14] In fact, in general elections, this has happened 108 times. Only five of these races were for the Senate. In addition to the Smith-Cormier race in 1960, Democrat Barbara Mikulski (MD) defeated Republican Linda Chavez in an open-seat race in 1986. In 1998, Senator Patty Murray (D-WA) defeated Republican Linda Smith. In 2002, Senator Mary Landrieu (D-LA) defeated Republican Suzanne Terrell, and Senator Susan Collins (R-ME) defeated Democrat Chellie Pingree.

Since 1972, there have been eighty-three general House and Senate elec-tions with two women candidates. All but sixteen of these, 81 percent, occurred after 1990. As table 5.1 shows, unlike the general trends discussed in chapter 2, there is no slow and steady increase in these numbers since 1972. During the 1970s and 1980s, the average number of general elections with two women candidates was two. In 1992, the number jumped to six. One of the races that received a great deal of attention in 1992 was the Democratic pri-mary for the Senate in New York. The primary featured two male candidates, Robert Abrams, the state attorney general, and Al Sharpton, the flamboyant boxing promoter and preacher, along with two female candidates, Elizabeth Holtzman, the youngest woman to serve in the House, and Geraldine Ferraro, a former member of the House and vice presidential candidate. Ferraro and Holtzman targeted their campaigns almost exclusively against each other, and the race became known as "the mother of all cat fights."[15] About a month before the primary, when Ferraro had a commanding lead in the polls, the *Village Voice* ran a story entitled "Gerry and the Mob."[16] Part of the story focused on an incident that occurred during her 1984 vice presidential campaign, when it was revealed that Ferraro's husband had rented space to a child pornographer with mob ties. She pledged to evict him, but he remained in the building for three more years. The day after the *Village Voice* article was published, Holtzman held a press conference outside the empty building

---

[13] The little research that does exist provides conflicting findings. Robert Bernstein's analysis of the 1992 and 1994 elections found that a woman had a substantial edge in winning an open-seat primary when she was the lone female candidate running against two or more men; in pri-maries with multiple women candidates, a woman was less likely to win; Robert Bernstein, "Why Are There So few Women in the House?" *Western Political Quarterly* 39 (1986): 155–64. Richard Fox, however, in his assessment of 1992 California congressional races, found just the opposite; in primaries with multiple women candidates, all of the women tended to do better than the men; Richard Fox, *Gender Dynamics in Congressional Elections* (Thousand Oaks, Calif.: Sage, 1997). See also Burrell, 1992; Bernstein, 1997.

[14] Here, it is especially important to note that we are only referring to the two major parties. Prior to the 1950s, many women ran as third-party candidates.

[15] Karen Foerstel and Herbert Foerstel, *Climbing the Hill: Gender Conflict in Congress* (Westport, Conn.: Praeger Press, 1996), 75.

[16] The article claimed that she and her husband had ties to twenty-four mafia figures. For exam-ple, two of Ferraro's campaign supporters were named "One-Eyed Charlie" and "Billy the Butcher"; Helen Dewar, "NY Senate Primary Gets Muddy Near the Wire," *Washington Post*, August 30, 1992, A3. See also Bruce Frankel, "Anything Goes in NY Primary," *USA Today*, September 11, 1992, p. 10A.

Table 5.1 General Elections in House and Senate Races with Two Women Candidates

Year	Female Incumbent Defeats Female Challenger	Female Challenger Defeats Female Incumbent	Open Seats	Total
1970	0	0	0	0
1972	2	0	0	2
1974	3	0	0	3
1976	1	0	0	1
1978	2	0	0	2
1980	2	0	0	2
1982	1	0	2	3
1984	2	0	0	2
1986	3	0	0	3
1988	3	0	0	0
1990	0	0	0	0
1992	2	0	4	6
1994	9	2	0	11
1996	3	0	1	4
1998	13	0	1	14
2000	10	0	1	11
2002	7	1	2	10
2004	8	0	3	11
Total	**69**	**3**	**14**	**83**

Sources: Data collected by the authors and from the Center for American Women and Politics, *Woman versus Woman Fact Sheet, 2004* (New Brunswick, N.J.: Rutgers University, 2005), http://www.rci.rutgers.edu/~cawp/Facts/CanHistory/WomVWom.pdf (accessed July 12, 2005).

and demanded that Ferraro "come clean."[17] During one of the debates, Holtzman said, "We need someone in the U.S. Senate who knows how to get rid of a child pornographer."[18] Her attack ads became some of the most memorable of the campaign, with one of them stating, "Questions Gerry Ferraro won't answer: collecting $340,000 from a child pornographer—after promising not to."[19] Abrams also attacked Ferraro for her less-than-clean past, but it was Holtzman who was criticized by some women's groups for her tactics.[20] Ultimately, Abrams narrowly won the primary, but was defeated by Republican Alfonse D'Amato in the general election.

---

[17] Dewar, 1992, A3.
[18] Jay Gallagher and Kyle Hughs, "Dirty Campaign Muddies Senate Contest in NY," *Chicago Sun-Times*, September 12, 1992, 36.
[19] Alessandra Stanley, "In Primary Race for Senate, Ads Are Costly and Caustic," *New York Times*, September 13, 1992, 1.
[20] Foerstel and Foerstel, 1996, 75–76.

Since 1994, the number of races with two women candidates has been relatively constant at around eleven. Table 5.1 also reveals that the vast majority of women candidates who face a female opponent are incumbents. Of the races since 1972 featuring two women in the general election, 84.2 percent have been elections with female incumbents facing female challengers. Many of these incumbents have faced female challengers several times. Incumbent Representatives Pat Schroeder (D-CO) and Nancy Johnson (R-CT), for example, faced a female challenger four times. Representatives Nancy Pelosi (D-CA), Carolyn Cheeks Kilpatrick (D-MI), Cynthia McKinney (D-GA), and Jane Harman (D-CA) faced female challengers three times. As expected, the incumbent almost always wins. Only three female challengers have defeated a female incumbent. All were cases in which a Republican challenger defeated a Democratic incumbent. In 1994, Linda Smith (R-WA) defeated incumbent Jolene Unsoeld (D-WA), and, as noted in chapter 2, Enid Greene Waldholtz (R-UT) defeated incumbent Karen Shepherd (D-UT). In 2002, Ginny Brown-Waite (R-FL) defeated incumbent Karen Thurman (D-FL) after redistricting substantially changed the district. As table 5.1 shows, very few general elections for an open seat feature two women candidates. Since 1972, there have only been seventeen open-seat races with two women candidates. In fact, prior to 1982, there was never an open-seat race with two women candidates in the general election.

"Equality" in the Electoral Arena

The conventional wisdom is that once they make the decision to run, women have achieved electoral parity with men. Although women are less likely to consider running for office or to be encouraged to run, when women do run for office, they are as likely to win as men.[21] Women who challenge incumbents are not any more likely to win (or lose) than men who challenge incumbents. Female incumbents are reelected at the same rates as male incumbents. In fact, female House incumbents do slightly better; their overall reelection rate is 95.6 percent compared to 94.8 percent for men. As table 5.2 shows, over

---

[21] R. Darcy and Sarah Slavin Schramm, "When Women Run against Men," *Public Opinion Quarterly* 41 (1977): 1–12; Susan Welch et al., "The Effect of Candidate Gender on Election Outcomes in State Legislative Races," *Western Political Quarterly* 38 (1985): 464–75; Burrell, 1992; Barbara Burrell, *A Woman's Place Is in the House: Campaigning for Congress in the Feminist Era* (Ann Arbor: University of Michigan Press, 1994); R. Darcy, Susan Welch, and Janet Clark, *Women, Elections, and Representation*, 2nd ed. (Lincoln: University of Nebraska Press, 1994); Ronald Keith Gaddie and Charles Bullock, "Congressional Elections and the Year of the Woman: Structural and Elite Influences on Female Candidates," *Social Science Quarterly* 76 (1995): 749–62; Richard Seltzer, Jody Newman, and Melissa Voorhees Leighton, *Sex as a Political Variable* (Boulder, Colo.: Lynne Rienner Publishers, 1997); Barbara Palmer and Dennis Simon, "Breaking the Logjam: The Emergence of Women as Congressional Candidates," in *Women and Congress: Running, Winning, and Ruling*, ed. Karen O'Connor (Binghamton, N.Y.: Haworth Press, 2001); but see Richard Fox, Jennifer Lawless, and Courtney Feeley, "Gender and the Decision to Run for Office," *Legislative Studies Quarterly* 26 (2001): 411–35; and Richard Fox and Zoe Oxley, "Gender Stereotyping in State Executive Elections: Candidates Selection and Success," *Journal of Politics* 65 (2003): 833–50.

Table 5.2 Reelection Rates for Male and Female Incumbents in the House

Redistricting Period	Reelection Rates for Male Incumbents (%)	Reelection Rates for Female Incumbents (%)	Male Incumbents Reelected with Safe Margin (%)	Female Incumbents Reelected with Safe Margin (%)	Average Two-Party Vote for Male Incumbents (%)	Average Two-Party Vote for Female Incumbents (%)
1956–1960	93.1	95.2	79.8	88.1	61.5	63.1
1962–1970	93.6	95.9	84.8	95.9	63.6	67.5
1972–1980	94.0	95.6	86.8	91.2	65.8	71.6
1982–1990	96.5	100.0	90.1	95.0	66.6	68.8
1992–2000	95.6	93.9	88.4	85.5	65.3	66.9
2002–2004	98.8	98.2	96.2	92.0	67.4	67.6
Overall	**94.8**	**95.6**	**87.2**	**90.1**	**65.0**	**67.7**

the last five decades, female incumbents have generally outperformed male incumbents. In fact, between 1982 and 1990, female incumbents had a perfect track record, winning all 101 of their campaigns. During this redistricting period, sixty-five male incumbents lost. In 2004, female incumbents also had a perfect record; all fifty-seven female House incumbents won, as did all five female incumbents in the Senate. Eight male House incumbents lost.[22] Thus, as far as winning reelection is concerned, female incumbents have reached electoral parity with men.

Moreover, female incumbents tend to win with larger electoral margins. Slightly more female incumbents earn the status of a safe seat than their male incumbents. In other words, male incumbents are slightly more likely to face a competitive general election. Female incumbents are likely to win with slightly larger shares of the two-party vote than their male counterparts. On average, female incumbents win 67.7 percent of the vote, almost three percentage points higher than male incumbents, who win 65.0 percent of the vote. In every redistricting period, women won with higher margins than men. During the 1970s, this difference was nearly six percentage points.

This suggests that there is a level playing field for male and female candidates, at least in terms of outcomes. Female incumbents actually do slightly better in terms of reelection rates. They are more likely to come from a safe seat and win with a greater share of the two-party vote. Once in office, it appears that the political glass ceiling is gone. But what does the broader competitive arena look like? Are female incumbents as likely to get a "free pass" as men and face no competition at all? Table 5.1 shows that most of the general elections featuring two women candidates are races with a female incumbent and female challenger. Are female incumbents as likely to face a female challenger as male incumbents? Do women tend to run against women more often than they run against men?

Understanding the Competitive Environment

Despite parity in electoral success, campaigns with women candidates are fundamentally different than those where only men compete for nomination and election. In particular, there are differences in (1) how the media cover the campaigns of female candidates, (2) how voters perceive and evaluate male and female candidates, and (3) how candidates formulate campaign strategy in light of the stereotypes present in media coverage and voter perceptions.

---

[22] Seven of these men lost House races, while one male Senate incumbent lost; Senate Minority Leader Tom Daschle lost his reelection bid in South Dakota to Republican John Thune. Four of the male House incumbents in Texas lost due to the unprecedented redistricting that occurred in 2003. One of the other male House incumbents, Phil Crane (R-IL), lost to a woman, Melissa Bean.

Media Coverage

Reporting on campaigns has been found to vary substantially depending on the gender of the candidate. Media coverage is often "the bane of the political woman's existence."[23] It is still "an artifact of this country's age-old but unresolved debate over the women citizens' proper roles versus 'proper women's' place."[24] As Eleanor Roosevelt put it, "If you're going to be a woman in public life, you've got to have skin as thick as a rhinoceros."[25]

Press secretaries for female members of Congress consistently report that the media tend to stress that their bosses are women first and representatives second. As one press secretary put it, "The next time [our local paper] puts together a story that doesn't mention she's a mom with young children it will be a first."[26] In contrast, press secretaries for male members of Congress generally complain about the way the media cover issues and legislation their representative sponsored. News stories are still substantially more likely to mention a woman's marital status and her age than a man's.[27] Women who run for the U.S. Senate actually receive less media coverage than their male counterparts.[28] And when they do receive coverage, the content tends to reinforce sex role stereotypes and traditional attitudes about women's roles, particularly in campaigns for higher-level offices.[29]

In fact, media coverage of women in elective office does not appear to have changed much over the last hundred years. Beginning with the first woman to serve in Congress, female candidates have always complained about the "soft news" focus in which their wardrobe, hairstyles, femininity, and family relationships receive more emphasis than their political experience

---

[23] Linda Witt, Karen Paget, and Glenna Matthews, *Running as a Woman: Gender and Power in American Politics* (New York: Free Press, 1995), 184.

[24] Witt, Paget, and Matthews, 1995, 182.

[25] Quoted from David Niven and Jeremy Zilber, "'How Does She Have Time for Kids and Congress?' Views on Gender and Media Coverage from House Offices," in *Women and Congress: Running, Winning, and Ruling,* ed. Karen O'Connor (New York: Haworth Press, 2001), 149.

[26] Quoted from Niven and Zilber, 2001, 154.

[27] Diane Bystrom et al., *Gender and Candidate Communication* (New York: Routledge, 2004), 179.

[28] Kim Fridkin Kahn and Edie Goldenberg, "Women Candidates in the News: An Examination of Gender Differences in U.S. Senate Campaign Coverage," *Public Opinion Quarterly* 55 (1991): 180–99; and Bystrom et al., 2004. See also Pippa Norris, "Women Leaders Worldwide: A Splash of Color in the Photo Op," in *Women, Media, and Politics,* ed. Pippa Norris (New York: Oxford University Press, 1997); Martha Kropf and John Boiney, "The Electoral Glass Ceiling? Gender, Viability, and the News in U.S. Senate Campaigns," in *Women and Congress: Running, Winning and Ruling,* ed. Karen O'Connor (New York: Haworth Press, 2001); and Niven and Zilber, 2001.

[29] Witt, Paget, and Matthews, 1995; and Niven and Zilber, 2001. See also Kim Fridkin Kahn, "Characteristics of Press Coverage in Senate and Gubernatorial Elections: Information Available to Voters," *Legislative Studies Quarterly* 20 (1995): 23–35; Kim Fridkin Kahn, *The Political Consequences of Being a Woman* (New York: Columbia University, 1996); Susan Carroll and Ronnee Schreiber, "Media Coverage of Women in the 103rd Congress," in *Women, Media, and Politics,* ed. Pippa Norris (New York: Oxford University Press, 1997); Shanto Iyengar et al., "Running as a Woman: Gender Stereotyping in Political Campaigns," in *Women, Media, and Politics,* ed. Pippa Norris (New York: Oxford University Press, 1997); Pat Schroeder, *Twenty-four Years of House Work and the Place Is Still a Mess* (Kansas City, Mo.: Andrews McMeel, 1999); and Eleanor Clift and Tom Brazaitis, *Madam President* (New York: Scribner, 2000).

or issue positions.[30] Throughout her career in Congress, Representative Jeannette Rankin (R-MT) was frustrated by her media coverage. She was constantly asked about her wardrobe and often portrayed as "a lady about to faint."[31] Once, when an Associated Press reporter appeared in her office, she told him to "go to hell."[32] The woman who followed Rankin in 1921 was lambasted by the press. There is no doubt that Representative Alice Robertson (R-OK) was very different from Rankin; she was an ardent antisuffragist and made it very clear that she would have voted for the United States' entry into World War I. The press, however, went well beyond comparing their policy positions. The *New York Times*, for example, wrote, "She is no tender Miss Rankin. . . . [She has] never wore a pair of silk stockings and won't wear high-heeled shoes."[33]

Even today, examples of this kind of media coverage are not hard to find. During the 1992 Illinois Senate race, the front page of the *New York Times* ran a story contrasting Democrat Carol Moseley Braun with Republican Richard Williamson: "She is commanding and ebullient, a den mother with a cheerleader's smile; he, by comparison, is all business, like the corporate lawyer he is."[34] Buried deep in the story, which was written by a female journalist, readers were told that Moseley Braun was also a lawyer with service as a U.S. attorney.[35] When Elizabeth Dole was running for president in 2000, the *Detroit News* remarked that her "public speaking style looks and sounds like Tammy Faye Baker meets the Home Shopping Network."[36] During the 2002 campaign, Ellen Goodman wrote an op-ed piece for the *Boston Globe* on Chellie Pingree, the Democrat who was challenging incumbent Senator Susan Collins (R-ME). In the second sentence, Goodman describes what Pingree wore on the campaign trail that day: "The 47-year-old Democrat . . . is heading down the Maine Turnpike, speed-talking and dressed in a light-blue turtleneck sweater."[37] Alison Roberts, a journalist for the *Sacramento Bee*, covered the 2005 campaign of Doris Matsui (D-CA):

> Doris Matsui, who is 60, is running to succeed her husband in Congress. As she talks about her loss and her new plans less than a week after her

---

[30] Kathleen Hall Jamieson, *Beyond the Double Bind: Women and Leadership* (New York: Oxford University Press, 1995); Maria Braden, *Women Politicians and the Media* (Lexington: University of Kentucky Press, 1996); Fox, 1997; Niven and Zilber, 2001; Bystrom et al., 2004; and Marie Wilson, *Closing the Leadership Gap: Why Women Can and Must Help Run the World* (New York: Viking, 2004).

[31] Witt, Paget, and Matthews, 1995, 184–85. See also Kevin Giles, *Flight of the Dove: The Story of Jeannette Rankin* (Beaverton, Ore.: Touchstone Press, 1980), 83.

[32] Quoted from Witt, Paget, and Matthews, 1995, 186.

[33] Quoted from Foerstel, 1999, 231.

[34] Isabel Wilkerson, "Black Woman's Senate Race Is Acquiring a Celebrity Aura," *New York Times*, July 29, 1992, 1.

[35] Witt, Paget, and Matthews, 1995, 181.

[36] Quoted from Wilson, 2004, 36.

[37] Ellen Goodman, "Racing All Out to Win Maine," *Boston Globe*, October 13, 2002, D11.

husband was buried, her manner is open and energetic. She sits on the edge of her living room couch, looking as though she might jump up at any moment. She is petite, dressed stylishly in a black sweater, a black-and-white nubby wool skirt and fine gold jewelry. Her delicate appearance belies the steadiness of her candidate's stance.[38]

As Representative Susan Molinari (R-NY) explained, "There I'd be, in a war zone in Bosnia, and some reporter—usually female—would comment on how I was dressed, then turn to my male colleague for answers to questions of substance."[39]

Wardrobe aside, women who cry—or even allegedly cry—cause a media frenzy. When Rankin cast her vote against World War I in 1917, the front page of the *New York Times* ran a headline that read, "Miss Rankin—Sobbing—Votes No."[40] (See figure 5.1.) Rankin's biographer did note that as she read her sixteen-word statement on the House floor, "[t]ears wandered down her cheeks."[41] The *New York Times*, however, reported that she "sank back to her seat . . . pressed her hands to her eyes, threw her head back and sobbed,"[42] which was patently false. Moreover, the paper neglected to mention that many of the male members, regardless of how they voted, were also weeping.

Fast-forward seventy years later. In September 1987, Representative Pat Schroeder (D-CO) held a press conference in Denver announcing that she was dropping out of the Democratic presidential primary. When she came to the part of her speech when she said she would no longer be running, tears momentarily ran down her face. The photo of her crying has become one of the most famous in presidential politics.[43] As Schroeder put it, "Those seventeen seconds were treated like a total breakdown."[44] Her tears were the subject of weeks of media coverage and debate. In fact, she noted that even after all of her years of service in Congress, "Anytime I go to any city to talk, that's the first piece of film the TV stations pull out. They've just decided that's the only thing I've ever done that counted."[45]

Even in the twenty-first century, a woman candidate crying was big news. In 2002, when Governor Jane Swift (R) announced she would not run for reelection, the front page of the *Massachusetts Telegram and Gazette* featured a photo of her wiping a tear from her eye. During her entire press conference, which lasted over thirty minutes, Swift teared up for about

---

[38] "Electing to Carry On: Grief Fuels Matsui's Bid for Congress," January 22, 2005, E1.
[39] Susan Molinari, *Representative Mom: Balancing Budgets, Bill, and Baby in the U.S. Congress* (New York: Doubleday, 1998), 7.
[40] "Miss Rankin—Sobbing—Votes No," *New York Times*, April 6, 1917, 1.
[41] Giles, 1980, 83.
[42] "Miss Rankin—Sobbing—Votes No," 1917, 1.
[43] See for example Clift and Brazaitis, 2000; and Schroeder, 1999.
[44] Schroeder, 1999, 185.
[45] Witt, Paget, and Matthews, 1995, 205.

DEBATE LASTED 16½ HOURS

One Hundred Speeches Were Made—Miss Rankin, Sobbing, Votes No.

ALL AMENDMENTS BEATEN

Resolution Will Take Effect This Afternoon with the President's Signature.

KITCHIN WITH PACIFISTS

Accession of the Floor Leader Added Others to the Anti-War Faction.

Special to The New York Times.

WASHINGTON, Friday, April 6.—At 3:12 o'clock this morning the House of Representatives by the overwhelming vote of 373 to 50 adopted the resolution that meant war between the Government and the people of the United States and the Imperial German Government.

Fig. 5.1 Press coverage of Jeannette Rankin's WWI vote.

thirty seconds as she was thanking her staff, yet that was the photo the paper ran above the fold. Even the *Boston Globe* referred to the event as her "tearful State House news conference."[46] Swift said she dropped out because of the challenge she would face in the primary from Mitt Romney, former head of the Salt Lake City Olympic Committee. She stated that she could not balance

---

[46] Frank Phillips, "Shake-up in the Governor's Race: Swift Yields to Romney Saying 'Something Had to Give,' Exits Race for Governor," *Boston Globe*, March 20, 2002, A1.

Miss Rankin Votes " No."

Miss Jeanette Rankin, the woman Representative from Montana, had been absent from the House most of the evening, but took her accustomed place while the roll call was in progress. When her name was called she sat silent. " Miss Rankin," repeated the clerk. Still no answer. The clerk went on with his droning, and floor and galleries buzzed.

On the second roll call Miss Rankin's name was again called. She sat silent as before. The eyes of the galleries were turned on her. For a moment there was breathless silence. Then Miss Rankin rose. In a voice that broke a bit but could be heard all over the still chamber she said:

" I want to stand by my country, but I cannot vote for war. I vote no." The " No " was scarcely audible.

And the maiden speech of the first woman Congressman ended in a sob. She was .deeply moved and big tears were in her eyes.

Fig. 5.1 (*Continued*)

running in a tough primary with her responsibilities as governor and her family; "I am sure there isn't a working parent in America that hasn't faced it, that when the demands of the two tasks you take on both increase substantially, something has to give."[47] Swift had gained national attention as the first woman to give birth while governor and was dogged by bad press during much of her term. When she decided not to run for reelection, citing family reasons, the *Lowell (Mass.) Sun* ran a front-page story entitled "Swift Sent Women a Bad Message."[48]

Interestingly, with the help of friends and constituents, Schroeder has collected stories of prominent political men crying. She calls it her "sob sister file." It includes the story of George Washington's farewell meeting with his Revolutionary War generals, who all cried around the dinner table.[49] Her file also includes President George H. W. Bush, Russian leader Mikhail Gorbachev, Lieutenant Colonel Oliver North, General Norman Schwarzkopf, President Ronald Reagan, Chile's General Augusto Pinochet, Senator John Sununu, and several male professional athletes. Schroeder argues that "crying is almost a ritual that male politicians must do to prove

---

[47] Phillips, 2002, A1.
[48] Jennifer Fenn, "Swift Sent Women a Bad Message," *Lowell (Mass.) Sun*, March 22, 2002.
[49] Schroeder, 1999, 186.

they are compassionate, but women are supposed to wear iron britches."[50] Crying helps men, but just proves that women are too emotional for politics.[51]

Over the last thirty years, while cultural attitudes about women running for office have changed substantially, and while more and more women have run for political office, it seems that media coverage of women candidates has remained constant. Female candidates may win at rates equal to their male counterparts, but the media still reinforce sex role stereotypes and portray them in a way that can disadvantage their campaigns. In other words, except in unusual circumstances like the 1992 election when being a woman was an advantage, they do not receive equal press coverage. In order to achieve equal rates of success, female candidates may have to work harder to counteract the stereotypes typically found in their coverage.

Voter Perceptions

Media coverage of campaigns involving female candidates tends to reinforce stereotypes held by voters. Male and female candidates are often perceived as having different leadership traits and different levels of competence in handling issues. Women are viewed as being more compassionate, trustworthy, and willing to compromise. Men are seen as more assertive, aggressive, and self-confident.[52] In addition to personality traits, there are

---

[50] Schroeder, 1999, 187.

[51] One exception to this is Edmund Muskie's 1972 Democratic presidential campaign. In late February, a week before the New Hampshire primary, Muskie was leading in the polls by a two to one margin, and was considered the man to beat. The *Manchester (N.H.) Union Leader* then published stories attacking his wife and accusing him of racial slurs against New Hampshire's French Canadian population. Muskie appeared live on the *CBS Evening News* to respond to the charges. Anchor Roger Mudd opened the story, stating, "Senator Edmund Muskie today denounced William Loeb, the conservative publisher of the Manchester, New Hampshire, *Union Leader,* as 'liar' and a 'gutless coward,'" and then cut to Muskie, standing on a flatbed truck in front of the paper's offices as the snow fell, crying, his voice breaking, barely able to speak. Muskie later explained that the moment "changed people's minds about me. . . . They were looking for a strong, steady man, and here I was weak." He won the primary, but only by nine points. In the wake of this episode, Muskie's campaign floundered. He came in fourth in the next primary in Florida, and by the end of April dropped out of the race; Theodore H. White, *The Making of the President, 1972* (New York: Atheneum Publishers, 1973), 84–87.

[52] Mark Leeper, "The Impact of Prejudice on Female Candidates: An Experimental Look at Voter Inference," *American Politics Quarterly* 19 (1991): 248–61; Deborah Alexander and Kristi Anderson, "Gender as a Factor in the Attribution of Leadership Traits," *Political Research Quarterly* 46 (1993): 527–45; Clyde Brown, Neil Heighberger, and Peter Shocket, "Gender-Based Differences in Perceptions of Male and Female City Council Candidates," *Women & Politics* 13 (1993): 1–17; Leonie Huddy and Nayda Terkildsen, "The Consequences of Gender Stereotypes for Women Candidates at Different Levels and Types of Office," *Political Research Quarterly* 46 (1993): 503–25; Leonie Huddy and Nayda Terkildsen, "Gender Stereotypes and the Perception of Male and Female Candidates," *American Journal of Political Science* 37 (1993): 119–147; Burrell, 1994; David Niven, "Party Elites and Women Candidates: The Shape of Bias," *Women & Politics* 19 (1998): 57–80; and Kira Sanbonmatsu, "Gender Stereotypes and Vote Choice," *American Journal of Political Science* 46 (2002): 20–34.

perceived differences in "issue ownership," the issues on which men and women are viewed as more competent.[53] Women candidates are typically seen as more competent on issues such as education, health care, rights issues, the environment, and welfare, while men are seen as more competent on issues such as taxes, budgets, crime, national defense, and foreign policy.[54]

Voter perceptions of a particular candidate's ideology are also strongly related to the gender of that candidate. Compassion issues such as education, health care, and welfare are largely associated with the Democratic Party and liberal policy positions. In contrast, the Republican Party is generally considered more competent to deal with issues like taxes, national defense, and crime.[55] These general party associations interact with gender. Female Democrats are perceived as more liberal than they actually are, and female Republicans are perceived as less conservative than they actually are.[56]

Thus, like political party labels, the gender of the candidate acts as a cue for voters.[57] Just knowing this small bit of information, voters "make inferences about a candidate's issue positions, policy competencies, ideological

[53] John Petrocik, "Issue Ownership in Presidential Elections, with a 1980 Case Study," *American Journal of Political Science* 40 (1996): 825–50; Jeffrey Koch, "Gender Stereotypes and Citizens' Impression of House Candidates' Ideological Orientations," *American Journal of Political Science* 46 (2002): 453–62; and Fox and Oxley, 2003.

[54] Leeper, 1991; Alexander and Andersen, 1993; Huddy and Terkildsen, 1993, "The Consequences"; Huddy and Terkildsen, 1993, "Gender Stereotypes"; Carroll, 1994; Michael Delli Carpini and Ester Fuchs, "The Year of the Woman? Candidates, Voters, and the 1992 Elections," *Political Science Quarterly* 108 (1993): 29–36; Karen Kaufman and John Petrocik, "The Changing Politics of American Men: Understanding the Sources of the Gender Gap," *American Journal of Political Science* 43 (1999): 864–87; Kathy Dolan, "Electoral Context, Issues, and Voting for Women in the 1990s," in *Women and Congress: Running, Winning and Ruling*, ed. Karen O'Connor (New York: Haworth Press, 2001); Sanbonmatsu, 2002, "Gender Stereotypes"; Fox and Oxley, 2003; and Bystrom et al., 2004; but see Kathy Dolan, *Voting for Women: How the Public Evaluates Women Candidates* (Boulder, Colo.: Westview Press, 2004). For a review of this literature, see Michelle Swers, "Research on Women in Legislatures: What Have We Learned, Where Are We Going?" in *Women in Congress: Running, Winning, Ruling*, ed. Karen O'Connor (Binghamton, N.Y.: Haworth Press, 2001).

[55] Petrocik,1996.

[56] Alexander and Anderson, 1993; Huddy and Terkildsen, 1993, "Gender Stereotypes"; and Jeffrey Koch, "Do Citizens Apply Gender Stereotypes to Infer Candidates' Ideological Orientations?" *Journal of Politics* 62 (2000): 414–29.

[57] Monika McDermott, "Voting Cues in Low-Information Elections: Candidate Gender as a Social Information Variable in Contemporary U.S. Elections," *American Journal of Political Science* 41 (1997): 270–83; Monika McDermott, "Race and Gender Cues in Low-Information Elections," *Political Research Quarterly* 51 (1998): 895–918; Koch, 2000, 2002; Richard Lau and David Redlawsk, "Advantages and Disadvantages of Cognitive Heuristics in Political Decision Making," *American Journal of Political Science* 45 (2001): 951–71; Sanbonmatsu, 2002, "Gender Stereotypes"; Lonna Rae Atkeson, "Not All Cues Are Created Equal: The Conditional Impact of Female Candidates on Political Engagement," *Journal of Politics* 65 (2003): 1040–61; and David King and Richard Matland, "Sex and the Grand Old Party: An Experimental Investigation of the Effect of Candidate Sex on Support for a Republican Candidate," *American Politics Research* 31 (2003): 595–612; but see Seth Thompson and Janie Steckenrider, "The Relative Irrelevance of Candidate Sex," *Women & Politics* 17 (1997): 71–92.

leanings, and character traits."[58] Gender provides a shortcut that helps voters "*estimate* the views of candidates."[59] Because women running for office, especially statewide office, are still a rare event, voters are more likely to rely on gender as a cue.[60] Gender cues are especially salient when women are a "novelty," such as in a primary election with a woman candidate running against several male competitors.[61] A 1994 survey found that two-thirds of voters felt that women had a tougher time than men getting elected to public office. Even voters who said they would vote for a woman candidate predicted she would lose.[62] Whether they actually are or not, women candidates may still be perceived as vulnerable by voters. If nothing else, it is clear that gender and party interact and have an impact on voter perceptions of a candidate's qualifications, issue positions, and ideology.

Campaign Strategy

Our discussion suggests that successful female candidates must adapt their campaign strategies to account for gender stereotypes about their character traits, issue competence, and ideology, as well as the media coverage that reinforces sex role stereotypes.[63] In essence, women face particular challenges in their "presentation of self."[64] According to Richard Fenno's classic work, *Homestyle: House Members in Their Districts*, this is the fundamental act of campaigning in which candidates place themselves in the "immediate physical presence of others" and "make a presentation of themselves."[65] In other words, candidates cultivate their images. The presentation of self is both verbal and nonverbal. The nonverbal is critical, particularly for women, since it may enhance or undermine the credibility given to verbal presentations and the level of trust that audiences place in the candidate.[66] For example, Mary Beth Rogers, the campaign manager for Ann Richards's successful run for Texas governor in 1990, explained that the main goal of the campaign was to portray her as a mother, former teacher, and "compassionate outsider" as well as a savvy and tough politician. Television ads featured Richards with her father, promising that she would get tough on

---

[58] Koch, 2000, 414.

[59] McDermott, 1997, 271.

[60] Koch, 2002, 460. See also Atkeson, 2003.

[61] Koch, 2002, 455.

[62] Seltzer, Newman, and Leighton, 1997, 76.

[63] See also Mandel, 1981.

[64] Richard Fenno, *Home Style: House Members in Their Districts* (Boston: Little Brown, 1978), 898.

[65] Fenno, 1977, 898.

[66] For example, in her first unsuccessful campaign for the Senate in 1974, Barbara Mikulski realized that "one of my problems is that I don't fit the image of a U.S. senator. You know, an Ivy-League-looking male, over 50 and over six feet tall"; quoted from Mandel, 1981, 36. Instead, she was a "round, short, fuzzy-haired Polish woman from Southeast Baltimore"; Mandel, 1981, 36. So as part of her campaign, she went on a diet. She said, "It showed people I could keep my mouth shut. . . . But it also showed them that when I make up my mind to do something, I can follow a goal"; quoted from Mandel, 1981, 36.

insurance companies that were shirking their responsibilities for people like her "daddy."[67]

It is from this presentation of self that voters draw inferences about the leadership traits of candidates. For the woman who seeks elective office, the challenge is to "craft a message and a public persona" establishing that "she can be as clear and independent a decision maker as any man, but more caring and trustworthy."[68] As one political consultant explained, in appearing before the public, women candidates "can't afford not to be nice, [or they will] immediately be branded as a bitch."[69] Thus, "[T]he woman candidate has to maintain some level of the traditional altruistic and a political above-it-all demeanor expected of a lady, all the while beating her opponents in what sometimes seems the closest thing to blood sport that is still legal."[70]

Women candidates must also account for the "political mood" or temper of the times, both nationally and locally, in formulating their campaign message and issue agendas. There are two important ways that political mood can affect women's success. The first pertains to the problems and issues deemed most important by their constituency and the degree to which these concerns mesh with voter perceptions of issue competency. If the focus rests on compassion issues, as it did in 1992, female candidates will be advantaged. In such circumstances, when women candidates use sex role expectations to their advantage, run on compassion issues, and target women voters, they are substantially more likely to win.[71] To the extent that the political mood and agenda focus on budgets and economic policy or foreign and defense policy, as they did in 2002,

---

[67] Richards was able to walk this fine line with a great deal of success in 1990. George W. Bush, however, effectively neutralized this in 1994 and was able to portray her as an "insider"; Sue Tolleson-Rienhart and Jeanie Stanley, *Claytie and the Lady: Ann Richards, Gender, and Politics in Texas* (Austin: University of Texas Press, 1994); and Jeanie Stanley, "Gender and the Campaign for Governor," in *Texas Politics: A Reader*, 2nd ed., ed. Anthony Champagne and Edward Harpham (New York: W. W. Norton, 1998). Other women have also attempted to combine these two images, including Dianne Feinstein (D-CA), who ran for governor on the slogan "Tough but Caring"; Celia Morris, *Storming the Statehouse: Running for Governor with Ann Richards and Dianne Feinstein* (New York: Charles Scribner's Sons, 1992). See also Theodore Sheckels Jr., "Mikulski vs. Chavez for the Senate from Maryland in 1986 and the 'Rules' for Attack Politics," *Communication Quarterly* 42 (1994): 311–26; and Julie Dolan, "A Decade after the Year of the Woman: Female Candidates' Success Rates in the 2002 Elections" (paper presented at the Southern Political Science Association Annual Meeting, January 2005, New Orleans).

[68] Witt, Paget, and Matthews, 1995, 214.

[69] Quoted from Witt, Paget, and Matthews, 1995, 214.

[70] Witt, Paget, and Matthews, 1995, 214.

[71] The quintessential example is Patty Murray, who ran as the "mom in tennis shoes." See Witt, Paget, and Matthews, 1995; Iyengar et al. 1997; Leonard Williams, "Gender, Political Advertising, and the 'Air Wars,'" *Women and Elective Office: Past, Present and Future*, ed. Sue Thomas and Clyde Wilcox (New York: Oxford University Press, 1998); Sanbonmatsu, 2002, "Gender Stereotypes"; Paul Herrnson, J. Celeste Lay, and Atiya Kai Stokes, "Women Running 'as Women': Candidate Gender, Campaign Issues, and Voter-Targeting Strategies," *Journal of Politics* 65 (2003): 244–55; and Shauna Shames, "The 'Un-Candidates': Gender and Outsider Signals in Women's Political Advertisements," *Women & Politics* 25 (2003): 115–47; but see Jerry Perkins and Diane Fowlkes, "Opinion Representation versus Social Representation; or Why Women Can't Run as Women and Win," *American Political Science Review* 74 (1980): 92–103.

women must formulate strategies to weaken the stereotypes and establish perceptions of issue competency on these traditional male issues. Second, there are times when the political mood is especially restive toward "politics as usual" and incumbents. Women can take advantage of being perceived as "outsiders" and as more honest during election cycles when events and scandals call into question the trustworthiness of politicians.[72] Thus, the campaign strategies employed by female candidates must take these factors into consideration. If they do not, female candidates could be substantially disadvantaged at the polls.

Implications for the Competitive Environment

These three factors—media coverage, gender stereotypes, and campaign strategy—suggest important implications for the electoral competition that women might face and lead us to draw several conclusions. Female candidates, including female incumbents, might be perceived as more vulnerable in the electoral arena than male candidates.[73] Despite the increasing presence of women in the electoral arena, a female nominee or incumbent remains a novelty. From 1992 to 2000, a woman won the Democratic nomination for the House at least once in 176 districts (40.5 percent); voters in the remaining 259 districts (59.5 percent) never saw a female Democratic nominee. In other words, during that entire eight-year period, there were no female Democratic candidates in a general election in almost two-thirds of all districts. The nomination of a female Republican is even more of a rare event. For the same period, there were female Republican nominees in only 113 districts (26.0 percent), and no female nominees in 322 districts (74.0 percent). This is particularly important, because reliance on gender stereotypes is stronger in exactly these circumstances, when candidates are perceived as novelties.[74]

Moreover, as much as a candidate's gender serves as a cue for voters, it can serve as a cue for potential opponents. Male candidates typically reformulate their campaign strategies when they run against women, and many plan campaign activities that target women voters.[75] In its August–September 1990 issue, *Campaigns and Elections*, a widely read trade magazine, ran an article entitled "How to Defeat Women and Blacks," advising men to "steal their opponent's rainbow" by quickly and specifically raising women's issues or compassion issues in order to "[b]eat your opponent to her strongest issue."[76]

---

[72] Burrell, 1994; Kahn, 1996; and Sanbonmatsu, 2002, "Gender Stereotypes."

[73] See for example Allison Stevens, "The Strength of These Women Shows in Their Numbers," *CQ Weekly*, October 25, 2003, 2625.

[74] Koch, 2002.

[75] In a survey of California State Senate campaign managers, Richard Fox found that eighteen of twenty-three (78 percent) campaign managers for male candidates said that they changed their strategy when it became apparent they would face a female opponent; Fox, 1997, 49.

[76] David Beiler, "How to Defeat Women and Blacks," *Campaigns & Elections*, August–September 1990. See also Fox, 1997; and Carole Chaney, "Running against a Woman: Advertising Strategies in Mixed-Sex Races for the United States Senate and Their Impact on Candidate Evaluation" (paper presented at the Western Political Science Association Annual Meeting, 1998, Los Angeles).

The very next issue of the magazine featured a piece by Sharon Rodine, president of the National Women's Political Caucus, entitled "How to Beat Bubba." Rodine observed, "We know that women are targeted more often due in great part to their perceived vulnerability in raising money and seeking seats which have been held by men for years."[77] She argues that if women "run as women," this can be used against them. If a woman candidate builds her campaign around stereotypes in order to win, this may actually limit her strategic choices and the types of responses she can use effectively. Thus, even though women win elective office as often as men do, women candidates, especially incumbents, may be initially perceived as easier to defeat and may face a more competitive environment.

A second implication is more positive. Conceivably, women candidates may foster competition in a different way, as role models for other women. In states with competitive female candidates, women citizens were more likely to discuss politics, have higher levels of political knowledge, and feel politically efficacious; viable women candidates "represent symbolic and substantive cues to women citizens that increase their political engagement."[78] The logical extension of this is that successful women candidates inspire other women to run. Beyond the role model effect, however, deciding to run against another woman can also be a strategic decision.[79] Against the backdrop of gender stereotypes, it is important to consider what the success of a woman winning a House seat signifies. It demonstrates that the female candidate was able to neutralize the stereotypes or make them work to her advantage. Her victory serves as a cue signaling that a woman can overcome the hurdles and compete successfully in that district.

Thus, gender stereotypes may work in a number of ways to stimulate competition. The novelty of female candidates may suggest vulnerability. In addition, female candidates as role models may inspire more women to run. A female incumbent may provide a "strategic signal" to other women about the probability of winning a district. Given all of this, do female incumbents face more competition to retain to their House seats than their male counterparts? Do female incumbents face more competition from female candidates?

---

[77] Sharon Rodine, "How to Beat Bubba," *Campaigns and Elections Magazine*, October–November, 1990.

[78] Atkeson, 2003, 1042. Research suggests that a female candidate may stimulate more voter participation among women. Susan Hansen, "Talking about Politics: Gender and Contextual Effects on Political Proselytizing," *Journal of Politics* 59 (1997): 73–103; and Angela High-Pippert, "Female Empowerment: The Influence of Women Representing Women," *Women & Politics* 19 (1998): 53–67.

[79] See for example Wilma Rule, "Why Women Don't Run: The Critical and Contextual Factors in Women's Legislative Recruitment," *Western Political Quarterly* 34 (1981): 60–77; Rosalyn Cooperman and Bruce Oppenheimer, "The Gender Gap in the House of Representatives," in *Congress Reconsidered*, 7th ed., ed. Lawrence Dodd and Bruce Oppenheimer (Washington, D.C.: CQ Press, 2001); Palmer and Simon, 2001; and Barbara Palmer and Dennis Simon, "Political Ambition and Women in the U.S. House of Representatives, 1916–2000," *Political Research Quarterly* 56 (2003): 127–138.

Explaining the Competitive Environment

On the surface, electoral outcomes for the U.S. House do indicate parity between male and female candidates. As table 5.2 showed, female incumbents actually do slightly better than male incumbents. This does suggest that there is gender equality, at least as far as the final outcome of an election is concerned. We expect, however, that given the disparity in press coverage and the way gender can affect voter perceptions and campaign strategies, that female candidates, particularly female incumbents, may be perceived as more vulnerable, and as a result may draw more competition than their male counterparts. In addition, female incumbents may have a "role model" effect and draw more female competition than their male counterparts.

While reelection rates show that there are no differences between male and female incumbents, there are, however, other aspects of the competitive environment that have not been explored. In addition to reelection rates, there are three other indicators of competition: no opponent in the primary, no major party opponent in the general election, and the "free pass" in which the incumbent has no opposition in both the primary and general elections. By examining these additional measures of competition, we produce a more complete and nuanced picture of the electoral environment.[80]

As table 5.3 shows, female incumbents are less likely to enjoy the luxury of having no opponent. In districts where women stand for reelection, there are slightly more contested primaries: 33.3 percent of districts compared to 29.4 percent of districts where men stand for reelection. Female incumbents also have fewer uncontested general elections: 9.6 percent compared to 16.3 percent for men. In fact, female incumbents are half as likely to get the "free pass"; while 11.9 percent of male incumbents had no competition in their primary or general elections, only 5.6 percent of women had no competition.

There are substantial partisan differences as well. Among Democratic incumbents, men and women are equally likely to face competition in their primary, 36.4 percent of men and 36.2 percent of women, but the parity ends there. Democratic female incumbents are substantially more likely to face major party opposition in the general election; the proportion of uncontested general elections (10.7 percent) is half the rate for men (21.1 percent). A similar result holds for the "free pass." Only 6.4 percent of Democratic female incumbents avoid competition throughout the election cycle, compared to 14.5 percent for Democratic males.

It should be noted that, in general, Republican incumbents face a less contentious primary arena than their Democratic counterparts: Democratic incumbents face primary challenges in 36.3 percent of their primaries, whereas the rate for Republicans is only 20.4 percent. But the patterns between

---

80 The full statistical tests are available in Barbara Palmer and Dennis Simon, "When Women Run against Women: The Hidden Influence of Female Incumbents in Elections to the U.S. House of Representatives, 1956–2002," *Politics and Gender* 1 (2005): 39–63.

Table 5.3 Uncontested Primary and General Elections among Incumbent Candidates for the House, 1956–2004

	Male Incumbents	Female Incumbents
All Incumbents		
Contested primary election	29.4%	33.3%*
	(2,627/8,930)	(190/571)
Uncontested general election	16.3%	9.6%***
	(1,486/9,122)	(56/586)
Uncontested primary and general elections	11.9%	5.9%***
	(1,065/8,930)	(37/571)
Democratic Incumbents		
Contested primary election	36.4%	32.2%
	(1,883/5,176)	(136/376)
Uncontested general election	21.1%	10.7%***
	(1,105/5,237)	(41/383)
Uncontested primary and general elections	14.5%	6.4%***
	(748/5,176)	(24/376)
Republican Incumbents		
Contested primary election	19.8%	27.7%**
	(744/3,754)	(54/195)
Uncontested general election	9.8%	7.4%
	(381/3,885)	(15/203)
Uncontested primary and general elections	8.4%	6.7%
	(317/3,754)	(13/195)

A t-test for the difference in proportions is used for each male-female comparison. *** $p < .001$, ** $p < .01$, and * $p < .05$.

Republican men and women are different in two ways. First, in contrast to the parity between men and women in Democratic primaries, female Republican incumbents are more likely to be challenged in a primary than their male counterparts, 27.7 percent versus 19.8 percent. Second, there are only slight differences in the rates of competition that male and female Republican incumbents face in the general election, 9.8 and 7.4 percent respectively. In addition, male and female Republican incumbents are also about equally as likely to receive a "free pass" and face no competition at either stage. Thus, while female Democratic incumbents face more competition in the general election, female Republican incumbents face more competition in their primaries. The interaction of gender and party is clear. Overall, at the primary stage, Republican male incumbents are the least likely to face primary competition. Female Democratic incumbents are the least likely of all to get a "free pass."

We also expect that the relationship between incumbent gender and competition should not be confined to contests within the party. If, as we hypothesize, female incumbents are perceived as vulnerable, then there should be greater competition for the nomination within the opposition party as well. As table 5.4 shows, competition for the opposition party nomination is significantly greater in districts with a female incumbent. When a female incumbent is running for reelection, there are contested primaries in the opposition party in 47.8 percent of the districts. When a male incumbent is running for reelection, there are contested primaries in the opposition party in 42.0 percent of the districts. For example, in 1976, Martha Keys, a Democratic incumbent from the 2nd District of Kansas, ran for her second term. She had won the open seat two years prior with 55.6 percent of the vote. She was the only Democrat in the Kansas delegation. In her reelection campaign, she ran unopposed in her own primary, but six Republicans, including one woman, ran in the opposition party primary. In the general election, she narrowly defeated Ross Freeman with 51.7 percent of the vote.

Once again, there are differences between the parties. When a female Democrat is the incumbent, 44.1 percent of Republican primaries are contested, compared to 38.6 percent of districts where the Democratic incumbent is male. Similarly, when a female Republican holds the House seat, 54.6 percent of the Democratic nominees are chosen in contested primaries, compared to 45.9 percent when the incumbent is a Republican male. Together, tables 5.3 and 5.4 show that female incumbents are associated with a more competitive electoral environment; they face more contested races than their male colleagues and, at the same time, foster more contested primary races within the opposition party.

Table 5.4 Contested Primary Races for the House within the Opposition Party, 1956–2004

	Districts with Male Incumbents	Districts with Female Incumbents
All opposition contests in districts where an incumbent seeks reelection	42.0% (3,163/7,535)	47.8%** (250/523)
Contested Republican primaries in districts with Democratic incumbent seeking reelection	38.6% (1,579/4,086)	44.1%* (150/340)
Contested Democratic primaries in districts with Republican incumbent seeking reelection	45.9% (1,584/3,449)	54.6%* (100/183)

The cell entries represent the proportion of contested primaries. A t-test for the difference in proportions is used for each male-female comparison. ** $p < .01$ and * $p < .05$.

While all of this suggests that female incumbents face more competition than male incumbents in general, do they draw other women into the campaign? In other words, are women more likely to run against women than men? Table 5.5 reports the proportion of contested primaries in which women challenged an incumbent of their own party and an incumbent of the opposition party. Additionally, to provide a composite picture of female challengers, we combine the first two rows of the table and report the total proportion of women seeking the nomination in districts held by male and female incumbents. The table shows that female incumbents foster additional female candidacies in a district. Among all incumbents, the percentage of female incumbents being challenged by a woman in their own party primary, 15.4 percent, exceeds the rate at which women challenge male incumbents, 10.5 percent. This intraparty gender effect is more pronounced among Democrats than Republicans. Female Democrats are challenged by women in 16.9 percent of contested primaries, while male Democrats are challenged by women in 11.3 percent of the contests. Among Republicans, the pattern still holds, but the difference is not significant. Women challenge female Republicans in 9.3 percent of the contests, while male incumbents face a female opponent in 8.7 percent of the contested Republican primaries.

Table 5.5 also reveals that female incumbents seeking reelection influence the gender distribution of candidates seeking the nomination within the opposition party. Women are almost twice as likely to seek the nomination of the opposition party in districts with a female incumbent (23.5 percent) than in districts with a male incumbent (13.2 percent). Moreover, within the opposition party, while the numbers are small, the incidence of two or more women competing for the nomination is greater in districts with female incumbents than in districts with male incumbents, 3.5 percent compared to 1.3 percent. Republican women seek the nomination in 20.3 percent of the districts with a female Democratic incumbent, compared to 14.8 percent of the primaries in districts held by male Democrats. Female Democrats seek the nomination in 22.4 percent of the primary elections in districts with a female Republican incumbent, compared to only 10.5 percent of the contests in districts held by male Republicans. The aggregate picture of primary elections for the U.S. House of Representatives, presented in the third row of table 5.5, is clear. The presence of additional female candidates is significantly greater in districts where a female incumbent holds the seat, regardless of party. This suggests that female incumbents do provide, as role models or as testaments to the "winability" of the district, a signal that leads other women to run for the seat.

Moreover, within the opposition, not only do women seek the nomination more frequently in districts held by female incumbents, but they win the nomination more frequently in these districts as well. Table 5.6 presents the percentage of nominations won by female candidates in the opposition party. Across all of these opportunities, the success rate for

Table 5.5 Female Competition in Contested Primary Races for the House, 1956–2004

	All Male Incumbents	All Female Incumbents	Male Democratic Incumbents	Female Democratic Incumbents	Male Republican Incumbents	Female Republican Incumbents
Within Incumbent Party						
Incumbent faces a primary challenge from a female candidate	10.5% (267/2,551)	15.4%* (27/175)	11.5% (216/1,883)	16.9%* (23/136)	8.7% (65/744)	9.3% (5/54)
Within Opposition Party						
Female candidate seeks nomination within the opposition party	13.2% (1,173/8,890)	23.5%*** (126/536)	10.9% (581/5,320)	23.3%*** (91/390)	16.8% (656/3,909)	23.2%** (47/203)
Within Incumbent and Opposition Party (Sum of Rows 1 and 2)						
Proportion of elections with a female challenger for the nomination	12.6% (1,440/11,411)	21.5%*** (153/711)	14.8% (825/5,570)	20.3%** (63/310)	10.5% (615/5,871)	22.4%*** (90/410)

A t-test for the difference in proportions is used for each male-female comparison. *** p < .001, ** p < .01, and * p < .05.

Table 5.6 Women Winning the Nomination of the Opposition Party in Districts Where an Incumbent Is Seeking Reelection, 1956–2004

Opposition Party	Districts Held by Male Incumbent	Districts Held by Female Incumbent
All opposition nominations, Democrats and Republicans, in districts where an incumbent seeks reelection	7.2% (667/9,229)	13.8 %*** (82/593)
Democrats running in districts with a Republican incumbent seeking reelection	9.8% (384/3,909)	14.3%* (29/203)
Republicans running in districts with a Democratic incumbent seeking reelection	5.3% (283/5,320)	13.6%*** (53/390)

The cell entries represent the proportion of nomination opportunities won by female candidates. These opportunities include contested primaries, uncontested primaries, and convention nominations. A t-test for the difference in proportions is used for each male-female comparison. *** p < .001, ** p < .01, and * p < .05.

women in districts with a female incumbent is double the rate in districts with male incumbents. The relationship also holds for both Democrats and Republicans. In fact, the Republican difference in success rates, 13.6 percent versus 5.3 percent, is larger than the rate among female Democrats seeking the nomination in Republican-held districts. The results in table 5.6 lend further credence to our earlier observation that the presence of a female incumbent may serve as a signal about the electoral prospects for women in a district. Because more women seek and win nominations in districts with a female incumbent, the presence of a female incumbent is likely to be a salient factor in the strategic decisions women make about where to run.

An additional question that arises from our analysis is whether the effect of female incumbents on the competitive environment varies with the level of electoral security. Table 5.7 presents seven measures of the electoral environment for marginal male and female incumbents.[81] There are significant differences between safe female incumbents and their male counterparts on all seven indicators; safe female incumbents face a more competitive electoral environment. In districts with female incumbents, there are substantially fewer uncontested general elections, (11.2 percent versus 18.8 percent for men), more contested primaries (33.1 percent versus 29.7 percent for men), and fewer "free passes" (7.6 percent versus 13.8 percent for men). In this sense, women actually enjoy less of the electoral security that is conventionally attributed to holding a safe seat. In addition, women from safe districts face more primary challenges from women than their male counterparts.

---

[81] In this analysis, we rely upon the conventional definition of safe and marginal districts. A marginal district is one in which the incumbent won with less than 55 percent of the two-party vote in the previous election.

Table 5.7 Electoral Competition for Incumbents Seeking Reelection, 1956–2004

	Safe Male Incumbent	Safe Female Incumbent	Marginal Male Incumbent	Marginal Female Incumbent
Uncontested general election	18.8% (1,443/7,656)	11.2%*** (56/498)	2.9% (43/1,466)	0% (0/88)
Incumbent faces contested primary	29.7% (2,236/7,515)	33.1%* (162/488)	27.6% (391/1,415)	33.7% (28/83)
Incumbent not contested in primary or general election	13.8% (1,034/7,515)	7.6%*** (37/488)	2.2% (31/1,415)	0% (0/83)
Incumbent challenged by female in party primary	10.8% (242/2,236)	15.4%* (25/162)	10.0% (39/391)	10.7% (3/28)
Contested primary in opposition party	39.0% (2,394/6,140)	44.0%* (194/440)	55.1% (769/1,395)	67.5%* (56/83)
Female seeks nomination in opposition party	12.7% (989/7,739)	20.4%*** (103/504)	16.6% (248/1,490)	39.3%*** (35/89)
Female wins nomination in opposition party	7.1% (551/7,739)	12.7%*** (64/504)	7.8% (116/1,490)	20.2%*** (18/89)

A t-test for the difference in proportions is used for each male-female comparison. *** $p < .001$, ** $p < .01$, and * $p < .05$.

Safe female incumbents also stimulate more competition within the opposition party. There were contested primaries in the opposition party in 44.0 percent of the districts with safe female incumbents, while there were contested primaries in the opposition party in 39.0 percent of the districts with safe male incumbents. Safe female incumbents also promote greater participation by women within the opposition party. In 20.4 percent of the districts with safe female incumbents, women ran in the opposition party's primary. This occurred in only 12.7 percent of the districts with male incumbents. Moreover, women were more likely to win the opposition party primary in these districts; female candidates in opposition party primaries won the nomination in 12.7 percent of the districts with safe female incumbents, while they won in 7.1 percent of the districts with safe male incumbents. Our analysis suggests that not only do safe female incumbents have more competition than safe male incumbents, but also the competition is more likely to be female.

A remarkable illustration is found in the electoral career of Republican Representative Connie Morella. Morella was first elected in 1986 from Maryland's 8th District, which wraps around the northern half of Washington, D.C. A large proportion of her constituents were federal employees, and the district has always leaned Democratic. As a result, throughout her career, Morella was one of the most liberal Republicans in the House. As table 5.8 shows, only in 1996 did she face any major competition for renomination. She was never challenged by a Republican woman. However, there always was a great deal of competition within the Democratic primary. In 1996, for

Table 5.8 Representative Connie Morella (R-MD) and Her Competition

Year	Her Primary Opponents	Democratic Primary Opponents	Female Democratic Primary Opponents	Her Vote Total in the General Election (%)
1986*	2	7	1	52.9
1988	0	5	1	62.7
1990	1	3	0	76.8
1992	0	8	0	72.5
1994	1	5	0	70.3
1996	3	9	2	61.3
1998	1	7	1	60.3
2000	0	5	3	53.1
2002	0	4	1	48.3

*Open seat.

example, there were nine candidates in the Democratic primary, even though Morella won the previous election with over 70 percent of the vote. Several of the challengers in the Democratic primary were women, but none of them ever won the nomination. The level of competition is quite surprising in light of the "safeness" of her district. Despite the fact that Morella was a Republican in a Democratic district, she was quite popular among her constituents. Until 2000, she consistently won reelection with at least 60 percent of the vote. In fact, her average two-party vote for all of her successful reelection campaigns was 65.3 percent, well over the safe margin of 55 percent. During the redistricting cycle in the wake of the 2000 U.S. Census, Maryland's state legislature substantially redrew her district, making it even more Democratic. As a result, in 2002, State Senator Chris Van Hollen won a four-way primary that included one woman, and then went on to defeat Morella in one of the most expensive and highly contested races of the year.[82] He won with only 51.7 percent of the vote.

There have only been thirty-seven safe female incumbents who enjoyed a "free pass" and had no competition in their primary or general elections. Six of these races (16.2 percent) were in 2004: Representatives Marsha Blackburn (R-TN), Eddie Bernice Johnson (D-TX), Stephanie Tubbs Jones (D-OH), Sheila Jackson Lee (D-TX), Hilda Solis (D-CA), and Diane Watson (D-CA).[83] The lone Republican, Representative Blackburn, was running for her second term. Although the Democratic Party did not field an opponent, she spent

---

[82] Jacki Koszczuk and H. Amy Stern, eds., *CQ's Politics in America, 2006* (Washington, D.C.: CQ Press, 2005), 485.

[83] Seven women, the most in any election cycle, enjoyed "free passes" in the 1998 midterm election: Maxine Waters (D-CA), Tillie Fowler (R-FL), Karen Thurman (D-FL), Ileana Ros-Lehtinen (R-FL), Carrie Meek (D-FL), Nita Lowey (D-NY), and Eddie Bernice Johnson (D-TX).

over $575,000 on her campaign to fight "those who would oppose freedom and would oppose strengthening democracy."[84] Of the five Democrats, four are African American and one is Latina; they all came from majority-minority districts where the total proportion of blacks, Hispanics, and Asians exceeds 80 percent. All of these districts voted overwhelmingly Democratic in the 2004 presidential election.[85] This suggests that women of color, who tend to come from racially gerrymandered districts, may be more secure electorally than white women. In the aggregate, however, the number of safe female incumbents who face no competition is substantially lower than the number of safe male incumbents.

The environment for marginal female incumbents is even more competitive. As table 5.7 shows, no marginal female incumbent has been unopposed in the general election over the five decades of our study. In contrast, forty-three marginal male incumbents had no opponents. Similarly, there are no marginal female incumbents who enjoyed the "free pass." Thirty-one marginal male incumbents have. While these numbers are small, it is quite surprising that marginal female incumbents *always* have competition.

With respect to competition within the opposition party, there are also substantial differences between men and women from marginal districts. As expected, marginal districts are more competitive than safe districts in general, but there is a clear gender effect; 67.5 percent of marginal districts with female incumbents had contested primaries in the opposition party, compared to only 55.2 percent of the marginal districts with male incumbents. Representative Stephanie Herseth (D-SD), for example, who won a special election in the summer of 2004 with only 50.6 percent of the two-party vote, saw seven Republicans competing to challenge her reelection in the fall.[86] Moreover, marginal female incumbents were more than twice as likely to draw female candidates into the opposition primary. In 39.3 percent of the districts with marginal female incumbents, women ran in the opposition primary, compared to 16.6 percent of the districts with marginal male incumbents. And women were almost three times as likely to win the opposition primary in districts with marginal female incumbents. Women won the opposition primary in 20.2 percent of districts with marginal female incumbents, while they won in only 7.8 percent of districts with marginal male incumbents. As table 5.8 reveals, in marginal districts, female incumbents not only stimulate more competition within the opposition party, but also draw more women of the opposition party into the fray.

---

[84] "Marsha Blackburn: Campaign Finance/Money-Contributions-Congressman-2004," http://www.opensecrets.org/politicians/summary.asp?CID=N00003105&cycle=2004 (accessed July 3, 2005); and Bartholomew Sullivan, "Safe Territory: Redrawing of Congressional District Lines Puts Incumbents in Driver's Seat," *Memphis Commercial Appeal*, October 27, 2004, B1.

[85] Koszczuk and Stern, 2005.

[86] None of them were women.

Conclusion

In 1986, after serving five terms in the House, Barbara Mikulski (D-MD) won an open Senate seat with 61 percent of the vote. Despite the fact that she won her seat by a margin conventionally considered safe, in her reelection campaign of 1992, fifteen Republicans ran in the opposition primary. Even more astonishing was that six candidates challenged her in the Democratic primary. She won the primary easily with 77 percent of the vote, and then went on to trounce Republican Alan Keyes in the general election with 71 percent of the vote. But even that performance was not sufficient to scare off competition. In 1998, ten Republicans fought for the nomination, and two Democrats challenged her in the Democratic contest. Mikulski won her primary with 84 percent of the vote and won the general election with 71 percent of the vote. Finally, in 2004, "her electoral strength [was] finally beginning to sink in"; she ran uncontested in her own primary, and only one Republican, a little-known state senator, threw his hat in the ring to challenge her.[87]

Chapters 3 and 4 suggest that women make the same strategic calculations as men with regard to pursuing congressional careers. And we began this analysis by showing that male and female incumbents win reelection at equal rates. We also show, however, that if we look more deeply at the competitive environment, the political glass ceiling reappears. While there are variations between the parties, women running for reelection face a more competitive environment than their male counterparts in two ways. First, female incumbents face more competition in the primary and general elections. They are more likely to be challenged within their own party's primary, and they foster more competition in the opposition party's primary. They are less likely to face no competition in the general election. They are also less likely to get the "free pass" and face no opposition in the primary and general elections. In fact, female incumbents with the least electoral security, those from marginal districts, *always* face competition.

Second, the presence of a female incumbent encourages more women to run. Female incumbents face more challenges from female candidates in primary elections. Within the opposition party in particular, more women run as challengers. Interestingly, it appears that female incumbents actually help their female opponents. Women running in opposition primaries were more likely to win in districts held by female incumbents. Ultimately, this shows that, despite comparable reelection rates, female incumbents have to work harder than male incumbents to retain their seats.

Our results thus reveal that female incumbents have a "hidden influence." Their presence increases the entry and participation of female candidates in House elections. The more women who serve in the House of Representatives, the more women run. On one hand, this enhances the representative character of House elections. It also has a secondary and salutary effect of increasing

---

[87] Stevens, 2003.

awareness and activity among female voters within a district.[88] On the other hand, given where these women are more likely to run—in districts with female incumbents—the overall number of women in the House will not necessarily increase under these circumstances. Female candidacies are disproportionately concentrated in districts already represented by women. Once a woman is elected, she faces higher probabilities of being challenged for renomination by a woman and facing a female opponent in the general election. In House elections from 1956 to 2004, for example, there are seventy-nine instances of female challengers running against female incumbents. In these contests, incumbency maintains its supremacy; female incumbents lost to a female challenger in only four of those seventy-nine elections (5.1 percent).[89] As a result, the increase in competition associated with female incumbents does not trigger changes in the gender composition of the House. While the presence of female incumbents encourages more women to run, incumbency continues to act as a "political glass ceiling," impeding the increase in the number of women who serve in Congress.

---

[88] Hansen, 1997; and Atkeson, 2003.

[89] It is worth noting that female challengers defeated male incumbents in 25 of 636 opportunities for a victory rate of 3.9 percent.

6

Where Women Run
Women-Friendly Districts

Two major conclusions emerge from our analysis in chapter 5. First, women face a more competitive environment than men when seeking reelection. Second, female incumbents are more likely than their male counterparts to face female challengers. The implication is that female candidates tend to cluster in particular districts. What explains this? Can we identify the districts that are more likely to elect women? Do women run and win elections in districts that are different than those that elect men?

Congressional districts in the United States vary widely in their demographic characteristics. Candidates rely heavily on demographic data to create their campaign strategies, and they often hire consulting firms, like the National Committee for an Effective Congress, to provide them with detailed demographic data and suggestions for targeting voters in their districts.[1] However, we know very little about the demographic characteristics of the districts where women have been successful candidates. But even a cursory analysis of the geographic distribution of the current women in Congress suggests that there is a distinct political geography to the districts they represent: twenty-five of the sixty-six women in the 109th Congress (2005 session), or 37.9 percent, are from California and New York. Female members of the House are not randomly distributed across the country. As we noted in chapter 1, even the women elected in the mid-1950s tended to come from urban districts and large cities.

In this chapter, we draw from the research on the relationship between the demographic character of districts and electoral success. There are particular demographic characteristics that make a House district predictably

---

[1] http://www.ncec.org/about/index.html (accessed July 5, 2005). U.S. Census data at the congressional-district level are also available to anyone at no charge; see http://factfinder.census.gov/home/saff/main.html?_lang=en.

Democratic or Republican. Democratic districts tend to be liberal, urban, racially diverse, and blue collar or working class; Republican districts tend to be conservative, suburban or rural, and wealthier. Our analysis shows that there are particular demographic characteristics that make a House district more or less likely to elect a woman. In effect, there are districts that are "women-friendly." Moreover, the characteristics that make a district women-friendly are not identical to those associated with party victories. Female Democratic House members tend to win election in districts that are more liberal, more urban, more diverse, more educated, and much wealthier than those won by male Democratic members of the House; they come from much more compact, "tonier," upscale districts than their male counterparts. Female Republican House members tend to win election in districts that are less conservative, more urban, and more diverse than those electing male Republicans; they come from districts that are "less Republican." These results, however, only hold true for white women. The African American women in Congress, all of whom have been Democrats, represent districts that are quite similar to those electing African American men.

Based upon our analysis of district characteristics, we create an index of women-friendliness. This index helps predict where women will run and the likelihood that they will win. Women are more likely to seek and win the nomination for the House in districts that are women-friendly, particularly female Democrats. Moreover, we show that the number of women-friendly districts has increased over the last three redistricting cycles, suggesting that the opportunities for women are expanding. On the other hand, these opportunities may not be equally shared by women in both parties. The districts that have elected Republican women are strikingly similar to the districts that have elected Democratic men. The districts where Republican women are most likely to win the primary because they are female are the districts where they will have a hard time winning the general election because they are Republican.

Demographic Characteristics and Women Candidates

The use of demographic characteristics in predicting electoral success has been an integral part of the academic study of elections and representation.[2] District-level characteristics, such as urban population, income, and racial diversity, are important predictors of primary competition and voter turnout.[3] Demographics have been used to explain and predict the outcome of presidential elections.[4] These factors have also taken center stage in the study of redistricting and, in particular, racial and partisan gerrymandering.[5] The first response of House incumbents to questions about their districts is usually a description of the demographics of their constituencies: the boundaries of the district, its socioeconomic and racial makeup, and its partisan and ideological leanings. As Richard Fenno noted in *Home Style*, "Every congressman, in his mind's eye, sees his geographic constituency in terms of some special configuration of such variables."[6] For example, one typical member of Congress described his district this way:

> It's a middle America district. It is poorer than most, older than most, more rural than most. It is basically progressive. It's not a conservative district; it's a moderate district. It is a heavily Democratic district—the third most, or second most, Democratic in the state. It is very concerned with bread and butter issues. It is environmentally conscious as far as

---

[2] See for example V. O. Key, *Southern Politics in State and Nation* (New York: A. A. Knopf, 1949); Kevin Phillips, *The Emerging Republican Majority* (New York: Anchor House, 1969); Richard Scammon and Ben Wattenberg, *The Real Majority* (New York: Coward-McCann, 1970); John Sullivan, "Political Correlates of Social, Economic and Religious Diversity of the American States," *Journal of Politics* 35 (1973): 70–84; Morris Fiorina, *Representatives, Roll Calls, and Constituencies* (Lexington, Mass.: D.C. Heath, 1974); Jon Bond, "The Influence of Constituency Diversity on Electoral Competition in Voting for Congress, 1974–1978," *Legislative Studies Quarterly* 8 (1983): 201–17; Charles Bullock and David Brady, "Party, Constituency, and Roll-Call Voting in the U.S. Senate," *Legislative Studies Quarterly* 8 (1983): 29–43; Benjamin Page et al., "Constituency, Party, and Representation in Congress," *Public Opinion Quarterly* 48 (1984): 741–56; Robert Erikson, Gerald Wright, and John McIver, *Statehouse Democracy: Public Opinion and Policy in the American States* (New York: Cambridge University Press, 1993); Earl Black and Merle Black, *The Vital South* (Cambridge, Mass.: Harvard University Press, 1992); Earl Black and Merle Black, *The Rise of Southern Republicans* (Cambridge, Mass.: Harvard University Press, 2002); and John Judis and Ruy Teixeira, *The Emerging Democratic Majority* (New York: Scribner, 2002).

[3] See for example Robert Dahl and Edward Tufte, *Size and Democracy* (Stanford, Calif.: Stanford University Press, 1973); Gordon Black, "Conflict in the Community: A Theory of the Effects of Community Size," *American Political Science Review* 68 (1974): 1245–61; Raymond Wolfinger and Steven Rosenstone, *Who Votes?* (New Haven, Conn.: Yale University Press, 1980); Steven Rosenstone and John Hansen, *Mobilization, Participation, and Democracy in America* (New York: Macmillan, 1993); and Paul Herrnson and James Gimpel, "District Conditions and Primary Divisiveness in Congressional Elections," *Political Research Quarterly* 48 (1995): 117–34.

[4] One early work, *Candidates, Issues, and Strategies*, presented simulations of the 1960 and 1964 presidential elections; Ithiel de Sola Pool, Robert Abelson, and Samuel Popkin, *Candidates, Issues, and Strategies* (Cambridge, Mass.: MIT Press, 1965). The analysis included pooling a large number of national surveys from several organizations and the use of demographic factors to create 480 distinct voter profiles. This book prompted publication of a novel, *The 480*, by Eugene Burdick (New York: McGraw-Hill, 1964), coauthor of William Lederer and Eugene Burdick, *The Ugly American* (New York: Norton, 1958), and Eugene Burdick and Harvey Wheeler, *Fail Safe* (New York: McGraw-Hill, 1962). In *The 480*, Burdick implicitly critiqued the simulated use of voter profiles and warned of future campaigns "when all crucial decisions would be made by a 'people machine'"; John Kessel, "Review of Candidates, Issues and Strategies," *Midwest Journal of Political Science* 10 (1966): 515–18, 515.

[5] See for example Bernard Grofman, Robert Griffin, and Amihai Glazer, "The Effect of Black Population on Electing Democrats and Liberals to the House of Representatives," *Legislative Studies Quarterly* 17 (1992): 365–79; Andrew Gelman and Gary King, "Enhancing Democracy through Legislative Redistricting," *American Political Science Review* 88 (1994): 541–59; Andrew Gelman and Gary King, "A Unified Method of Evaluating Electoral Systems and Redistricting Plans," *American Journal of Political Science* 38 (1994): 514–54; Kevin Hill, "Do Black Majority Districts Aid Republicans?" *Journal of Politics* 57 (1995): 384–401; Charles Cameron, David Epstein, and Sharyn O'Halloran, "Do Majority-Minority Districts Maximize Substantive Black Representation in Congress?" *American Political Science Review* 90 (1996): 794–812; and David Lublin, "Racial Redistricting and African-American Representation," *American Political Science Review* 93 (1999): 183–86.

[6] Richard Fenno, *Home Style: House Members in Their Districts* (Boston: Little Brown, 1978), 2.

rural districts go. . . . It is a basic working-class district with pockets of professional leadership.[7]

Some districts are more homogeneous than others, but no member of Congress sees "an undifferentiated glob" within the district boundaries.[8] Fenno found, in fact, that when describing their districts, the vast majority of members provided demographic information before they described the political leanings of their constituents, if they provided an evaluation of the partisanship of the district at all.[9]

The conventional wisdom among academics, political consultants, and candidates is that there are particular configurations of demographic characteristics associated with typical Democratic and Republican districts:

> Democrats receive strong support from lower socioeconomic groups, blue collar workers, minority ethnic and religious groups and central city voters, while Republicans receive their largest support from higher socioeconomic groups, white collar workers, whites, Protestants, and suburban voters.[10]

The relationship between the characteristics of a constituency and its voting habits is anchored in electoral history and flows from the strategies that the Democratic and Republican Parties devise for building winning coalitions. Party appeals to voters are not undifferentiated. Instead, platforms and proposed policies are designed to target and win the loyalties of voting blocs. Since the time of Franklin Roosevelt, a vital part of the Democratic Party's coalition has been ethnic, working-class voters residing in large cities such as Boston, New York, Philadelphia, Pittsburgh, Cleveland, Detroit, Milwaukee, and Chicago. Similarly, Republicans built their coalition by advocating the interests of the business and professional classes as well as rural America. In more recent times, support for the Democrats among African Americans, Hispanics, and women is, in part, a response to the party's advocacy of civil rights, while Republicans have made substantial inroads among social conservatives and Evangelical Christians, particularly in the South.

To illustrate the characteristics of "party-friendly" districts, the presidential election results of 2000 can be used to identify the twenty strongest Democratic districts and the twenty strongest Republican districts. The average vote for President George W. Bush in the Democratic top twenty was 14.0 percent, compared to 72.7 percent in the Republican top twenty. Within the Democratic districts, the average proportions of African American and Hispanic

---

[7] Fenno, 1978, 2.
[8] Fenno, 1978, 3.
[9] Fenno, 1978, 3.
[10] William Koetzle, "The Impact of Constituency Diversity upon the Competitiveness of U.S. House Elections, 1962–1996." *Legislative Studies Quarterly* 23 (1998): 562–73.

residents were 44.2 and 20.9 percent respectively; the comparable proportions for the Republican districts were 4.5 percent African American and 11.1 percent Hispanic. Median income in the Democratic districts was $34,973 compared to $45,014 in the Republican districts. The proportion of urban residents was 100 percent in the Democratic districts and 71.1 percent in the Republican districts. Thirteen of the twenty Republican districts are located in the South, while only one southern district fell into the Democrats' top twenty. This comparison shows that there are relatively clear, identifiable demographic characteristics associated with the party identification of a district. In addition, the ideology—liberalism or conservatism—of a constituency is related to its demographic character as well.[11]

Given that we can identify party-friendly districts, there are two possibilities with respect to the impact of these factors on the success of female candidates. First, those women elected to the House may find success in districts that conform to the conventional party profile of districts. In this instance, there would be nothing unique about districts that elect women to the House. Party would trump gender, in that female and male Democratic members would be elected from demographically similar districts, as would female and male Republican members. Alternatively, women may be elected from districts where one or more characteristics do not conform to the standard partisan profile; female and male Democratic members would be elected from demographically distinct districts, as would female and male Republican members. If this is the case, then "women-friendly" and "party-friendly" denote different kinds of districts.

Is there any theoretical reason to expect that districts electing Democratic and Republican women would be different from the standard partisan profile? As discussed in chapter 5, the gender of a candidate is a critical factor that influences media coverage, how voters perceive candidates, and campaign strategy. Women are viewed as being more compassionate, trustworthy, and willing to compromise. Men are seen as more assertive, aggressive, and self-confident. In addition to these personality traits, voters perceive differences in "issue ownership," the issues on which men and women are viewed as more competent. Women candidates are typically seen as more competent on compassion issues—education, health care, rights issues, the environment, and welfare. Men are seen as more competent on issues such as taxes, budgets, crime, national defense, and foreign policy. Most importantly for our analysis here, voter perceptions of candidates' ideology are strongly related to gender. Female Democrats are perceived as more liberal than they actually are, and female Republicans are perceived as less conservative than they actually are.[12] This implies that party identification and gender interact.

---

[11] Phillip Ardoin and James Garand, "Measuring Constituency Ideology in U.S. House Districts: A Top-Down Simulation," *Journal of Politics* 65 (2003): 1165–89.

[12] Alexander and Anderson, 1993; Huddy and Terkildsen, 1993, "Gender Stereotypes"; and Jeffrey Koch, "Do Citizens Apply Gender Stereotypes to Infer Candidates' Ideological Orientations?" *Journal of Politics* 62 (2000): 414–29.

Because there are certain demographic characteristics that predict the partisanship of a district, we explore the extent to which these factors predict whether a woman will win that congressional seat. There is a great deal of partisan and ideological variation across districts. This implies that particular districts, because of their demographic composition, may be more or less receptive to the perceived leadership traits of women, to agendas emphasizing compassion issues, and to a candidate's ideology perceived to be on the more liberal (or less conservative) side of the spectrum.

Understanding the Political Geography of Women's Success

There are surprisingly few analyses of the geography and demography of congressional districts and their impact on women's success. The most noteworthy feature of the published research is the lack of uniformity.[13] As a result, we know very little about the districts *where* women win. To explore the impact of political geography on women's success, we examine four categories of demographics: (1) partisanship and ideology, (2) geographic factors, (3) race and ethnicity, and (4) socioeconomic factors.

Partisanship and Ideology

At present, there are nearly twice as many Democratic women than Republican women in Congress. This suggests that party plays a role in the electoral success of women. But what exactly is that role? Party is the most important cue in the voting booth: Democratic voters overwhelmingly vote for Democratic candidates, and Republican voters overwhelmingly vote for Republican candidates.[14] For example, in the 2004 presidential election, a national exit poll found that 89 percent of those identifying themselves as Democrats voted for John Kerry, and 93 percent of those identifying themselves as Republicans voted for George W. Bush.[15] Party labels provide voters with a shortcut that is

---

[13] There is substantial variation in the unit of analysis, the dependent variables, and statistical methods. There is also some research on state legislatures; Wilma Rule, "Why Women Don't Run: The Critical and Contextual Factors in Women's Legislative Recruitment," *Western Political Quarterly* 34 (1981): 60–77; Wilma Rule, "Why More Women Are Legislators: A Research Note," *Western Political Quarterly* 43 (1990): 437–48; Carol Nechemias, "Geographic Mobility and Women's Access to State Legislatures," *Western Political Quarterly* 38 (1985): 119–31; and Carol Nechemias, "Changes in the Election of Women to U.S. State Legislative Seats," *Legislative Studies Quarterly* 12 (1987): 125–42. For a review of this literature, see Dennis Simon and Barbara Palmer, "The Political Geography of Women-Friendly Districts, 1972–2000" (paper presented at the Southern Political Science Association Annual Meeting, January 2005, New Orleans).

[14] See for example Angus Campbell et al., *The American Voter* (New York: Wiley, 1960); Richard Lau and David Sears, eds., *Political Cognition* (Hillsdale, N.J.: L. Erlbaum Associates, 1986); Wendy Rahn, "The Role of Partisan Stereotypes in Information Processing about Political Candidates," *American Journal of Political Science* 37 (1993): 472–96; Michael Delli Carpini and Scott Keeter, *What Americans Know about Politics and Why It Matters* (New Haven, Conn.: Yale University Press, 1996); and Richard Lau and David Redlawsk, "Advantages and Disadvantages of Cognitive Heuristics in Political Decision Making," *American Journal of Political Science* 45 (2001): 951–71.

[15] www.cnn.com/ELECTION/2004/pages/results/states/US/P/oo/epolls.0.html (accessed June 10, 2005).

used to infer candidate positions and make evaluations about their willingness to support a candidate.

We also know that gender is a cue for voters as well. As noted in chapter 5, voters use gender to evaluate candidates. There are, however, very few studies that explore how these two cues interact, but the results are suggestive.[16] One study of the 1972 election found that Republican women ran in districts that leaned Democratic; in other words, Republican women won nomination in districts where they were less likely to win.[17] In 1993, the Republican Network to Elect Women (RENEW) sponsored a poll of 820 randomly selected adults. Each respondent was read an identical description of a Republican candidate, but half of the sample was told the candidate was male, and the other half was told the candidate was female. As expected, in the aggregate, substantially more Republican respondents said they would be "very likely" to vote for the candidate (47.1 percent) than Democratic respondents (19.6 percent).[18] However, the survey found that Republican female candidates "have serious problems within their own party."[19] Respondents who identified themselves as Republicans were less likely to support the female candidate than the male candidate. When asked to compare identical profiles, male Republicans' support for the profile dropped by nearly fourteen percentage points when told the candidate was a female.[20] Overall, Republican women candidates actually did better among Democratic and Independent voters. This illustrates how the cues of party and gender can interact. The research also implies that Republican women will be more effective as candidates in swing districts or in districts where crossover voting is more likely, districts that are distinct from those that regularly elect Republican males.[21]

As a measure of district partisanship, we use the proportion of the two-party vote won by the Republican candidate in the most recent presidential election; higher percentages indicate that the district is more Republican, while lower percentages indicate that the district is more Democratic.[22] Using the 2000 election as an example, the vote for President Bush ranged from

---

[16] For a review of this literature, see Richard Matland and David King, "Women as Candidates in   Congressional Elections," in *Women Transforming Congress*, ed. Cindy Simon Rosenthal (Norman: University of Oklahoma Press, 2002); and David King and Richard Matland, "Sex and the Grand Old Party: An Experimental Investigation of the Effect of Candidate Sex on Support for a Republican Candidate," *American Politics Research* 31 (2003): 595–612.

[17] R. Darcy and Sarah Slavin Schramm, "When Women Run against Men," *Public Opinion Quarterly* 41 (1977): 1–12; but see Barbara Burrell, *A Woman's Place Is in the House: Campaigning for Congress in the Feminist Era* (Ann Arbor: University of Michigan Press, 1994).

[18] King and Matland, 2003, 601.

[19] King and Matland, 2003, 604.

[20] King and Matland, 2003, 604.

[21] King and Matland, 2003, 605.

[22] A variety of measures of district partisanship have been used in other studies. See for example Darcy and Schramm, 1977; and Burrell, 1994.

5.2 percent in the 16th District of New York to 78.0 percent in the 8th District of Texas.[23] The average vote across all congressional districts was 49.1 percent.

We measure the ideology of a district using a composite score created by political scientists Phillip Ardoin and James Garand. A positive score indicates that the district is more conservative, while a negative score indicates that the district is more liberal.[24] For the decade from 1992 to 2000, the most conservative district was the 10th District of North Carolina, with a score of 35.5; the most liberal district was the 16th District of New York, with a score of –46.7. The average score across all congressional districts was 10.7. We expect that female members of Congress are elected in districts that have a different partisan and ideological profile than those that elect males.

Geographic Factors

District size has been hypothesized to affect the success of women candidates. The logic is that the larger the House district, measured in square miles, the harder it is to represent. Because constituents are dispersed in larger districts, more time is required to keep in contact with them. This is a particular problem for women. Women are generally under more time constraints than men because they are usually the primary caregivers of children even when they serve in public office.[25] Women are more likely to juggle the roles of spouse, parent, and elected official than their male counterparts. Thus, women are going to encounter more "geographic immobility" than men.[26] A study done in the early 1980s, for example, found that women state legislators were more likely to run in districts closer to the state capital. It would also follow that women would come from smaller, more geographically compact districts.[27]

In the 109th Congress (2005 session), the smallest House district in the country was New York's 11th District in Brooklyn, only twelve square

---

[23] Democrat Jose Serrano represents the 16th District of New York. Based upon the 2000 U.S. Census, it is the poorest district in the nation with a median income of $19,311; 30.3 percent of the residents are African American and 68.2 percent are Hispanic. The congressman from the 8th District of Texas is Republican Kevin Brady. The median income in his district is $60,619; 5.2 percent of the residents are African American, and 13 percent are Hispanic.

[24] District ideology is a composite score that includes the Democratic vote for president in the district, location in the Deep South, and the proportion of district residents who are blue-collar workers, homeowners, and urban residents. The scores are available at http://www1.app-state.edu/~ardoinpj/research.htm (accessed July 20, 2005). Unfortunately, this measure is only available for two of the three redistricting periods we analyze.

[25] Virginia Sapiro, "Private Costs of Public Commitments or Public Costs of Private Commitments? Family Roles versus Political Ambition," *American Journal of Political Science* 26 (1982): 265–79; Richard Fox, "Gender, Political Ambition and the Decision Not to Run for Office," Center for American Women and Politics, 2003, http://www.rci.rutgers.edu/~cawp/Research/Reports/Fox2003.pdf; and Jennifer Lawless and Richard Fox, *It Takes a Candidate: Why Women Don't Run for Office* (New York: Cambridge University Press, 2005).

[26] Nechemias, 1985. One study found that populous states with small legislatures had smaller proportions of women state legislators, which also suggests that district size acts as a constraint; Emmy Werner, "Women in the State Legislatures," *Western Political Quarterly* 19 (1968): 40–50.

[27] We measure geographic size by the total square miles of the district; these data were obtained from the U.S. Census and are reported in the Adler data set.

miles. The seat was held by Democratic Representative Major Owens, an African American man who has been reelected eleven times. Democratic Representative Carolyn Maloney is from the smallest district represented by a woman, the 14th District of New York, the third smallest district in the nation. At fifteen square miles, the district covers parts of Manhattan and Queens. Apart from those states sending only one representative to the House, the largest district in the nation is the 2nd District of Nevada, at 105,635 square miles. The district is represented by Republican Jim Gibbons. Male House members come from districts that average 1,836 square miles, while female House members come from districts that average only 410 square miles. In fact, women represent six of the nation's twenty smallest districts—almost one-third.[28] None of the six districts is larger than 60 square miles. Of the twenty largest districts in the nation, women represent two states in at-large seats, Republican Representative Barbara Cubin of Wyoming and Democratic Representative Stephanie Herseth of South Dakota. If the five at-large representatives are eliminated (there is one each for five states), the only woman elected from one of the twenty largest districts in the nation is Republican Representative Cathy McMorris, elected for the first time in 2004 from Washington's 5th District, at 23,166 square miles. Thus, we expect that the women in the House will, on average, represent smaller districts than the men in the House.

One of the more consistent findings of past research is that women in Congress are more likely to represent urban districts.[29] Women are more likely to be recruited to run for office in urban areas because there is a "larger pool of activist women who are potential candidates" than in rural areas.[30] There are also more seats and thus more opportunities to run in areas with higher populations.[31] Democratic women in particular tend to rely on women's groups for campaign support, and these organizations tend to be located in larger urban centers.[32] EMILY's List, for example, has major offices in Washington, D.C. and Los Angeles. The Women's Campaign Fund has offices in Washington, D.C. and New York. In addition, women are more likely to be

---

[28] In addition to Maloney, they are Democrat Nydia Velazquez from New York's 12th District (20 square miles), Democrat Diane Watson from California's 33rd District (48 square miles), Democrat Maxine Waters from California's 35th District (55 square miles), Democrat Loretta Sanchez from California's 47th District (55 square miles), and Democrat Lucille Roybal-Allard from California's 34th District (59 square miles).

[29] Barbara Burrell, "Women Candidates in Open-Seat Primaries for the U.S. House: 1968–1990," *Legislative Studies Quarterly* 17 (1992): 493–508; Darcy and Schramm, 1977; Irene Diamond, *Sex Roles in the State House* (New Haven, Conn.: Yale University Press, 1977); Rule, 1981; Susan Welch, "Are Women More Liberal than Men in the U.S. Congress?" *Legislative Studies Quarterly* 10 (1985): 125–34; and Welch et al., "The Effect of Candidate Gender on Election Outcomes in State Legislative Races," *Western Political Quarterly* 38 (1985): 464–75; but see Emmy Werner, "Women in the State Legislatures," *Western Political Quarterly* 19 (1968): 40–50; and Jeane Kirkpatrick, *Political Woman* (New York: Basic Books, 1974).

[30] Darcy and Schramm, 1977, 8.

[31] Rule, 1981, 71.

[32] Darcy and Schramm, 1977, 8.

recruited and do well electorally in urban areas because these constituencies are most receptive to agendas emphasizing social welfare issues. These issues, which include funding for after-school programs, aid to dependent children, and other public assistance programs, are often major concerns in urban districts. Because women are perceived to be "better" on these issues, they are more likely to run and win.[33] Based upon the 2000 U.S. Census, there are forty-nine House districts in which the proportion of urban residents is 100 percent; there are twenty districts where the proportion of urban residents is less than 40 percent. The 5th District of Kentucky, at 21.3 percent, is the least urban in the country. It is represented by Republican Harold Rogers. More generally, in House elections from 1956 to 2002, the average percent of urban residents in districts that elected Republican women was 73 percent, compared to 64.5 percent in districts that elected Republican men. Among Democrats, the averages were 85.7 percent for women and 71.4 percent for men. Given that district size and urbanization are related, we expect that women will have a higher probability of winning in districts that have a larger proportion of their population living in urban areas.[34]

Cultural traditionalism has also been found to be an important predictor of women's success. As we explained in chapter 3, women in the South were especially discouraged from running for office. Historically, the barriers that kept women out of the political arena included the region's nonegalitarian heritage, support for restricting women's political and social roles, and rejection of women's suffrage and the Equal Rights Amendment.[35] We found that of the 180 careerist women to serve in the House, only thirty-two, 17.8 percent, were elected from southern states; nine of the thirty-two women were African American. We expect, then, that regional differences help explain the success of women.[36] Female candidates will be more likely to seek and to win House seats in districts outside the South.

Race and Ethnicity

Numerous studies of congressional districts have examined the impact of race and ethnicity. One analysis of women in Congress during the 1980s found that the diversity of the district had no impact on the success of women candidates.[37] Another study of women in Congress during the 1970s found, however, that women members tended to win in districts that were more racially and ethnically diverse; their districts had a higher percentage of African Americans and a higher percentage of immigrants.[38] This makes sense, given that voter registration among African Americans increased in the wake of the

---

[33] Rule, 1981, 65.
[34] We use the data provided by the U.S. Census in the Alder data set.
[35] Rule, 1981, 63.
[36] Here, we use the same classification of states in the South as we did in chapter 3.
[37] Burrell, 1984.
[38] Welch, 1985.

Voting Rights Act of 1965.[39] In many states, these populations tend to reside in urban areas.

Beyond the racial and ethnic makeup of a district, there is clear evidence about the impact of the race and ethnicity of candidates. Like party and gender, the race and ethnicity of a candidate operate as cues for voters.[40] Moreover, taking the race and ethnicity of the candidate as well as the constituency into account is especially important since white and black districts may have different profiles, especially in light of the 1990s round of districting and the creation of majority-minority districts in several states. In 1982, Congress amended the Voting Rights Act of 1965, mandating that minorities be able to "elect representatives of their choice."[41] The theory was that increasing the number of minorities in a district would increase the number of minorities elected to the House: minority voters are much more likely than white voters to vote for minority candidates.[42] In fact, one study suggests that "only the percentage of blacks and Latinos in the district alters the probability of an African American winning election to the House."[43] Thus, in 1992, the first round of elections under the new mandate, fifteen new districts were created to maximize the number of African American constituents. This produced the largest increase in the number of African Americans elected to the House in history. In addition, ten new districts were created to maximize the number of Hispanic constituents, which also resulted in the largest increase in the number of Hispanics in the House.[44]

---

[39] The Voting Rights Act of 1965 dramatically increased black voter registration in the South; Edward Carmines and James Stimson, *Issue Evolution: Race and the Transformation of American Politics* (Princeton, N.J.: Princeton University Press, 1989), 49. Within six months of its passage, over 75,000 African Americans were added to voter registration roles. In 1963, only 43 percent of blacks were registered to vote; by 1968, 62 percent of blacks were registered to vote; Marsha Darling, "African-American Women in State Elective Office in the South," in *Women and Elective Office: Past, Present and Future,* ed. Sue Thomas and Clyde Wilcox (New York: Oxford University Press, 1998), 154. See also Jerald David Jaynes and Robin Williams, eds., *A Common Destiny: Blacks and American Society* (Washington, D.C.: National Academy Press, 1989).

[40] See for example David Lublin, *The Paradox of Representation: Racial Gerrymandering and Minority Interests in Congress* (Princeton, N.J.: Princeton University Press, 1997); and Lau and Redlawsk, 2001.

[41] Quoted from David Canon, *Race, Redistricting, and Representation: The Unintended Consequences of Black Majority Districts* (Chicago: University of Chicago Press, 1999), 1.

[42] See for example Bernard Grofman and Lisa Handley, "Minority Population Proportion and the Black and Hispanic Congressional Success in the 1970s and 1980s," *American Politics Quarterly* 17 (1989): 436–45; Lisa Handley and Bernard Grofman, "The Impact of the Voting Rights Act on Minority Representation: Black Office Holding in Southern State Legislatures and Congressional Delegations," in *Quiet Revolution in the South: The Impact of the Voting Rights Act, 1965–1990,* ed. Chandler Davidson and Bernard Grofman (Princeton, N.J.: Princeton University Press, 1994); Lublin, 1997; and Canon, 1999.

[43] Lublin, 1997, 40.

[44] Lublin, 1997, 22–23. See also Carol Swain, *Black Faces, Black Interests: The Representation of African-Americans in Congress* (Cambridge, Mass.: Harvard University Press, 1993); Cameron, Epstein, and O'Halloran, 1996; Kenny Whitby, *The Color of Representation: Congressional Behavior and Black Interests* (Ann Arbor: University of Michigan Press, 1997); and Richard Fleisher and Jon Bond, "Polarized Politics: Does It Matter?" in *Polarized Politics: Congress and the President in a Partisan Era,* ed. Jon Bond and Richard Fleisher (Washington D.C.: CQ Press, 2000).

Thus, the diversity of the district as well as the race and ethnicity of the candidate must be taken into account. As discussed in chapter 3, until the 1960s, many white women obtained legislative seats at the state and national levels upon the death of a husband. Very few black women have taken this route to office;[45] nearly all won election without the advantages bestowed by a deceased husband.[46] In the wake of the Civil Rights and Women's Rights Movements, black women made much faster gains than white women in obtaining elective office, particularly at the local and state levels.[47]

At the national level, as table 6.1 shows, only thirty women of color have served in the House, and most of them were elected very recently. In the 109th Congress (2005 session), there were twelve African American women. The only woman of color to serve in the Senate was Carol Moseley Braun (D-IL) from 1992 to 1998. The first African American woman to serve in Congress, Shirley Chisholm, was elected in 1968. Chisholm had been the second black woman to serve in the New York State Assembly. After two terms in the state legislature, she decided to run for Congress when a constituent who was on welfare visited her home, offered her a campaign donation of $9.62 in change from a bingo game she won, and pledged to raise money for her every Friday night.[48] Chisholm noted, "When I decided to run for Congress, I knew I would encounter both anti-black and antifeminist sentiments. What surprised me was the much greater virulence of the sex discrimination. . . . I was constantly bombarded by both men and women exclaiming that I should return to teaching, a woman's vocation, and leave politics to men."[49] While there have been three African American Republican men to serve in Congress since Reconstruction,[50] there has yet to be a black Republican woman elected to Congress. In 2004, in Virginia's 3rd District, Republican Winsome Sears (see figure 6.1) ran unsuccessfully against incumbent Democrat Bobby Scott, an African American man who ran unopposed in his last several elections. Sears was the first African American Republican elected to the Virginia General Assembly.

---

[45] Of the widows who won a seat in the House, only one, Representative Cardiss Collins (D-IL), was African American.

[46] Jewel Prestage, "Black Women State Legislators: A Profile," in A Portrait of Marginality: The Political Behavior of American Women, ed. Marianne Githens and Jewel Prestage (New York: David McKay, 1977); Jewel Prestage, "The Case of African American Women and Politics," PS: Political Science and Politics 27 (1994): 720–21; and Gary Moncrief, Joel Thompson, and Robert Schuhmann, "Gender, Race and the State Legislature: A Research Note on the Double Disadvantage Hypothesis," Social Science Journal 28 (1991): 481–87.

[47] Herrington Bryce and Alan Warrick, "Black Women in Electoral Politics," in A Portrait of Marginality: The Political Behavior of American Women, ed. Marianne Githens and Jewel Prestage (New York: David McKay, 1977); R. Darcy and Charles Hadley, "Black Women in Politics: The Puzzle of Success," Social Science Quarterly 69 (1988): 629–45; and Darling, 1998.

[48] Karen Foerstel, Biographical Dictionary of Congressional Women (Westport, Conn.: Greenwood Press, 1999), 55.

[49] Foerstel, 1999, 54.

[50] Senator Ed Brooke of Massachusetts, who served from 1967 to 1979, Representative Gary Franks, who served from the 5th District of Connecticut from 1991 to 1997, and Representative J. C. Watts, who served from the 4th District of Oklahoma from 1995 to 2002.

Table 6.1 Women of Color Elected to the House

Name	Dates of Service

African Americans

Shirley Chisholm (D-NY)	1969–1983
Yvonne Brathwaite Burke (D-CA)	1973–1979
Cardiss Collins (D-IL)	1973–1997
Barbara Jordan (D-TX)	1973–1979
Barbara-Rose Collins (D-MI)	1982–1985
Katie Hall (D-IL)	1982–1985
Maxine Waters (D-CA)	1991–present
Carrie Meek (D-FL)	1993–2003
Corrine Brown (D-FL)	1993–present
Eddie Bernice Johnson (D-TX)	1993–present
Cynthia McKinney (D-GA)	1993–2003; 2005–present
Sheila Jackson Lee (D-TX)	1995–present
Juanita Millender-McDonald (D-CA)	1995–present
Julia Carson (D-IN)	1997–present
Carolyn Cheeks Kilpatrick (D-MI)	1997–present
Barbara Lee (D-CA)	1997–present
Stephanie Tubbs Jones (D-OH)	1999–present
Diane Watson (D-CA)	2001–present
Denise Majette (D-GA)	2003–2005
Gwen Moore (D-WI)	2005–present

Asian Pacific Islanders

Patsy Mink (D-HI)	1965–1977, 1990–2002
Patricia Saiki (R-HI)	1987–1991
Doris Matsui (D-CA)	2005–present

Latinas

Ileana Ros-Lehtinen (R-FL)	1989–present
Lucille Roybal-Allard (D-CA)	1993–present
Nydia Velazquez (D-NY)	1993–present
Loretta Sanchez (D-CA)	1997–present
Grace Napolitano (D-CA)	1999–present
Hilda Solis (D-CA)	2001–present
Linda Sanchez (D-CA)	2003–present

Sources: Center for American Women and Politics, *Women of Color in Elective Office, 2005* (New Brunswick, N.J.: Rutgers University, 2005); and *U.S. Congress Handbook* (Washington, D.C.: Votenet Solutions, 2005).

Fig. 6.1 Winsome Sears talks with Dvora Lovinger at a fundraiser during her 2004 House campaign. Sears was the first African American Republican elected to the Virginia General Assembly. Photo by Barbara Palmer.

The first Cuban American to be elected to Congress, Representative Ileana Ros-Lehtinen (R-FL), is also the only female Republican Latina to be elected to Congress. Ros-Lehtinen won a highly contested special election for Democrat Claude Pepper's seat after he died in 1989. Born in Havana, Ros-Lehtinen immigrated to the United States when she was seven. While she tends to vote with the conservative wing of the Republican Party in Congress the vast majority of the time, because of her background and constituency, she often breaks party lines on immigration issues.[51] Another Hispanic Republican woman ran in 2004; Becky Armendariz Klein unsuccessfully ran in the Texas 25th District against Lloyd Doggett, a Democratic incumbent whose district was substantially redrawn by the Republican-controlled state legislature in 2003. The new district was 70 percent Hispanic, was 350 miles long, and shared a nickname as one of the "fajita districts." During the campaign, Armendariz Klein caused a small media storm when she referred to Doggett as a "gringo."[52] She lost with 31 percent of the vote, but Doggett spent almost $2 million to win the seat.[53]

As measures of district diversity, we use the percentage of residents who identified themselves in the U.S. Census as African American, Hispanic, or Latino, and foreign-born.[54] Across the time frame of our study, districts that elected women were, on average, 13.5 percent black, 9.3 percent Hispanic, and

---

[51] Her American Conservative Union score in 2004 was 80 percent and indicates high agreement with the positions of this conservative group; www.vote-smart.org/issue_rating_category.hph?can_id=H0851103 (accessed June 15, 2005).

[52] Jaime Castillo, "Words Such as 'Gringo,' 'Smear' Flying in Doggett-Klein Race," *San Antonio (Texas) Express-News*, July 24, 2004, 3B.

[53] http://www.opensecrets.com (accessed June 15, 2005).

10.4 percent foreign-born; the comparable averages for districts electing men were 11.1 percent black, 6.3 percent Hispanic, and 5.7 percent foreign-born. Thus, we expect that female House members will run and be elected in districts that are more racially diverse than those of their male counterparts. In addition, we expect that African American and Hispanic House members will be elected in districts that have a substantially higher proportion of people of color. If gender and race interact, then female African American and Hispanic representatives will be elected from districts that are different from those that elect male African American and Hispanic representatives as well as those that elect white female representatives.

Socioeconomic Factors

Several socioeconomic factors are thought to influence the success of women candidates. Women in Congress tend to be elected in wealthier districts.[55] One line of reasoning suggests that lower incomes make legislative service more attractive to men; because politics is an option for men, it "becomes more relevant when men's opportunities in other occupations [are] limited. . . . When income levels are greater for men, other occupations become more attractive even when state legislative salaries are high."[56] As a measure of income, we use the relative medium income of the congressional district, expressed as a percent of the national median.[57] Values greater than 100 percent represent districts over the national median, and values less than 100 percent are those below the national median. The magnitude of the measure conveys the degree to which a district is rich or poor compared to all congressional districts in a given redistricting period. For example, according to the 2000 Census, the poorest congressional district is the 16th District of New York, with a median income of $19,311, and the wealthiest is the 11th District of Virginia, with a median income of $80,397. Across all

---

[54] For African Americans and foreign-born residents, we use the data provided by the U.S. Census in the Adler data set. For Hispanics or Latinos, we use the data provided by the U.S. Census, compiled by David Lublin; available at http://www.american.edu/dlublin/research/data.htm.

[55] Rule, 1981; Welch, 1985; Nechemias, 1987; and Burrell, 1994.

[56] Rule, 1981, 69.

[57] More specifically, simply using the median income in each district could be problematic given the upward trend in the measure over the decades of our analysis. For example, the median income across all congressional districts was $9,555 in the period 1972–1980; this increased to $19,701 during the period 1982–1990 and increased again to $34,114 for the 1992–2000 districting period. Median income across all congressional districts in the 2000 U.S. Census was $41,060. To control for this drift, we used these national median values from each redistricting period and then divided each district's median by the national median. Thus, the measure expresses median income in the district as a proportion of the median across all districts for each redistricting period. The interpretation of the measure is easy. Values greater than 100 percent represent districts over the national median, and values less than 100 percent are those below the national median. The magnitude of the measure conveys the degree to which a district is rich or poor compared to all congressional districts in a given redistricting period. Over the time frame of our analysis, the values of the relative income measure range from 42.7 to 188.2 percent.

congressional districts, median income is $41,060. Using our measure, the relative income in New York's 16th is 47.0 percent of the national average, and in Virginia's 11th it is 196 percent of the national average. We expect that as the median income of a district increases, the likelihood that a female candidate would win should also increase.

Income and education are highly correlated, so it is not surprising that women in Congress tend to be elected in districts that have higher education levels.[58] People with more education are more likely to support a more egalitarian view of women and less likely to hold traditional attitudes about gender roles.[59] In addition, women with more education are more likely to run for office, and consequently, districts with higher levels of education should be more fertile recruiting grounds.[60] To measure education, we use the proportion of residents age twenty-five or older who completed four or more years of college.[61] According to the 2000 Census, the proportion of residents with college degrees is lowest in two districts, both of which are represented by men: California's 20th, represented by Democrat Jim Costa, and Texas' 29th, represented by Democrat Gene Green. The district with the highest education level, at 57 percent, is the 14th District of New York, represented by Democrat Carolyn Maloney. We anticipate that as the proportion of residents with college degrees increases in a district, women should be more likely to win a House seat.

Related to income and education are indicators of social class. There is evidence that women are likely to be more successful in middle-class districts than in blue-collar, working-class districts.[62] Women residing in middle-class districts are more likely to "have occupations that provide opportunities to run for office."[63] Moreover, the traditionalist and less-than-accepting attitudes toward female candidates among labor leaders and white ethnic groups influential in Democratic Party politics have also served as a barrier to women candidates.[64] Until relatively recently, "party slating of candidates by ethnic background appear[ed] to be reserved for the sons of ethnics."[65] For the decade from 1992 to 2000, the 17th District of Ohio is among those that are the most blue collar. Historically, the core of this district is Youngtown and

---

[58] Nechemias, 1987; and Allison North Jones and Ellen Gedalius, "Martinez 'Humbled to Be' U.S. Senator," *Tampa Tribune*, November 4, 2004.

[59] See for example Susan Welch and Lee Sigelman, "Changes in Public Attitudes toward Women in Politics," *Social Science Quarterly* 63 (1982): 312–21.

[60] Burrell, 1994.

[61] We use the proportion of residents age twenty-five or older who completed four or more years of college. The data were gathered by the U.S. Census and are contained in the Lublin data set.

[62] Nechemias, 1987; and Susan Welch and Donley Studlar, "The Opportunity Structure for Women's Candidacies and Electability in Britain and the United States," *Political Research Quarterly* 49 (1996): 861–74.

[63] Welch and Studlar, 1996, 863.

[64] Welch and Studlar, 1996, 869. See also Kira Sanbonmatsu, "Political Parties and the Recruitment of Women to State Legislatures," *Journal of Politics* 64 (2002): 791–809.

[65] Rule, 1981, 64.

surrounding areas in Mahoning and Trumbull Counties.[66] Once the home of numerous steel mills, the district is heavily unionized, with the General Motors Assembly Plant in Lordstown now a major employer. Since 1936, five men have represented the district, four Democrats and one Republican.[67] Between 1956 and 2004, only four Democratic women sought the nomination in the district and none were successful. During the same time period, only three Republican women entered campaigns for the seat; two won the nomination but were soundly defeated in the general election.[68] In constrast, with only 2.8 percent of its residents employed in blue-collar jobs from 1992 to 2000, the 14th District of New York has one of the smallest working-class constituencies in the nation. The district includes the Upper East Side of Manhattan and is home to "people with more accumulated wealth than anywhere else in the world."[69] Democrat Carolyn Maloney has represented this district since 1992. In both 1998 and 2000, Maloney defeated female Republicans to retain her seat.[70] Between 1972 and 2000, the proportion of blue-collar workers across all districts ranged from 2.3 to 26.3 percent; the national average was 9.5 percent. Given that social class is correlated with income and education, we expect that women will do better in districts with fewer blue-collar workers.[71]

One final demographic characteristic that we add to this mix could cut either way: the school-age population in a district. Given that women candidates are perceived as more competent on issues involving education and children, the parents of school-age children might be more likely to vote for a woman candidate: the more parents in a district, the more likely a woman would win the district. On the other hand, families with school-age children might have more traditional attitudes about women. Women with children are less likely to work outside the home full-time than women without children. There are three districts whose school-age population exceeds 24 percent: the 15th District of Texas, represented by Democrat Ruben Hinojosa; the 1st District of Utah, represented by Republican Rob Bishop; and the 3rd District of Utah, represented by Republican Chris Cannon. Among the districts with the lowest school-age population are New York's 14th, represented by Maloney,

---

[66] Michael Barone and Richard Cohen, *Almanac of American Politics, 2004* (Washington, D.C.: National Journal, 2003), 1293–96.

[67] Michael Kirwan (D, 1937–1970), Charles Carney (D, 1970–1979), Lyle Williams (R, 1979–1983), James Traficant (D, 1983–2003), and Tim Ryan (D, 2003–present).

[68] In 1970, Democrat Charles Carney defeated Republican Margaret Dennison, 58–42 percent; in 2002, Democrat Tim Ryan won the three-way contest with 51 percent of the total vote to 34 percent for Republican Ann Womer Benjamin. James Traficant, who had been expelled from Congress, earned 15 percent of the vote as an independent candidate.

[69] Barone and Cohen, 2003, 1138.

[70] In 1998, Maloney defeated Stephanie Kupferman, 77.0 to 23.0 percent; in 2000, she defeated C. Adrienne Rhodes with 76.3 percent of the vote.

[71] We use the data provided by the U.S. Census in the Adler data set. It should be noted that the proportion of blue-collar workers contained in the Adler data differs from those reported in other sources.

and Florida's 22nd, represented by Republican Clay Shaw. Overall, the average school-age population across all House districts is 15.5 percent. Because women remain the primary caregivers to children, the number of school-age children in a district should have some impact on women's electoral success.[72]

Explaining the Political Geography of Women's Success

There are particular demographic characteristics that determine whether a district will elect a Democrat or a Republican. Are there particular demographic characteristics that influence whether a district will elect a man or a woman? We expect that the success of female candidates will vary with these four types of demographic measures in a district: its partisanship and ideology, its geography, its racial and ethnic makeup, and its socioeconomic characteristics. Beginning with the 1972 election cycle, district lines are regularly redrawn every ten years in response to the Census.[73] For each redistricting decade, we identified those districts that are reliably Democratic or Republican and those that have the characteristics of swing districts. We defined a core Democratic district as one in which the Democratic candidate for the seat won at least four of the five elections in the ten-year period. Similarly, core Republican districts are defined as those in which the Republican candidate won at least four of five elections in the decade. The remaining districts, where the parties split 3–2 during the decade, are treated as swing districts.[74] Overall, our data encompass thirty years and include 1,305 districts; 153 of these elected women.

Party, Race, and Gender

Table 6.2 reports the number of districts that elected only white candidates during the redistricting period and the number of districts that elected a black or Hispanic at least once during the decade. Of the 681 districts classified as core Democratic districts, African American candidates were elected in 11.4 percent (78), and Hispanic candidates were elected in 4.7 percent (32). In

---

[72] The specific measure of school-age children is the proportion of residents enrolled in public elementary and high schools; these data were gathered by the U.S. Census and are contained in the Adler data set.

[73] We begin with the 1972–1980 period for two reasons. First, several measures that we use, including the Hispanic population, were not available for earlier periods. Second, because of the "one person, one vote" rulings of the Supreme Court, the decade from 1962 to 1970 was chaotic as far as district boundaries are concerned. A number of states redraw their boundaries in mid-decade, and a handful of states redrew them two or more times.

[74] This exercise entails aggregating our database for each redistricting period. We then have observations for 435 districts in each of these three periods (n = 1,305). Given our definitions, 681districts are classified as core Democratic and 487 are classified as core Republican. In 989 of the 1,168 (85.0 percent) core districts, the party held the seat for all five elections in the districting period. Of the 179 districts that split 4–1, 158 of them (88.0 percent) involved four consecutive wins for one party or the other. We adopted the 4–1 criterion for defining a core district based on these proportions. It does not seem plausible to define a swing district as one where a party won four consecutive elections in a decade.

Table 6.2 District Partisanship, Race, and Gender, 1972–2000

Party and Race	Districts in All Three Redistricting Periods	Districts Electing a Woman
Core Democratic Districts		
Electing white Democrat only	83.8% (571)	8.8% (50/571)
Electing African American Democrat	11.4% (78)	29.5% (23/78)
Electing Hispanic Democrat	4.7% (32)	12.5% (4/32)
Percentage of all districts (total)	52.2% (681)	11.3% (77)
Swing Districts		
Electing white candidates only	97.1% (133)	20.3% (27/133)
Electing African American candidate	2.2% (3)	0% (0/3)
Electing Hispanic candidate	1.0% (1)	100% (1/1)
Percentage of all districts (total)	10.5% (137)	20.4% (28)
Core Republican Districts		
Electing white Republican only	98.6% (480)	7.5% (36/480)
Electing African American Republican	0.5% (2)	0% (0/2)
Electing Hispanic Republican	1.0% (5)	20.0% (1/5)
Percentage of all districts (total)	37.3% (487)	7.6% (37)

swing districts, only three African American candidates were elected—all of them male. Democratic Representative Mike Espy won Mississippi's 2nd District in 1986, making him the first African American to be elected from Mississippi since the Reconstruction. He gave up his seat in 1993 when he was appointed secretary of agriculture by President Bill Clinton, but resigned from that post a year later after allegations that he took illegal gifts from lobbyists.[75] Republican Representative Gary Franks was first elected in 1990 to Connecticut's 5th District. Franks, who was often lambasted by members of the Congressional Black Caucus, lost his 1996 reelection bid in a close race to a former state senator, Democrat Jim Maloney.[76] Democratic Representative Cleo Fields was first elected in 1992 in the 4th District of Louisiana, a district that became known as the "Mark of Zorro" because of its unusual Z-shape.

---

[75] Espy was indicted on thirty-nine counts of accepting illegal favors from corporations and deceiving investigators, including an allegation that, along with his brother (who ran for his open seat) and another friend, he received $35,000 worth of favors, including tickets to the Super Bowl and the NBA playoffs; "Grand Jury Indicts Espy on 39 Counts," *CQ Weekly,* August 30, 1997, 2033. After a four-year investigation that cost $17 million, a jury acquitted Espy on all counts; Susan Page and Mimi Hall, "Verdict Could Kill Law That Made Case Possible; Espy Acquittal Puts Heat on Independent Counsel Statute," *USA Today,* December 3, 1998, 18A.

[76] See for example Guy Gugliotta, "Defeated Rep. Franks Accused of 'Uncle Tomism,'" *Washington Post,* November 21, 1996b, A15.

Fields actually helped to create the district when he was a state senator and chair of the senate redistricting committee.[77] In 1995, the U.S. Supreme Court held that the district was an unconstitutional racial gerrymander, and Fields decided not to run in the redrawn district in 1996.[78] Republican John Cooksey won the seat.

Only one Hispanic has won in a swing district. In 1996, Democrat Loretta Sanchez defeated nine-term Republican incumbent, Representative Robert "B-1 Bob" Dornan, by 984 votes. Dornan challenged the results and claimed that "the election was stolen through rampant illegal voting by noncitizens."[79] A fourteen-month investigation by the House Oversight Committee concluded that there were voting irregularities, but not enough to affect the outcome. Dornan challenged Sanchez in her 1998 reelection bid in what turned out to be the most expensive House race of the election cycle.[80] He lost badly, with only 39 percent of the vote. His election-night concession speech turned into a tirade in which he spoke of a "fog of evil that has rolled across our country," and his daughter's boyfriend got into a fistfight with a police officer.[81]

Only two African Americans were elected in core Republican districts, Representatives Gary Franks from Connecticut's 5th District and J. C. Watts from Oklahoma's 4th District. Five Hispanics were elected in core Republican districts, one woman and three men: Representatives Ileana Ros-Lehtinen (R-FL), Lincoln Diaz-Balart (R-FL), Henry Bonilla (R-TX), and Manuel Lujan (R-NM), who served from 1969 until 1989, and thus held the seat during two redistricting periods. Only 6 percent of all minority candidates to serve between 1972 and 2000 were elected in core Republican districts. Thus, the partisan makeup of a district is related to the success of minority candidates. Minority candidates are almost entirely from core Democratic districts.

Core Democratic districts were also more likely to elect women than core Republican districts, 11.3 percent compared to 7.6 percent, but the percentage of swing districts electing women, 20.4 percent, surpasses both of these. However, when we look at the interaction of race and gender, there were few minority women elected from swing or core Republican districts. Core Democratic districts were far more likely to elect black (29.5 percent) and Hispanic

---

[77] Dave Kaplan, "Louisiana: Redrawn Map Still Feature[s] Two Minority Districts," *CQ Weekly*, April 20, 1983.

[78] Joan McKinney, "Reapportionment Reaction," *The Advocate*, Baton Rouge, Louisiana, December 1, 1996, 13B.

[79] Jacki Koszczuk, "Proof of Illegal Voters Falls Short, Keeping Sanchez in House," *CQ Weekly*, February 7, 1998, 330.

[80] The two candidates spent more than $6.4 million. Much of the election centered around the issue of abortion. Dornan, who is of Irish descent, called himself the "true Latino candidate" because of his pro-life position; "Sanchez Claims Victory in Nation's Most Expensive Race," Associated Press, November 4, 1998, BC cycle.

[81] Larry Gerber, "Dornan Loses Solidly, Not Quietly," Associated Press, November 4, 1998, AM cycle.

(12.5 percent) women than white women (8.8 percent). This suggests that the partisanship of a district interacts with both the gender and race of the candidate. In other words, minority women come from districts with different partisan leanings than white women.

Given that the race of winning candidates is related to partisanship in the district, our analysis will take race and gender into account. We conduct two separate analyses, examining those core Democratic and Republican districts that elected only nonminority candidates to the House, and those core districts that elected African Americans.[82] We further divide these sets of districts into two sets again: those that elected a woman at least once during a redistricting period, and those that elected only men during the redistricting period. For each set, we calculated the average of our eleven demographic measures.[83]

White Women in Core Democratic and Republican Districts

As table 6.3 shows, the core Democratic and Republican districts electing white women have different demographic characteristics. In fact, the results for core Democratic districts are dramatic and clearly demonstrate that the districts electing women are distinct.[84] In core Democratic districts, eleven of the twelve demographic factors are different for districts electing men than districts that elected a woman.

With respect to partisanship and ideology, core Democratic districts that elected a woman lean more to the left than those that elected only men. Given our measure of partisanship, Republican share of the presidential vote, we would expect these numbers to be lower in core Democratic districts compared to core Republican districts. But there is a substantial gender gap; the average Republican share of the presidential vote in districts electing only men was ten percentage points higher than the districts that have elected a woman. A similar gap is evident in the measure of district ideology. The average ideology score of those core Democratic districts electing men is 11.0, nearly identical to

---

[82] Unfortunately, it was not possible to compare Hispanic men and women since only six Hispanic women have been elected to Congress.

[83] We use the median values rather than means, because the distribution of several of the demographic variables is substantially skewed. These include ideology, district size, the measures of diversity (African American, Hispanic, and foreign-born), along with the proportion of residents with a college degree. When data are skewed, the median offers a more satisfactory measure of central tendency in a distribution.

[84] In the table, the asterisk next to the median value of the demographic variable for women denotes that the difference in medians between these groups is statistically significant. We used the Mann-Whitney test, which is the nonparametric counterpart of the difference-in-means test. It is used in the analysis because it involves less stringent assumptions about the distribution of the variables. The conventional difference-in-means test assumes that the data are drawn from a normal distribution. As noted previously, this assumption is not reasonable when dealing with distributions that are skewed. Essentially, the Mann-Whitney procedure tests for differences in the medians of the distribution where the null hypothesis is that the medians are equal; Robert Winkler and William Hays, *Statistics: Probability, Inference and Decision*, 2nd ed. (New York: Holt, Rinehart, and Winston, 1975), 848–55.

Table 6.3 Characteristics of Core Democratic and Republican House Districts, 1972–2000 (Districts Electing African Americans and Hispanics Not Included)

	Core Democratic Districts Electing Only Males during Decade (521)	Core Democratic Districts Electing a Female during Decade (50)	Core Republican Districts Electing Only Males during Decade (444)	Core Republican Districts Electing a Female during Decade (36)	Do Districts Electing Female Democrats Differ from Those Electing Female Republicans?
Partisanship and Ideology					
Republican share of presidential vote	50.8%	40.8%***	57.4%	49.9%*	Yes***
Simulated ideology of district*	11.0	1.6***	18.3	15.5*	Yes***
Geography					
District size in square miles	1,836.0	409.5***	3,615.0	1,622.0	Yes***
Urban residents	76.0%	94.7%**	62.6%	72.6%	Yes***
South	33.0%	10.0%***	28.8%	8.3%**	No
Race and Ethnicity					
African American residents	6.4%	7.3%	3.8%	3.4%	Yes**

Hispanic residents	1.5%	3.7%***	1.5%	2.4%	No
Foreign-born residents	3.4%	6.8%***	2.9%	5.4%**	Yes*
Socioeconomic				
Relative median income	99.4%	109.7%***	101.8%	112.1%***	No
College degrees	12.4%	17.6%***	15.4%	19.9%*	No
School-age population	19.9%	16.1%***	18.8%	17.5%*	No
Blue-collar workers	9.6%	7.8%***	8.3%	6.6%*	No

*1982–2000 only. The level of significance is denoted as follows: *** $p < .001$, ** $p < .01$, and * $p < .05$.

the overall mean of 10.7. The mean ideological score in those core Democratic districts electing women, 1.6, is significantly to the left of those electing only men. This suggests that the core Democratic districts that elect women produce greater margins for Democratic presidential candidates and, ideologically, are more liberal than the districts electing only men.

With respect to geography, core Democratic districts electing women are smaller, more urban, and nonsouthern. In fact, as mentioned earlier, the districts that elected a white women are, on average, less than one-fourth the size of the districts that elected white men, only 409.5 square miles compared to 1,836.0 square miles. As table 6.3 shows, core Democratic districts that elected a woman are overwhelmingly the smallest of the four categories of districts. As mentioned earlier, women represent six of the nation's twenty smallest districts; all six of these women are Democrats. Given this result, it should come as no surprise that core Democratic districts that elected a woman are almost entirely urban, while districts that elected men are only 76.0 percent urban. Core Democratic districts that elected a woman are also less likely to be in the South.

In terms of the racial and ethnic makeup, there are no measurable differences between core Democratic districts with respect to the size of their black populations, but this should come as no surprise, given that this analysis focuses on nonminority candidates. But core Democratic districts electing white women are more diverse, with larger Hispanic and foreign-born populations. The numbers are small, but they are distinct; core Democratic districts electing a woman have almost twice the proportion of Hispanic and foreign-born residents.

The results thus far show that, while core Democratic districts that have elected a white woman are different from those that have only elected men, these factors conform to characteristically Democratic districts and partisan expectations. In other words, all of these demographic measures are in the expected range for Democratic districts, but white women are elected from "more Democratic" districts than their male counterparts.

However, three of the four indicators listed under the socioeconomic category reveal that women are elected from districts that have characteristics atypical of their party. Core Democratic districts electing white women are wealthier than the districts that elected only men. In fact, there is a ten-point difference in the measure of median income. For example, in the redistricting period from 1992 and 2000, the "income advantage" in districts electing women was $3,500 per year. And although the differences are smaller, women are more likely to come from districts with a larger proportion of college graduates and a smaller blue-collar workforce. Interestingly, core Democratic districts electing men have the highest percentage of school-age children, while core Democratic districts electing women have the lowest percentage of school-age children. Thus, these results reveal that for Democrats, while districts that elect women are more liberal, urban, and racially diverse, as well as smaller, they are also more "upscale."

While the differences are not as sharp as those of the Democrats, core Republican districts electing white men and women are distinct as well. Table 6.3 shows that eight of the demographic characteristics are different for districts electing men from the districts that have elected a woman. In terms of partisanship and ideology, core Republican districts that elected a woman are not as far to the right as those districts that elected only men. There is nearly a ten percentage point gap in average support for Republican presidential candidates. Core Republican districts electing only men exhibit the highest average Republican share of the presidential vote of the four categories of districts, 57.4 percent. Core Republican districts that elected a woman had an average 49.9 percent Republican share of the presidential vote. In this respect, core Republican districts that elect women are remarkably similar in their presidential voting patterns to core Democratic districts that elected only men. This suggests that districts electing Republican women are more moderate and less partisan than Republican districts that elect only men.

Turning to geography, while core Republican districts are larger than core Democratic districts, core Republican districts that elected a woman are less than half the size of the districts that elect only male Republicans, 1,622 square miles compared to 3,615 square miles.[85] Of the nation's one hundred largest districts in the 109th Congress (2005 session), only three were represented by women—all Republicans. Along with Representative Cathy McMorris from Washington's 5th District, there were Republican Representative Jo Ann Emerson from Missouri's 8th District and Republican Representative Shelley Moore Capito from West Virginia's 2nd District. Core Republican districts electing a woman have a substantially larger urban population; core Republican districts electing a woman are 72.6 percent urban, while core Republican districts electing men are only 62.6 percent urban. Districts that elected a Republican woman are also primarily outside of the South. Core Republican districts in general are not as racially and ethnically diverse as core Democratic districts. Among the core Republican districts, we find that there are no differences in the proportion of African American and Hispanic residents in districts that have elected only men and districts that have elected a woman. Districts that elected a woman, however, do have larger foreign-born populations, indicating that they are slightly more diverse. This leads to the conclusion that women are elected in core districts that are "less" stereotypically Republican. In fact, there are four measures—the Republican share of the presidential vote, district size, urbanization, and foreign-born residents—where the core Republican districts that elected women look more like the core Democratic districts that elected men.

The socioeconomic factors highlight some interesting differences as well. Like core Democratic districts that elected a white woman, core Republican districts that elected a white woman are significantly wealthier than districts

---

[85] This difference is not statistically significant.

electing only males. As in the case of Democrats, districts electing Republican women are 10 percent wealthier than those electing men. For the 1992–2000 period, the median income in core Republican districts electing women was $38,242 compared to $34,728, a difference of $3,514. Core Republican districts that elected a woman are the wealthiest of the four categories of districts. These districts are also more educated; almost 20 percent of residents have college degrees, also the highest proportion of all four categories. Core Republican districts that elected a woman have smaller school-age populations than districts that have elected only men. They also have a lower proportion of blue-collar workers, once again the smallest of all four categories, only 6.6 percent on average.

Overall, table 6.3 reveals the differences and similarities among core Democratic and Republican districts electing white women. The last column of the table shows that, with respect to partisanship and ideology, women of both parties represent districts that are more liberal than those of their male counterparts, but it is important to keep in mind that core Democratic districts electing a woman are still more Democratic and liberal than core Republican districts electing a woman. And while women of both parties represent districts that are smaller than their male counterparts', core Democratic districts electing women are the smallest, about one-fourth the size of core Republican districts electing women. Core Democratic districts electing women are more urban than core Republican districts electing women and are, albeit slightly, more racially and ethnically diverse. For six of the eight measures, there are differences between the core Democratic districts electing a woman and core Republican districts electing a woman. Thus, with respect to partisanship and ideology, geography, and diversity, the core Democratic and Republican districts electing women are distinct. These distinctions, however, fall in line with the expected partisan characteristics. In other words, on these measures, there are differences between the core Democratic districts electing women and the core Republican districts electing women, but these differences can be explained by "party friendliness."

On the other hand, as the last column of table 6.3 also shows, the socioeconomic makeup of core Democratic and Republican districts electing white women is virtually identical. These districts have the same relative median incomes, the same proportion of the population with college degrees, the same proportion of school-age children, and the same proportion of blue-collar workers. In other words, women are elected in districts that are distinct from the districts men represent. And these particular measures can arguably be thought of as indicators of more progressive attitudes about women's roles. Thus, "party-friendly" and "women-friendly" are not the same concept. Women-friendly districts have their own unique political geographies.

White Women in Swing Districts

Over the three decades included in our analysis, there were 133 nonminority districts where a party won two or three elections in the redistricting period. There are 309 elections where male Democrats won, 33 elections where female Democrats won, 297 elections where male Republicans won, and 20 elections where female Republicans won.

Like core Democratic districts, table 6.4 shows that there are significant differences on eleven of our twelve measures between swing districts that elected white male Democrats and swing districts that elected white female Democrats. Swing districts won by a female Democrat are more supportive of Democratic presidential candidates and are more liberal. Once again, with respect to geography, these districts are substantially smaller: roughly half the size of swing districts electing male Democrats, only 1,348 square miles compared to 2,655 square miles. In addition, they have a higher percentage of urban residents, 72.3 percent compared to 66.8 percent respectively. Swing districts in the South are one-third as likely to elect a Democratic woman as they are to elect a Democratic man. With respect to diversity, swing districts where a Democratic woman won have higher percentages of Hispanic and for-eign-born residents; they are more diverse. The swing districts that elected female Democrats are "more" Democratic in their partisanship and ideology, geography, and diversity.

The biggest differences among these districts are their socioeconomic char-acteristics. Swing districts electing a Democratic woman are wealthier than districts electing Democratic men. Again using the national median for 1992–2000, median income in swing districts won by male Democrats is $33,943; for female Democrats, it is $41,551, a difference of $7,608. Swing districts won by a Democratic woman are the wealthiest of all four categories. In addition, the swing districts where Democratic women were elected had almost twice as many residents with college degrees, 25.3 percent compared to only 13.4 percent, once again the highest of all four categories. These districts also have a smaller school-age population and only half as many blue-collar workers. Thus, the swing districts that elect Democratic men are quite different from those that elect Democratic women; their socioeconomic indi-cators are "less" Democratic.

In the case of the swing districts that elected Republicans, there are signifi-cant differences between the districts that elected white men and women on ten of the twelve measures. Here, swing districts won by a female Republican are less supportive of Republican presidential candidates and are less conser-vative. Their geographic characteristics are also distinct. Swing districts that elected Republican women are one-sixth the size of the districts that elect their male counterparts, only 541 square miles compared to 3,712 square miles. These districts are also almost entirely urban, while the districts electing male Republicans are only 63.7 percent urban. Republican women are also elected

Table 6.4 Characteristics of Swing Districts in House Elections, 1972–2000 (Districts Electing African Americans and Hispanics Not Included)

	Swing Districts Won by Male Democrats (309)	Swing Districts Won by Female Democrats (33)	Swing Districts Won by Male Republicans (297)	Swing Districts Won by Female Republicans (20)	Do Districts Electing Female Democrats Differ from Those Electing Female Republicans?
Partisanship and Ideology					
Republican share of presidential vote	55.0%	47.3%**	55.8%	48.9%**	No
Simulated ideology of district*	15.7	9.6***	16.2	9.3***	No
Geography					
District size	2,655.0	1,348.0**	3,712.0	541.0*	No
Urban residents	66.8%	72.3%**	63.7%	93.6%***	No
South	30.7%	9.1%***	28.6%	30.0%	Yes*
Race and Ethnicity					
African American residents	4.1%	5.2%	4.1%	8.5%	No

Hispanic residents	1.4%	2.9%***	1.4%	3.7%**	No
Foreign-born residents	3.0%	6.0%***	2.9%	5.9%**	No
Socioeconomic					
Relative median income	99.5%	121.8%***	99.8%	119.1%**	No
College degrees	13.4%	25.3%***	13.3%	19.7%***	No
School-age population	21.2%	16.0%***	20.9%	16.5%***	No
Blue-collar workers	9.2%	5.4%***	9.2%	5.8%***	No

*1982–2000 only. The level of significance is denoted as follows: *** $p < .001$, ** $p < .01$, and * $p < .05$.

from districts that are more diverse than those electing male Republicans; in fact, the proportions of blacks, Hispanics, and foreign-born in districts electing female Republicans are more than twice the proportions in districts electing male Republicans. This demonstrates that swing districts won by Republican women are "less" Republican on these measures.

The socioeconomic characteristics of the swing districts electing Republican men and women are also quite different. Republican women are elected in swing districts that are wealthier. Using the national median for 1992–2000, the median income in swing districts electing Republican men was $34,046; the median income in swing districts electing Republican women was $40,630, a difference of $6,584. These Republican women are elected in swing districts that have a higher proportion of residents with college degrees, fewer school-age children, and fewer blue-collar workers than the swing districts Republican men come from. Thus, Republican women are elected in swing districts that have more characteristically Republican socioeconomic factors.

As the last column of table 6.4 shows, there are strong similarities among swing districts that elect white women candidates of either party. In fact, in almost all respects, the swing districts that elect Democratic and Republican women are virtually identical. Swing districts that have elected a woman of either party are similar in their partisanship and ideology, their geography, their racial and ethnic makeup, and their socioeconomic characteristics. As such, there are no party-friendly characteristics that separate the kinds of swing districts that elect white Democratic and Republican women. In swing districts, the only differences that matter are those that make a district women-friendly. Combined with our analysis of core Democratic and Republican districts, this provides considerable evidence that districts electing nonminority women to the House are unique and distinct from districts that have elected only men.

African American Women and Core Democratic Districts

African American men were elected in fifty-five core Democratic districts, and African American women were elected in twenty-three core Democratic districts.[86] As table 6.5 illustrates, unlike the findings for white women, there are very few differences in the makeup of these districts. Both African American men and women are elected from districts with very low levels of support for Republican presidential candidates, only 20.4 and 23.4 percent respectively. In addition, the ideological scores demonstrate that these districts are distinctly to the left and among the most liberal. Geographically, these districts are quite small and are 100 percent urban. Male and female African Americans are equally likely to be elected from districts in the South; about one-third of the

---

[86] We do not examine core Republican districts here because, as mentioned earlier, no Republican African American woman has been elected to the House, and there have been only two Republican African American men.

Table 6.5 Characteristics of Core Democratic Districts Electing African Americans, 1972–2000

	Core Democratic Districts Electing Only African American Males during Decade (55)	Core Democratic Districts Electing an African American Female during Decade (23)	Do Democratic Districts Electing White Females Differ from Those Electing Black Females?
Partisanship and Ideology			
Republican share of presidential vote	20.4%	23.4%	Yes***
Simulated ideology of district*	−18.7	−12.7	Yes***
Geography			
District size in square miles	59.0	104.0	Yes**
Urban residents	100%	100%	Yes***
South	27.3%	34.8%	Yes*
Ethnicity			
African American residents	59.4%	49.4%*	Yes***
Hispanic residents	1.9%	8.2%*	Yes*
Foreign-born residents	4.9%	6.0%	No
Socioeconomic			
Relative median income	85.4%	78.9%	Yes***
College degrees	13.1%	11.1%	Yes**
School-age population	18.4%	18.6%	Yes*
Blue-collar workers	8.2%	9.0%	No

*1982–2000 only. The level of significance is denoted as follows: *** p < .001, ** p < .01, and * p < .05.

African Americans in the House are from the South. Finally, these core Democratic districts have similar socioeconomic profiles with no significant differences in income, education, school-age population, or blue-collar workers.

There are some noteworthy patterns with regard to the race and ethnicity of the constituents in these core Democratic districts. These districts have overwhelmingly larger proportions of people of color compared to the districts that elect white House members. But districts that elected African American men have a substantially larger proportion of black residents than districts that elected African American women, 59.4 percent compared to

49.4 percent, a ten-point gap. African American women, however, represent districts that have much larger Hispanic populations, 8.2 percent compared to 1.9 percent.

The last column of table 6.5 compares core Democratic districts that elected an African American woman to those core Democratic districts electing a white woman.[87] Clearly, black and white women are elected from Democratic constituencies that are quite distinct. There are significant differences between ten of the twelve characteristics, with African American women representing districts that are less Republican in their support for presidential candidates, more liberal, substantially smaller, more solidly urban, more diverse, poorer, less educated, and younger than the districts of their white female counterparts. Our analysis shows that failure to control for the race of the winning candidate would obscure the unique character of the districts that elect African American women and the districts that elect white women. In effect, African American women do not come from districts with the distinctly women-friendly socioeconomic characteristics that white women do. The districts that elect black women are virtually identical to the districts that elect black men. And these districts that African American House members represent are different than the districts electing white Democrats; they are the "most" Democratic districts in the analysis. In other words, they have the "party-friendliest" Democratic demographics.

The Index of Women-Friendliness

To further explore the impact of demographics on women's success, we develop an "index of women-friendliness" for each party based on the results of table 6.3. Here, we use eleven of the twelve demographic characteristics; we do not use the measure of simulated ideology, since it is only available from 1982 to 2000. In core Democratic districts, ten of the eleven remaining demographic characteristics have significantly different values in districts that elected a woman compared to districts that elected only men. Six of these demographic characteristics have greater values in the districts that have elected a woman: urban residents, median income, college graduates, and the proportion of African American, Hispanic, and foreign-born residents. In each congressional district, if the particular factor had a value greater than or equal to the average of the core Democratic districts that elected a woman, it is assigned a one. There are four demographic characteristics that have lower values in the districts that elected a woman: Republican vote for president, size of the district, school-age population, and blue-collar workforce. In each congressional district, if the particular factor had a value less than or equal to the average of the core Democratic districts that elected a woman, it is also

---

[87] These are based upon comparing the medians of core Democratic districts electing African American women (column 3 of table 6.6) and core Democratic districts electing white women (column 3 of table 6.3).

assigned a one.[88] Districts outside the South are also assigned a one. The idea is that assigning the value of one to a particular characteristic indicates that the district has that women-friendly attribute; the characteristic is different for districts that elected a woman compared to districts that elected only men. For example, the average size of core Democratic districts that elected a woman is 1,348 square miles. Any districts that are 1,348 square miles or smaller are assigned a one; districts greater than 1,348 square miles are assigned a zero. The average share of urban residents in core Democratic districts that elected a woman is 72.3 percent. Any districts that have 72.3 percent or more urban residents are assigned a one; districts whose urban population is smaller are assigned a zero. We used the same process for core Republican districts.

Our index of women-friendliness is calculated by summing these demographic characteristics and ranges from zero to eleven. Thus, for each congressional district, we have two indicators of the relative friendliness of a constituency—one for Democrats and one for Republicans. Among core Democratic districts, the median number of attributes in districts electing only men is three; for districts electing a woman, it is six. For Republican core districts, the median number of attributes in districts electing only men is four; for districts electing a woman, it is also six. For Democrats in swing districts, the median value of those electing only men is two, and for those electing women, it is six. Among Republicans in swing districts, those electing only men have a median number of four, while those electing women have a median number of seven. In sum, our measures perform well in encapsulating the differences highlighted in tables 6.3 and 6.4.

We can use this index to examine the success of women at all three stages of a campaign: running in a primary, winning a primary, and winning the general election. Table 6.6 reports the results for two electoral contexts: elections for open seats, and elections against an incumbent of the opposition party. The set of open seats includes districts where the sitting incumbent vacates the seat as well as those new seats created as a result of reapportionment. For each party, we collapse the eleven-point index into three categories, low (0–3 attributes), medium (4–7), and high (8–11). Those scoring low on the index are considered "ambivalent" toward women candidates, while those scoring high are "women-friendly." For the entire period of our analysis, there were 433 women-friendly districts, 157 for the Democrats and 276 for the Republicans.

As table 6.6 shows, the results are unambiguous. Where women decide to run in a primary is influenced by the friendliness of the district. For female Democrats in open-seat elections, the proportion of contests in which a woman seeks the party's nomination doubles from 29.5 percent in districts

---

[88] This index is constructed in a manner similar to building a party-friendly index. See for example Lewis Froman, *Congressmen and Their Constituencies* (Chicago: Rand McNally, 1963); and Koetzle, 1998.

Table 6.6 Women Running in Primaries, Winning Primaries, and Winning General Elections by the Friendliness Index, 1972–2000

Electoral Phase and Women-Friendly Index Value	Open Districts, Female Democrats	Open Districts, Female Republicans	Female Democrats in Districts with Republican Incumbents	Female Republicans in Districts with Democrat Incumbents
Ran in the Primary				
Women-Friendly Attributes				
Low: 0–3 attributes	29.5% (114/387)	17.0% (54/317)	17.7% (239/1,353)	10.8% (129/1,194)
Medium: 4–7 attributes	40.4% (108/267)	25.8% (72/279)	23.2% (206/889)	12.1% (174/1,437)
High: 8–11 attributes	61.2% (41/67)	36.8% (46/125)	35.9% (61/170)	20.9% (153/732)
Chi-square	27.71 ***	20.23 ***	34.32***	43.98***
Won the Primary				
Women-Friendly Attributes				
Low: 0–3 attributes	9.8% (38/387)	3.5% (11/317)	9.6% (130/1,353)	5.9% (71/1,194)
Medium: 4–7 attributes	17.6% (37/267)	8.6% (26/279)	15.1% (134/889)	7.1% (102/1,437)
High: 8–11 attributes	29.9% (20/67)	16.8% (21/125)	21.8% (37/170)	11.9% (87/732)
Chi-square	21.57 ***	22.53***	29.11***	23.85***
Won the General Election				
Women-Friendly Attributes				
Low: 0–3 attributes	2.6% (10/387)	2.2% (7/317)	0.4% (5/1,353)	0.1% (1/1,194)
Medium: 4–7 attributes	10.1% (27/267)	3.6% (10/279)	0.4% (4/889)	0.5% (7/1,437)
High: 8–11 attributes	19.4% (13/67)	4.8% (6/125)	3.5% (6/170)	0.0% (0/732)
Chi-square	31.67***	2.18	25.07***	6.70*

The proportions presented are the product of a 2 x 3 cross-tabulation. The test statistic is chi-square with 2 degrees of freedom. The level of significance is denoted as follows: *** $p < .001$, ** $p < .01$, and * $p < .05$.

ranked low on the index to 61.2 percent in those districts ranked high. The same pattern is evident for Republicans. In districts with open seats, female Republicans are twice as likely to run in a primary in districts that rank high on the women-friendliness index as they are to run in districts that rank low. There is a similar relationship in districts where an incumbent seeks reelection. When faced with the prospect of running against a Republican incumbent, Democratic women are twice as likely to seek the nomination of their party in districts that rank high on the women-friendliness index compared to those districts that rank low. The proportion of elections in which Democratic women seek the nomination increases from 17.7 percent in the least friendly districts to 35.9 percent in the most friendly. Once again, the same pattern holds for Republican women. In districts with a Democratic incumbent, the likelihood that a Republican woman will run in the primary increases from 10.8 percent in districts that rank low on the index to 20.9 percent in districts that rank high on the index.

Table 6.6 also demonstrates that winning a primary varies with the friendliness of the district. Among Democrats in open districts, the proportion of female nominees increases from 9.8 percent in districts that rank low on the index to 29.9 percent in districts that rank high. The increase among Republicans is from 3.5 to 16.8 percent. In other words, for both parties, the movement from the least friendly to the most friendly districts more than *triples* the likelihood of winning a primary. A similar but less dramatic relationship appears in districts where an incumbent is seeking reelection. The proportion of female Democrats winning the nomination in Republican-held districts increases from 9.6 to 21.8 percent. For Republicans in Democratic districts, the proportion of female primary winners increases from 5.9 to 11.9 percent. In sum, our index reveals that the decision of where to seek the nomination and the results of the resulting primaries systematically vary with the women-friendliness of the district. Women of both parties are more likely to seek and win the nomination in districts that are women-friendly. This holds in districts with open seats and in districts where an incumbent of the opposition party is running for reelection.

The last section of table 6.6 presents the proportion of women who won a general election contest. For female Democrats seeking an open seat, there is a strong association between winning and the value of our index. The proportion increases from 2.6 percent in the least friendly districts to 10.1 percent in the midrange districts and increases again to 19.4 percent in the friendliest districts. Thus, for Democratic women, the probability of winning an open seat depends upon the demographic character of the district. The relationship for Republican women in open seats is much weaker. The proportion increases from 2.2 percent in least friendly districts to only 4.8 percent in the most friendly.[89] The number of cases, however, is quite

---

[89] This relationship is not statistically significant.

small. Between 1972 and 2000, only twenty-three Republican women won open seats. The last comparison in table 6.6 is the set of general elections where a woman faced a sitting incumbent. The most striking aspect of these results is the small number of women who won, a testament to the strength of incumbency. Across the entire time frame of our analysis, only thirteen female Democrats and eight female Republicans defeated an incumbent member of the House. For the Democrats, winning is related to the friendliness of the district; the proportion of victories in the least friendly and midrange districts is 0.4 percent, and increases to 3.5 percent in the most friendly districts. There is no such increase for Republican women challenging Democrat incumbents; all of these proportions are less than 1.0 percent.

While women of both parties are more likely to run in and win a primary in districts that are women-friendly, it is important to point out the differences between women in the Democratic and Republican Parties. The proportions running in a primary, winning a primary, and winning a general election are lower among Republican women, although they appear to have more opportunities. There were 67 districts with open seats that scored high on the Democratic women-friendliness index. Female Democrats ran in 41, a rate of 61.2 percent. There were almost double the number of open districts that scored high on the Republican women-friendliness index, 125. But only 46 Republican women ran in these districts, a rate of 36.8 percent, about half the rate for Democratic women. Among districts with Republican incumbents seeking reelection, there were 170 that scored high on the women-friendliness index, and Democratic women ran in 61 of these primaries, 35.9 percent. There were four times as many Democratic incumbents who sought reelection in districts that scored high on the women-friendliness index, but Republican women entered only 153 of these primaries, 20.9 percent. At any rate, what we have shown is that open seats are not uniform in their likelihood to elect women. And female candidates, whether they run in open seats or against incumbents, are more likely to run in districts that are women-friendly.

Looking to the Future: Women-Friendly Districts and Their Implications

Our analysis demonstrates that the districts electing white women to the U.S. House of Representatives are distinct. There are demographic characteristics in a district, captured in our index of women-friendliness, that are related to where women run in primaries, win primaries, and, for female Democrats, win general elections. Although we have not ruled out a "role model effect," our analysis demonstrates that where women choose to run and the success of their campaigns vary systematically with the attributes included in our index. As a result, we can use our index of women-friendliness to speculate about possible opportunities for women candidates.

The Growth in Women-Friendly Districts

One way of assessing opportunities for women is to look at the growth of women-friendly districts. We examined those House districts with high scores on the index of women-friendliness, eight or more demographic characteristics, over the redistricting periods in our analysis. Table 6.7 shows that the number of women-friendly districts has increased over time.[90] In the redistricting period from 1972 to 1980, there were only 11 districts classified as women-friendly for the Democrats and 28 districts for the Republicans. During this decade, only 9.0 percent of all 435 districts could be classified as women-friendly. By the 1992 to 2000 period, women-friendly districts

Table 6.7 The Growth in Women-Friendly House Districts

Redistricting Period	Democratic Women-Friendly Districts	Republican Women-Friendly Districts
All House Districts		
1972–1980	2.5% (11/435)	6.4% (28/435)
1982–1990	12.4% (54/435)	20.9% (91/435)
1992–2000	21.1% (92/435)	36.1% (157/435)
Open Districts (Vacated)		
1972–1980	2.4% (6/246)	3.7% (9/246)
1982–1990	9.7% (16/165)	17.6% (29/165)
1992–2000	15.9% (40/251)	30.3% (76/251)
New Districts		
1972–1980	0% (0/18)	5.6% (1/18)
1982–1990	4.5% (1/22)	13.6% (3/22)
1992–2000	21.1% (4/19)	36.8% (7/19)

---

[90] No doubt, as we noted in chapter 1, in the redistricting that occurred in the 1960s in the wake of the U.S. Census and the U.S. Supreme Court's rulings in *Baker v. Carr* (1962) and *Wesberry v. Sanders* (1964), substantially more urban districts were created. Unfortunately, our demographic data do not go back far enough to fully explore this.

numbered 92 (21.1 percent) for the Democrats and 157 (36.1 percent) for the Republicans. In other words, the proportion of women-friendly districts jumped to 57.2 percent of all districts. Thus, the number of districts that afford women a greater likelihood for electoral success dramatically increased. This suggests that there are now substantial opportunities where women would be successful if they ran.

What explains the increase in women-friendly districts? Five of the demographic variables in our analysis have changed over the last three decades in a direction beneficial to women. Constituencies have grown more racially and ethnically diverse. Across all House districts, the median proportion of Hispanic residents has increased from 1.0 percent in the 1972–1980 period to 3.1 percent in the 1992–2000 period; similarly, the proportion of foreign-born residents has increased from 3.0 to 4.2 percent. In addition, the proportion of residents with college degrees has risen from 9.7 to 18.4 percent. At the same time, the school-age population has dropped from 23.7 to 15.6 percent, and the median proportion of blue-collar workers has declined from 13.3 to 6.7 percent. Thus, the changing demography of the United States has expanded political opportunities for women. As our nation becomes increasingly diverse and educated, women are increasingly likely to be successful as candidates.

At the same time, however, it is important to keep incumbency in mind. It is clear from table 6.7 that the number of opportunities to run in open seats that are women-friendly has dramatically increased. The total number of women-friendly seats that were open increased from 16 (6.0 percent) during the 1972–1980 period to 127 (47 percent) during the 1992–2000 period. In open seats that were vacated by an incumbent, the proportion of women-friendly districts is relatively low, 15.9 percent for the Democrats and 30.3 percent for the Republicans. Newly created districts are more likely to be women-friendly than those that were vacated, but only nineteen new districts were created in the 1992–2000 redistricting period. And overall, women-friendly open seats were only 5.8 percent of all House seats.

As a result, while demographic changes may be working in favor of women, incumbency is still a consistent barrier. Moreover, our analysis shows that, although open districts do provide the major electoral opportunity for women to win a seat in the House, the districts that come open in any given election do not afford equal opportunities. Not only does incumbency limit real political opportunities for women, but the seats that do come open may not always be receptive to female candidates. The "political glass ceiling" is a function of not simply incumbency, but also particular district-level characteristics that may discourage women from running and keep them from winning.

The Paradox for Republican Women

According to our index of women-friendliness, there are more districts classified as women-friendly for Republicans than for Democrats. As mentioned earlier, during the entire period of our study, there are a total of 157 districts friendly to female Democrats and 276 friendly to female Republicans. In the aggregate, then, there are almost twice as many Republican women-friendly districts than Democratic women-friendly districts. One reason, as noted in our discussion of table 6.3, is that the demographic differences between core Republican districts that elected only men and those that elected a woman are not as sharp or pronounced as the differences for the Democrats. More important, however, is the direction of the Republican differences. Districts grow more friendly toward Republican women as the Republican presidential vote declines, as ideology moves to the left, as Hispanic and foreign-born residents increase, and as the school-age population declines. In effect, as districts become friendlier to Republican women, they simultaneously grow more characteristic of Democratic districts.

This becomes particularly clear when we examine the partisanship of women-friendly districts. Table 6.8 shows that nearly 73 percent of the districts friendly to Democratic women are core Democratic districts; less than one-fourth fall into the core Republican category. In other words, almost three-quarters of the women-friendly Democratic districts are core Democratic districts. In those districts that are the most likely to elect a woman, party and gender interact to the advantage of Democratic women. The contrast with Republicans is striking. Over 58 percent of the districts friendly to Republican women are core Democratic districts; less than a third are core Republican districts. Thus, for Republican women, their gender is an advantage, but their party is a major disadvantage. These districts are more receptive to women but, at the same time, more likely to vote Democratic. Simply put, the districts where Republican women have the best opportunity to win a primary are the districts where their prospects in the general election are the lowest.

The Paradox for Democratic Women

The question arises as to whether female Democrats face a similar predicament in light of the atypical characteristics associated with women-friendly districts, in particular, the higher levels of wealth. Wealthier districts are

Table 6.8 The Partisan Character of Women-Friendly Districts, 1972–2000

Party	Women-Friendly Districts That Are "Core Democrat"	Women-Friendly Districts That Are "Swing"	Women-Friendly Districts That Are "Core Republican"
Democrats	72.6%	6.4%	21.0%
(157 total)	(114)	(10)	(33)
Republicans	58.7%	9.1%	32.2%
(276 total)	(162)	(25)	(89)

generally assumed to be more Republican. Thus, are Democratic women likely to have trouble in these districts? Our analysis in this chapter suggests no. In fact, the mixing of upscale congressional districts with Democratic or liberal politics does not appear to be an impediment to the political fortunes of Democratic women at all. Wealthier districts have grown less antagonistic toward Democratic presidential candidates over time. During the presidential elections of 1972, 1976, and 1980, 27.7 percent of those districts with relative median incomes of 110 percent or more gave a majority of the presidential vote to the Democratic candidate. In the presidential elections of 1984 and 1988, the proportion increased to 30.6 percent. For the elections of 1992, 1996, and 2000, the proportion again increased to 46.4 percent.

Moreover, the geographic location of these Democratic women-friendly districts is instructive. Many are located in the wealthier and highly professionalized sections of major American cities, such as New York, San Francisco, Los Angeles, and Chicago. These congressional districts resemble the "ideopolis" described in *The Emerging Democratic Majority* by John Judis and Ruy Teixeira.[91] The "ideopolis" is a label used to describe the emerging political economy of particular cities and metropolitan areas. These places, like Austin, Boulder, and the Silicon Valley, have developed postindustrial economies based on research and development, "soft technology," and "knowledge industries" like telecommunications or pharmaceuticals. Most of these cities include a major research university, such as the University of Wisconsin, Stanford, and Northwestern. Ideopolises attract well-paid, nonmanagerial professionals who, as a group, are ethnically diverse and culturally "libertarian and bohemian."[92] This growing "creative class" shares "a common ethos that values creativity, individuality, difference, and merit."[93] They choose to live in places that value tolerance and "diversity" in all its forms: "urban grit alongside renovated buildings, the commingling of young and old, long-time neighborhood characters and yuppies, fashion models and 'bag ladies.'"[94] As a result, the ideopolis has a substantially different political outlook than cities like Muncie, Fresno, or Memphis, which still rely on the manufacturing of cars and other industrial goods.[95] Ideopolises are becoming overwhelmingly Democratic in their voting patterns. For example, in the 2000 election, the Denver-Boulder area favored Al Gore 56 to 35 percent over George Bush. Overall, ideopolis counties in 2000 voted 58 percent Democratic.[96] If ideopolises continue to grow, then the redistricting process will reflect this growth, at least in part. Thus, we should see the number of districts that are friendly toward Democratic women candidates continue to grow as well.

---

[91] Judis and Teixeira, 2002.
[92] Judis and Teixeira, 2002, 73.
[93] Richard Florida, "The Rise of the Creative Class: Why Cities without Gays and Rock Bands are Losing the Economic Development Race," *Washington Monthly* 34 (2002): 15–26.
[94] These areas also tend to have very large gay populations; Florida, 2002.
[95] Judis and Teixeira, 2002, 72–73.
[96] Judis and Teixeira, 2002, 76.

Conclusion

Chapter 5 demonstrated that female incumbents tend to attract more female competition. One reason is that a successful female candidate may have a "role model" effect; she serves as a signal that a woman can win the district and may inspire other women to run. While that may be the case, we have shown here that it may actually be the district that inspires women to run. Between 1972 and 1980, female candidates won a total of 85 elections for the U.S. House of Representatives, but these victories were won in only 32 (7.4 percent) of the 435 congressional districts. After the redistricting cycle following the 1980 Census, the number of female victories increased to 119, with 38 districts (8.7 percent) electing a woman at least once. This proportion more than doubled during the districting regime in place from 1992 to 2000. During those years, women won 260 elections to the House in 83 (19.1 percent) districts. More districts are becoming women-friendly, and women are winning in more districts.

There are clear differences, at least among white members of Congress, between the districts that elected a woman and districts electing only men. Democratic women tend to represent districts that are upscale, diverse, and highly urbanized: "bohemian ideopolises." Republican women tend to represent districts that are also upscale, but also less conservative, more urban, and more diverse than their male counterparts: Democratic districts. In fact, the districts electing Republican women are quite similar to the districts electing Democratic men. As a result, Republican women face an uphill battle. Republican women thus seem to face a Catch-22: they can run in solidly Republican districts where they have less chance of winning because of their gender, or they can run in more moderate districts where they have less chance of winning because of their party affiliation.

Our index of women-friendliness reveals that the political glass ceiling is not simply a function of incumbency, but should also be understood in terms of opportunities. There is no doubt that, in general, women have a better chance of winning open seats than defeating an incumbent. But the number of open seats in a given election cycle is quite small, and once the demographics of these open seats are taken into account, the number of real opportunities for women to win these open seats is even smaller. A substantial number of districts, through 2010, are still unlikely to elect a woman.

7

Conclusions

We began our analysis with a central question: why has the pace of electing women to Congress been so slow? In her study of state legislators, Jeane Kirkpatrick argued that increasing the number of women in political office could only be achieved by changing "[s]ocial goals, beliefs about the identity and the role of men and women, [and] practices concerning socialization, education, political recruitment and family."[1] In other words, "both a cultural and a social revolution is required."[2] In addition to a change in the political culture, our analysis shows that there has been change in the political opportunity structure. While entering the pipeline is easier, the upper portions of the hierarchy are blocked. As demonstrated in chapter 2, just as the first women were running for Congress in the early twentieth century, the development of careerism made it more difficult for women to succeed. The system has evolved to the point where incumbents are now virtually unbeatable. And even open seats do not necessarily provide an electoral environment where female candidates can be successful.

The Picture Now: The Women of 2004

In 2004, seventy-nine women won election to Congress, sixty-five women in the House and fourteen in the Senate. After an acrimonious campaign, President George W. Bush earned a second term in office by defeating Democratic John Kerry of Massachusetts with 51.2 percent of the popular vote. The Republicans maintained control of the Congress with a 232–202 advantage in the House and a 55–45 majority in the Senate. Topping the national agenda was the "war on terror" with ongoing military operations in Afghanistan and Iraq. Cultural and social issues—abortion, stem cell research, religious

---

[1] Jeane Kirkpatrick, *Political Woman* (New York: Basic Books, 1974), 244.
[2] Kirkpatrick, 1974, 244.

displays in public spaces, and gay marriage—came to the forefront domestically.[3] During the summer of 2005, U.S. Supreme Court Justice Sandra Day O'Connor, an important swing vote on the Court—particularly in abortion cases—unexpectedly announced her retirement. Chief Justice William Rehnquist died that September, creating a second vacancy for President Bush to fill, guaranteeing that these cultural issues would continue to dominate public debate.

In the 109th Congress (2005 session), there was a major "gender gap" in the partisanship of the female members. Forty-two of the female House members were Democrats and twenty-three were Republicans; nine of the female senators were Democrats and five were Republicans. In the House, eleven women, all Democrats, were African American; six female Democrats and one female Republican were Hispanic. The most senior women serving in the House were Representatives Nancy Johnson (R-CT) and Marcy Kaptur (D-OH), both elected to their twelfth terms in 2004. Second in the line of seniority among women were Representatives Nancy Pelosi (D-CA) and Louise Slaughter (D-NY), who were serving their tenth terms in the House. In addition, thirty women of the House were beyond the midcareer point of five terms; eight women from the "class of 1992" were serving their seventh terms of office.

Our analysis in chapter 4 demonstrated that many of these women have risen to leadership positions in both the party and committee hierarchies. Democrat Nancy Pelosi was the minority leader. Republicans Judy Biggert (IL), Jo Ann Davis (VA), Nancy Johnson (CT), Sue Kelly (NY), Candice Miller (MI), Marilyn Musgrave (CO), Deborah Pryce (OH), Ileana Ros-Lehtinen (FL), and Heather Wilson (NM) served as the chairs of subcommittees. Democrats Jane Harman (CA), Juanita Millender-McDonald (CA), Louise Slaughter (NY), and Nydia Velazquez (NY) were ranking members of full committees. In the 85th Congress (1957 session), the fifteen women were regarded as novelties; in the 109th Congress (2005 session), eighty women, while far from proportionate, constituted a "presence," both on the floor and in committee rooms.

The Rules: No Longer a Man's Game

With seventy-nine women elected to the House and Senate in 2004, there is no doubt that progress has been made. Women made up 14.8 percent of Congress. On the other hand, one could still say that women have "a very small share, though a very large stake, in political power."[4] Cultural norms and gender role expectations have changed, but there are still remnants, particularly when it comes to raising children and housework. On the other hand, the

---

[3] See Morris Fiorina, *Culture War? The Myth of a Polarized America* (New York: Longman, 2005).
[4] Kirkpatrick, 1974, 3.

political pipeline is now open to women. In addition, redistricting and current demographic trends may actually provide opportunities for women.

Cultural Norms

Without doubt, cultural and social attitudes have changed since the 1950s. A college degree is now regarded as important to the futures of both men and women. In 2002, for example, 57 percent of bachelor's degrees awarded went to women.[5] Gone is the stigma of the working wife. In 2000, only 3 percent of the respondents in the National Election Study believed that a woman's place was in the home, down from 19 percent in 1972.[6] In 2003, the proportion of married women in the civilian workforce was 61 percent, compared to 29 percent in 1956.[7]

Politics is no longer off-limits to women. Since the 1970s, the political participation of women has increased substantially.[8] For the last two decades, voter turnout among women has consistently exceeded turnout among men by two to three percentage points. In the 2000 election, for example, 56 percent of women reported voting, compared to 53 percent for men; 7.8 million more women than men voted.[9] Women are as likely as men to engage in other kinds of political participation as well, including working on campaigns. In fact, women have more positive feelings than men about participating in campaigns, attending fundraisers, going door-to-door to meet with constituents, and dealing with the press.[10]

Despite these changes, the vestiges of the old cultural norms remain. In chapter 5, we emphasized the continued presence of gender stereotypes in evaluating character traits and issue competence. In addition, female candidates, regardless of party, are perceived as more liberal than male candidates. The effects of socialization remain as well. Women are still substantially less likely to think about running for office. Even when they have the same resumes as men, women are less likely to think they are qualified to run for office. They are also less likely to be told by others, even members of their own families, that they should run for office. For women, housework and child care still play major roles in their decisions to pursue political careers.[11] In contrast,

---

[5] U.S. Bureau of the Census, *Statistical Abstract of the United States, 2004–2005,* http://www.census.gov/prod/www/statistical-abstract-04.html (accessed August 1, 2005).

[6] http://www.umich.edu/~nes/nesguide/toptable/tab4c_1.htm (accessed August 2, 2005).

[7] U.S. Bureau of the Census.

[8] See for example M. Margaret Conway, Gertude Steurnagel, and David Ahern, *Women and Political Participation* (Washington, D.C.: CQ Press, 1997).

[9] Susan Carroll, "Women Voters and the Gender Gap," American Political Science Association, 2005, http://www.apsanet.org/content_5270.cfm (accessed July 25, 2005).

[10] Richard Fox, "Gender, Political Ambition and the Decision Not to Run for Office," Center for American Women and Politics, 2003, http://www.rci.rutgers.edu/~cawp/Research/Reports/Fox2003.pdf; Richard Fox, Jennifer Lawless, and Courtney Feeley, "Gender and the Decision to Run for Office," *Legislative Studies Quarterly* 26 (2001): 411–35; and Richard Fox and Jennifer Lawless, "The Impact of Sex-Role Socialization on the Decision to Run for Office" (paper presented at the Southern Political Science Association Annual Meeting, January 2002, Atlanta).

"Men pursue goals of whatever type with a singlemindedness absent in women"; women tend to consider the impact on their families.[12] This suggests that while women are no longer confined to "lickin' and stickin'" jobs on a campaign staff, they are still primarily responsible for raising children and doing most of the housework, and do not appear to be conscious of the fact that their skills and backgrounds make them qualified to run for office themselves.[13] On the up side, although women are not encouraged to run for office as often as men, when they are encouraged, they are as likely to consider running.[14] Thus, internships, mentoring programs, and other informal recruitment methods—for example, something as simple as telling more women they should run—could have a substantial impact on the number of female candidates.[15] (See figure 7.1.) Our results in chapter 5 emphasize a possible "role model" effect as well.

Entry Professions and the Pipeline

Over time, the backgrounds of the men and women who serve in Congress have converged. The career paths of women are becoming more like those of their male counterparts.[16] The entry professions of law and business are no longer blocked.[17] In fact, women have caught up to men in law school admissions. The proportion of law degrees awarded to women in 1956 was only 3.5 percent. In 2002, the proportion of law degrees awarded to women was 48.3 percent.[18] In 1971, only 3.9 percent of all MBA students were women. By 2002, 41.1 percent of all MBA students were women.[19] Women have substantially increased their numbers in lower-level political offices. For the last three decades, there has been a relatively steady increase in the number of women

---

[11] Fox, 2003; Fox, Lawless, and Feeley, 2001; and Lawless and Fox, 2005. See also Timothy Bledsoe and Mary Herring, "Victims of Circumstances: Women in Pursuit of Political Office," *American Political Science Review* 84 (1990): 213–23.

[12] Bledsoe and Herring, 1990, 221.

[13] Conway, Steuernagel, and Ahern, 1997.

[14] Fox, 2003.

[15] See for example Mark Rozell, "Helping Women Run and Win: Feminist Groups, Candidate Recruitment and Training," *Women & Politics* 21 (2000): 101–16.

[16] Joan Hulce Thompson, "Career Convergence: Election of Women and Men to the House of Representatives, 1916–1975," *Women & Politics* 5 (1985): 69–90; Irwin Gertzog, *Congressional Women: Their Recruitment, Integration, and Behavior*, 2nd ed. (Westport, Conn.: Praeger Press, 1995); Kathleen Dolan and Lynne Ford, "Change and Continuity among Women State Legislators: Evidence from Three Decades," *Political Research Quarterly* 50 (1997): 137–51; Kathleen Dolan and Lynne Ford, "Are All Women State Legislators Alike?" in *Women and Elective Office: Past, Present and Future*, edited by Sue Thomas and Clyde Wilcox (New York: Oxford University Press, 1998); and Nancy McGlen and Karen O'Connor, *Women, Politics and American Society*, 2nd ed. (Upper Saddle River, N.J.: Prentice Hall, 1998).

[17] Christine Williams, "Women, Law and Politics: Recruitment Patterns in the Fifty States," *Women & Politics* 10 (1990): 103–23; and Cynthia Fuchs Epstein, *Women in Law*, 2nd ed. (Chicago: University of Illinois Press, 1993).

[18] Dennis Simon, Barbara Palmer, and David Peterson, "Women in the Political Hierarchy: A Time Series Analysis" (paper presented at the Southern Political Science Association Annual Meeting, January 2004, New Orleans).

[19] http://www.census.gov/prod/2004pubs/04statab/educ.pdf (accessed July 25, 2005).

Fig. 7.1 Susannah Shakow, president of Women Under Forty Political Action Committee, speaks at an event for women interning on Capitol Hill, encouraging them to run for office. Photo by Barbara Palmer.

serving in state legislatures. In 1971, 4.5 percent of state legislators were women.[20] In 2005, 22.6 percent of state legislators were women.[21] The political pipeline is now open to women.

As table 7.1 illustrates, among the seventy-one women elected to the House in the twenty-first century, twelve women, 18.2 percent, were lawyers, slightly greater than the 12.7 percent among the women between 1916 and 1956.[22]

---

[20] Center for American Women and Politics, *Women in State Legislatures, 2002* (New Brunswick, N.J.: Rutgers University, 2002).

[21] It should be noted that since 1999, however, the proportion of women appears to have stalled at 22 percent; Center for American Women and Politics, *Women in Elective Office, 2005* (New Brunswick, N.J.: Rutgers University, 2005).

[22] Our count of women elected in 2002 and 2004 includes Democrat Patsy Mink (D-HI). Mink died on September 28, 2002, but was posthumously elected to the 108th Congress in November 2002.

Table 7.1 A Profile of the Seventy-one Women Elected to the House in the Twenty-first Century, 2002 and 2004

Background	Number of Women	Percentage
Lawyer	12	18.2
Prior Elective Office Experience		
Elected to local office	22	31.0
Elected to state house of representatives	33	46.5
Elected to state senate	19	26.8
Elected to statewide office	2	2.8
Other Political Experience		
Served in appointed administrative office	21	29.6
Served in party organization	11	15.5
Lateral Entry		
Widows	4	5.6
No prior elective office experience	5	7.0

While women have clearly caught up to men in terms of law school enrollment, this suggests that as a career, law still weighs less heavily for women entering the hierarchy of elective offices.[23] In fact, in recent elections, many women have been successful precisely because they have come from fields other than law, such as health and education.[24] On the other hand, almost one-third, 31.0 percent, of the women elected in 2002 and 2004 served in local political offices. Almost half were elected to their state house of representatives, and over one-fourth were elected to their state senate. Among all the women elected between 1916 and 1956, only 10.9 percent had served in local offices, 16.4 percent in the state house of representatives, and 1.8 percent in the state senate. Whereas Iris Blitch (D-GA) was the only woman to serve in both chambers during the 1916–1956 era, eleven women of the twenty-first century followed this route.[25]

---

[23] In the 109th Congress (2005 session), the proportion of all House members with law degrees was 38.6 percent; 42.3 percent of the male representatives had law degrees, while only 18.2 percent of the female representatives had law degrees. The proportion of all senators with law degrees was 58.0 percent; 54.0 percent of the male senators had law degrees, while 28.6 percent of the female senators had law degrees.

[24] McGlen and O'Connor, 1998.

[25] These include Republicans Ileana Ros-Lehtinen (FL), Barbara Cubin (WY), and Marilyn Musgrave (CO), along with Democrats Patsy Mink (HI), Carrie Meek (FL), Eddie Bernice Johnson (TX), Julia Carson (IN), Barbara Lee (CA), Hilda Solis (CA), Debbie Wasserman Schultz (FL), and Gwen Moore (WI).

Table 7.1 also reveals that 29.6 percent of the women elected in 2002 and 2004 had prior experience in administrative offices. The comparable figure from the 1918 to 1956 period was 18.2 percent. It also appears that as women gained access to the pipeline, the prominence of the party path to the House declined. From 1916 to 1956, 25.4 percent of the women elected to the House worked in party organizations. Among those elected in 2002 and 2004, only 15.5 percent, or eleven of seventy-one, served in party organizations. This suggests that women are now launching their political careers in lower-level elective office rather than serving apprenticeships in party organizations.

Finally, table 7.1 shows that only five women were elected in 2002 and 2004 without prior elective or administrative experience. Four of them were relatively young when they launched their political careers. Representatives Stephanie Herseth (D-SD) and Linda Sanchez (D-CA) ran for the House in 2002, Sanchez at the age of thirty-three and Herseth at the age of thirty-two. Representatives Melissa Bean (D-IL) and Loretta Sanchez (D-CA) pursued careers in business for a decade before running. Sanchez was elected to the House in 1996 at the age of thirty-seven, while Bean won election to the House in 2004 at the age of forty. The fifth woman, Representative Carolyn McCarthy, launched her campaign after a personal tragedy. In 1993, her husband was killed and her son injured in the Long Island Railroad massacre when a gunman opened fire on the passengers of a commuter train. In the wake of the incident, McCarthy lobbied Representative Dan Frisa (R-NY) to support stricter gun control measures; Frisa was not interested. In 1996, after contemplating a run against Frisa as a Republican, McCarthy was approached by the Democratic Party and encouraged to run as a Democrat. She defeated Frisa in the general election by sixteen percentage points.[26]

There is some evidence that, in general, lateral entry has increased over time, particularly into the Senate. In other words, the pipeline is becoming less relevant for all congressional candidates. There are increasing numbers of "amateur candidates" who have never run before and who spend a great deal of their own money or capitalize on their celebrity status to obtain high-level offices.[27] For example, some senators have come from prominent political families, such as Senators Robert Kennedy (D-NY), Edward Kennedy (D-MA), and Jay Rockefeller (D-WV). Senator George Murphy (R-CA) starred in four Broadway shows and forty-five motion pictures before he ran for the Senate in 1964.[28] Senator Bill Bradley (D-NJ) played professional basketball for the New York Knicks and then ran for the Senate in 1978. Two astronauts have served in the Senate, John Glenn (D-OH) and Harrison Schmidt (R-NM). Before his Senate bid in 1994, Fred Thompson had a long

---

[26] Karen Foerstel, *Biographical Dictionary of Congressional Women* (Westport, Conn.: Greenwood Press, 1999), 176–77.

[27] David Canon, *Actors, Athletes and Astronauts* (Chicago: University of Chicago Press, 1990).

[28] *Biographical Directory of the United States Congress*, http://bioguide.congress.gov/scripts/bio-display.pl?index=M001092 (accessed July 20, 1995).

career as an actor, with roles in *The Hunt for Red October, Cape Fear,* and *Die Hard II,* and guest appearances on *China Beach* and *Matlock.*[29] Thompson resigned from the Senate in 2002 and landed the role of District Attorney Arthur Branch on *Law and Order.*[30] None of these men ever ran for office before their Senate bids.

Among all eighteen women who were elected in their own right to the Senate, there are only two who bypassed the pipeline and ran for Senate as the first elective office they sought. Both of them are examples of political "celebrities." Senator Nancy Kassebaum (R-KS) was the daughter of former governor and presidential nominee Alf Landon (R-KS). Senator Hillary Clinton (D-NY) was a former first lady. Her experience on her husband's two presidential campaigns no doubt helped prepare her. A third woman, Senator Elizabeth Dole (R-NC), was also able to take advantage of her national name recognition when she ran for the Senate in 2002. The first political office she ever ran for was president, two years prior. In other words, 83.3 percent of all the women elected to the Senate had run for a lower-level office before they ran for the Senate. Of the fourteen women in the 109th Congress (2005 session), six (42.8 percent) were former House members.[31] This suggests that lateral entry for women is still relatively rare. On the other hand, increasing numbers of women are entering the traditional political pipeline.

The stereotype of the early women in Congress was the "bereaved widow"—drafted out of a sense of duty to squelch intraparty disputes, and expected to step aside after completing her husband's term. Women who were not widows were also lumped into this category. Thus, until relatively recently, the conventional wisdom was that the path to Congress for a woman was by stepping over her husband's dead body.[32] Our analysis shows, however, that even among widows, this stereotype did not apply to many women. Most congressional widows, especially those who pursued congressional careers, had a great deal of political experience either independently or with their husbands. In other words, a large proportion of widows had political ambitions of their own. Over time, congressional widows have come to look more like the women who ran without the benefit of a dead husband. Those widows who were reelected in 2002 and 2004 provide a case in point. Mary Bono (R-CA), Lois Capps (D-CA), and Jo Ann Emerson (R-MO) are serving their fifth terms in the 109th Congress. As we noted in chapter 3, the fourth widow, Doris Matsui (D-CA), is also seeking reelection.

Our analysis has also shown that women are as politically ambitious as their male counterparts: once elected, they are as careerist as men. The average

---

[29] "Thompson, Fred," in *CQ's Politics in America 2002, the 107th Congress* (Washington, D.C.: CQ Press, 2001), http://library.cqpress.com/congress/pia107-0453055379 (accessed July 25, 2005).

[30] http://www.nbc.com/Law_&_Order/bios/Fred_Thompson.html.

[31] Of the eighty-six men in the Senate, thirty-eight (44.2 percent) were former House members.

[32] Diane Kincaid, "Over His Dead Body: A Positive Perspective on Widows in the U.S. Congress," *Western Political Quarterly* 31 (1978): 96–104.

length of service in the House is longer for men than women, but the differ-ence can be explained by the fact that most women were elected in 1992 or later. The vast majority of women in Congress now seek long careers and are gradually accumulating the leadership roles and influence that come with long-term service. Some, however, decided to seek higher office. These women are quite strategic in deciding whether to run for the Senate, and they consider many of the same factors that men do. For both men and women, the decision to pursue a Senate seat systematically varies with the cost of running, the probability of winning, the value of a House seat, and whether they are "risk takers." Very few sitting female House members have made a run for the Senate, but very few sitting male House members make the attempt. We argue that, for both men and women, this is largely a function of opportunity: the power of incumbency, the longevity of incumbents, and the electoral calendar block the career ladder. This suggests that women in Congress have career goals and make strategic decisions that are similar to those of men.

The Politics of Redistricting

The pipeline theory is a "bottom-up" approach to explaining the integration of women into Congress; growth in the number of women in the preparatory professions will eventually cause growth in the number of women running for state and local offices, which will eventually cause growth in the number of women running for Congress. This implies a relatively steady and sequential pattern. And, as suggested above, there is evidence that the pipeline matters, especially for women candidates.[33] This approach, however, does not take into account opportunity—or lack thereof. Our analysis shows that the structure of elections and the electoral context matter a great deal. Movement through the pipeline is constricted not only by incumbency but also by district-level factors that make a constituency more or less likely to elect a woman. This suggests that the way district lines are drawn can have a substantial impact on the success of female candidates.

While the documented examples are few, there is one very direct way in which the drawing of district lines can affect women's success. If female (or male) state legislators are interested in running for Congress, they can serve on the committee in the state legislature responsible for redrawing dis-trict lines. This gives them the opportunity to create a House district that largely overlaps their current constituency, making the transition from state legislature to Congress much easier. For example, Eddie Bernice Johnson was elected to the Texas State Senate in 1986, the first African American to serve in

---

[33] Given that women are more likely to consider themselves as unqualified to run for office, it makes sense that they might be more likely to go through the traditional political pipeline more often than men and that we would see less lateral entry among women; Kathryn Pearson and Eric McGhee, "Strategic Differences: The Gender Dynamics of Congressional Candidacies, 1982–2002" (paper presented at the American Political Science Association Annual Meeting, September 2004, Chicago).

that chamber since Reconstruction. She chaired the Committee on Reapportionment and drew herself a House district that she ran for and won in 1992 with 72 percent of the vote.[34] Cynthia McKinney was elected to the Georgia House in 1988. She served on the Reapportionment Committee, drew herself a House district that was 60 percent black, and won the seat in 1992.[35] Having allies on these committees can also help. Ginny Brown-Waite, for example, served in the Florida State Senate for ten years and moved up the leadership ladder to become Republican whip. The Republican-controlled Redistricting Committee substantially changed the lines of incumbent Democratic Representative Karen Thurman's House district. The new district included all of Brown-Waite's state senate district and excluded the more liberal part of the district around the University of Florida.[36] Brown-Waite narrowly defeated Thurman by 1.7 percent. Ironically, Thurman played a key role in drawing the district ten years earlier in the previous round of redistricting. Thurman also served in the Florida State Senate and chaired the Committee on Congressional Reapportionment in 1990. Florida had gained a House seat, and Thurman was instrumental in making sure the new seat included most of her state senate district.[37]

The impact of redistricting on the political fortunes of female candidates has received very little, if any, systematic attention.[38] As we discussed in chapter 1, redistricting controversies in the 1960s focused on malapportionment and the resulting rural dominance in state legislatures. Debates in the 1990s focused upon racial gerrymandering and its impact on the representation of people of color in Congress.[39] In 1990, states were mandated to redraw congressional district lines to comply with the Justice Department's new rules regarding the creation of "majority-minority districts." A record number of

---

[34] Foerstel, 1999, 135.

[35] Foerstel, 1999, 181. This district was then the subject of a lawsuit filed by white voters challenging the constitutionality of "racial gerrymandering," and according to the Supreme Court in *Miller v. Johnson*, had to be redrawn. In 1996, she was reelected in her new district, which was now 65 percent white; J. L. Moore, "Majority-Minority District," in *Elections A to Z* (Washington, D.C.: CQ Press, 2003), http://library.cqpress.com/elections/elaz2d-156-7490-402760 (accessed July 25, 2005).

[36] "Brown-Waite, Ginny," in *CQ's Politics in America, 2006, the 109th Congress* (Washington, D.C.: CQ Press, 2005), http://library.cqpress.com/congress/document.php?id=pia109-Brown-Waite.

[37] Foerstel, 1999, 270.

[38] Interestingly, in 2001, Virginia State Senator Virginia Byrne accused the state legislature of "gender gerrymandering" and making it tougher for the women who had been elected in the northern part of the state to get reelected. Her colleague, Senator Linda Puller, agreed and said that in the latest round of redistricting, "They were harsher on us. It's still good ol' boys"; R. H. Melton, "Byrne Strikes a Nerve in Richmond; Fairfax Senator Says Colleagues Are Trying to Force Out Democratic Women," *Washington Post*, April 15, 2001, C5.

[39] See for example David Lublin, *The Paradox of Representation: Racial Gerrymandering and Minority Interests in Congress* (Princeton, N.J.: Princeton University Press, 1997); David Lublin, "Racial Redistricting and African-American Representation: A Critique of 'Do Majority-Minority Districts Maximize Substantive Black Representation in Congress?'" *American Political Science Review* 93 (1999): 183–86; Canon, 1999; and David Epstein and Sharyn O'Halloran, "A Social Science Approach to Race, Redistricting, and Representation," *American Political Science Review* 93 (1999): 187–91.

African Americans and Hispanics were elected to Congress in 1992. There is evidence, however, that racial gerrymandering has also had an unintended consequence: helping Republicans. One study found that four of the nine districts that switched from Democratic to Republican control in 1992 did so because of the creation of majority-minority districts.[40] In fact, some argue that racial gerrymandering actually gave Republicans the opportunity to take control of the House in 1994.[41] To create majority-minority districts, large numbers of African Americans are "packed" into a district. Because African Americans disproportionately vote Democratic, these seats elect Democratic House members by extremely large margins that, in essence, waste Democratic votes. Packing Democratic voters into one district creates opportunities for Republicans in other districts.[42] As a result, according to Michael McDonald, a professor at George Mason University and a redistricting consultant, racial gerrymandering has created an "unholy alliance" between minority and Republican House members.[43] Our analysis in chapter 6 showed that male and female African American representatives come from the most Democratic districts. There are, in fact, few differences between the districts that elect black male Democrats to the House and those that elect black female Democrats. This suggests that racially gerrymandered districts are equally as likely to elect men and women of color.

The latest round of redistricting after the 2000 U.S. Census has refocused the debate on incumbent protection. In fact, "[T]he nationwide theme of congressional line drawing was incumbent protection."[44] In 1992, eighty House members won their seats with less than 55.0 percent of the vote. In 2002, thirty-seven—fewer than half as many—House members won their seats with less than 55.0 percent of the vote. In 2000, the election cycle before the redistricting, there were fifty-seven House members who came from marginal seats. In 2002, after the redistricting, only three of these incumbent House members lost.[45] Incumbent protection plans are typically the product of bipartisan negotiations. For example, Republican Representative and Speaker of the House Dennis Hastert and Democratic Representative William

[40] Kevin Hill, "Do Black Majority Districts Aid Republicans?" *Journal of Politics* 57 (1995): 384–401.

[41] See for example Charles Bullock, "Affirmative Action Districts: In Whose Face Will They Blow Up?" *Campaigns and Elections* 16 (1995): 22–23; Lani Guinier, "Don't Scapegoat the Gerrymander," *New York Times Magazine*, January 8, 1995, 36; and Hill, 1995.

[42] Hill, 1995.

[43] Interview with Barbara Palmer, Washington, D.C., March 17, 2004.

[44] Gregory Giroux, "Remaps' Clear Trend: Incumbent Protection," *CQ Weekly*, November 3, 2001, 2627; Bob Benenson, Gregory Giroux, and Jonathan Allen, "Safe House: Incumbents Face Worry-free Election," *CQ Weekly*, May 17, 2002, 1274; and Richard Scammon, A. V. McGillivray, and R. Cook, "Analysis of the Elections of 2002," in *America Votes, 25* (Washington, D.C.: CQ Press, 2003), http://library.cqpress.com/elections.amvt25-181-9622-602649 (accessed July 25, 2005). See also Gary Cox and Jonathan Katz, *Elbridge Gerry's Salamander: The Electoral Consequences of the Reapportionment Revolution* (New York: Cambridge University Press, 2002).

[45] Connie Morella (R-MD), Bill Luther (D-MN), and Jim Maloney (D-CT); Scammon, McGillivray, and Cook, 2003, 2.

Lipinski, both from Illinois, brokered a deal that "protected the reelection prospects of almost every Illinois incumbent."[46] In 2001, their proposal sailed through a state legislature that was under divided control of the parties.[47] Even in California, where Democrats controlled the state legislature, incumbent protection was the goal. In addition to protecting almost all of the safe Democratic House members, the seven marginal Democratic House members were given safe seats, and nineteen of the twenty Republicans in the California House delegation were also protected.[48]

Seats are made safer by adding more constituents who identify with the House member's party; Democratic members are given more Democratic voters, and Republican members are given more Republican voters, typically until they reach the 55 to 60 percent range. In addition to being used in racial gerrymandering, "packing" is a technique in which seats are made overly safe (that is, beyond the 55 to 60 percent range) by the opposition party in an effort to waste votes in one district while creating opportunities for themselves in other districts.[49] This "partisan gerrymandering" became a flashpoint in Texas. In 2000, the state legislature was under divided party control and passed an incumbent protection plan. The state's congressional delegation was seventeen Democrats and fifteen Republicans, in spite of the fact that in the aggregate, voters in the state leaned Republican. In 2002, the Republicans gained control of both chambers and also held the governor's seat. In an unprecedented move, in May 2003, House Majority Leader Tom DeLay and Karl Rove, one of President Bush's closest advisors, proposed a new redistricting plan that would create twenty-two Republican seats. Historically, no state had redrawn its district lines at this point in the ten-year cycle unless under orders from the federal courts. In response to this re-redistricting plan, Democrats in the state legislature walked out and took up temporary residence in Oklahoma, out of reach of the state troopers and Texas Rangers. After a bitter fight, which included another walkout to New Mexico by Senate Democrats, the new map passed.[50] In 2004, the Texas congressional delegation included twenty Republicans and twelve Democrats.

What is the impact of incumbent protection or partisan gerrymandering on female candidates? Incumbent protection plans make it harder for any kind of turnover. If more incumbents are running for reelection in safe seats, it further limits opportunities for challengers, male or female. But whether seats are made safer for incumbents or even packed, the result is the same: districts become more extreme and less competitive. They have larger proportions of Democrats or Republicans. Our analysis in chapter 6 showed that female

---

46 Giroux, "Remaps," 2001, 2627.
47 Giroux, "Remaps," 2001, 2627.
48 Gregory Giroux, "California Democrats' Remap Puts Two of Their Own in Tough Spots," *CQ Weekly*, September 22, 2001, 2224.
49 Kenneth Jost, "Redistricting Disputes," *CQ Researcher*, March 12, 2004, 221–47.
50 Ronald Keith Gaddie, "The Texas Redistricting, Measure for Measure," in *Extensions: Congressional Redistricting*, ed. Ronald Peters (Norman: University of Oklahoma, 2004); and Jost, 2004.

Democratic candidates do better in districts that have more Democratic voters than the districts that elect male Democratic candidates. Female Democratic candidates can benefit from this kind of redistricting, provided that those additional elements that make a district women-friendly are included. On the other hand, the opposite is true for Republican women. The more Republican voters in a district, the less likely it is that a female Republican candidate will run and win. Female Republican candidates do better in more moderate or swing districts. If these districts are disappearing, our analysis suggests that opportunities for Republican women might disappear as well.

Another Option: Women-Friendly Districts

These redistricting strategies—the creation of majority-minority districts, incumbent protection, and partisan gerrymandering—potentially have indirect consequences for female candidates. On the other hand, it seems possible that "gender gerrymandering" could be a more direct method of increasing opportunities for women. In chapter 6, we found that women are more likely to run and win in districts that are women-friendly, districts that have particular demographic characteristics. Thus, another way of increasing the number of women in Congress might be to draw district lines taking into account these characteristics. Our analysis of women-friendly districts in chapter 6 focused on three redistricting periods, ending in 2000. Since states redrew their lines in 2002, we can use our index to determine the most and least friendly districts for women in the 2002–2010 period and look for potential opportunities for women candidates. Unfortunately, one of our measures of women-friendliness, school-age population, was not yet available, so in this analysis we use a ten-point scale.

Table 7.2 provides a list of the districts with high scores, defined as eight or more characteristics, on both the Democratic and Republican women-friendly indices. There were eighteen districts that fit this criterion; these are the eighteen districts in the nation that are the most women-friendly to both Democratic and Republican women candidates. Representative Nancy Pelosi (D-CA), the House Minority leader, represents the district that scored the highest on both indices. In fact, six of the districts are in California and another six are in New York; two-thirds of these districts are in two states.

But, as the table shows, not all women-friendly districts are held by women. In fact, ten of these districts, over half, are occupied by men. These are districts, however, where women would have a good chance of winning. Our earlier analysis emphasizes that while open seats are conventionally seen as the primary opportunities for women, open seats vary in their friendliness to women. Some districts can, in fact, be hostile to female candidates. Here, our index of women-friendliness suggests that there are male incumbents who might be vulnerable against a female candidate. In other words, these ten districts may offer real opportunities for women, opportunities that have, for the most part, been largely overlooked.

Table 7.2 The Friendliest Districts in the 109th Congress (2005 Session)

State and District	D Score	R Score	2005 Occupant	Party	Sex
CA-8	*10*	*9*	*Nancy Pelosi*	*D*	*Female*
NY-5	9	9	Gary Ackerman	D	Male
CA-9	*9*	*8*	*Barbara Lee*	*D*	*Female*
MA-8	9	8	Mike Capuano	D	Male
CA-12	8	10	Tom Lantos	D	Male
CA-15	8	10	Mike Honda	D	Male
CA-33	*8*	*8*	*Diane Watson*	*D*	*Female*
CA-36	*8*	*10*	*Jane Harman*	*D*	*Female*
IL-5	8	10	Rahm Emanuel	D	Male
IL-9	*8*	*8*	*Jan Schakowsky*	*D*	*Female*
MD-8	8	9	Chris Van Hollen	D	Male
NJ-8	8	9	Bill Pascrell	D	Male
NY-4	*8*	*9*	*Carolyn McCarthy*	*D*	*Female*
NY-8	8	9	Jerrold Nadler	D	Male
NY-14	*8*	*9*	*Carolyn Maloney*	*D*	*Female*
NY-17	8	8	Eliot Engel	D	Male
NY-18	*8*	*9*	*Nita Lowey*	*D*	*Female*
VA-8	8	8	Jim Moran	D	Male

Aside from the significant male presence in these eighteen women-friendly districts, what is most striking is the partisanship of the occupants. All eighteen are Democrats. Table 7.2 makes the challenges faced by Republican women all too clear. The districts that are friendliest to Republican women are Democratic districts. These are districts where a Republican woman is most likely to win a primary because she is a woman, but she will have trouble winning the general election because she is a Republican. This helps to understand why there are now nearly twice as many Democratic women as Republican women in the House.

While there were eighteen districts with high scores on both the Democratic and Republican women-friendly indices, there were 153 districts with low scores on both indices. In effect, 35.2 percent of the current House districts are unlikely to be receptive to women candidates through the 2010 elections. Table 7.3 lists the "lowest of the low," the thirty-four districts with scores of zero or one on both the Democratic and Republican women-friendly indices. Six districts have a score of zero on both indices. Only one is represented by a woman. In fact, Representative Virginia Foxx (R-NC) is the only woman

Table 7.3 The Most Unfriendly Districts in the 109th Congress (2005 Session)

State and District	D Score	R Score	2005 Occupant	Party	Sex
AL-4	0	0	Robert Aderholt	R	Male
KY-1	0	0	Edward Whitfield	R	Male
KY-2	0	0	Ron Lewis	R	Male
NC-11	0	0	Charles Taylor	R	Male
NC-5	*0*	*0*	*Virginia Foxx*	*R*	*Female*
OK-4	0	0	Tom Cole	R	Male
AR-3	0	1	John Boozman	R	Male
KY-4	0	1	Geoff Davis	R	Male
KY-5	0	1	Harold Rogers	R	Male
OK-3	0	1	Frank Lucas	R	Male
TN-1	0	1	William Jenkins	R	Male
TN-2	0	1	John Duncan	R	Male
TN-6	0	1	Bart Gordon	D	Male
VA-9	0	1	Frederick Boucher	D	Male
AL-1	1	0	Josiah Bonner	R	Male
AL-2	1	0	Terry Everett	R	Male
AL-5	1	0	Robert Cramer Jr.	D	Male
FL-1	1	0	Jeff Miller	R	Male
GA-1	1	0	Jack Kingston	R	Male
GA-9	1	0	Charlie Norwood	R	Male
KY-6	1	0	A. B. Chandler	D	Male
LA-4	1	0	Jim McCrery	R	Male
LA-5	1	0	Rodney Alexander	R	Male
LA-7	1	0	Charles Boustany	R	Male
MS-1	1	0	Roger Wicker	R	Male
MS-3	1	0	Charles Pickering	R	Male
MS-4	1	0	Gene Taylor	D	Male
NC-3	1	0	Walter Jones	R	Male
SC-3	1	0	J. Gresham Barrett	R	Male
SC-5	1	0	John Spratt	D	Male
TX-4	1	0	Ralph Hall	R	Male
VA-4	1	0	Randy Forbes	R	Male
VA-5	1	0	Virgil Goode	R	Male
VA-6	1	0	Bob Goodlatte	R	Male

on the entire list of 153, and she was first elected in 2004. Prior to running for the House, she served in the North Carolina Senate and on her local school board.[51] Her campaign for the House was particularly nasty. She ran in a crowded Republican primary that featured eight candidates competing to fill the open seat vacated by Republican Representative Richard Burr. She finished second to Winston-Salem City Councilman Vernon Robinson, an African American Republican, and faced him in a runoff election. Robinson ran television ads featuring a Pakistani man, Kamran Akhtar, who was caught by police in downtown Charlotte filming office buildings and charged with immigration violations. In the ad, Robinson states, "I'm Vernon Robinson and I approve this message because Akhtar didn't come here to live the American dream. He came here to kill you."[52] In another ad, he compared Foxx to Hillary Clinton: "Hillary Clinton voted for racial quotas, higher taxes, gay rights and the abortion bills. So did Virginia Foxx."[53] His aggressive tactics backfired, and Foxx won the runoff by ten percentage points. She then easily defeated her Democratic opponent, Jim Harrell, in the general election. More generally, it is noteworthy that all thirty-four of these low-scoring districts are southern. Republicans represent twenty-eight of these districts, or 82.3 percent.

The Political Glass Ceiling

The American electoral arena is unique: it is the only place in the United States where women and men engage in direct, public competition.[54] Sports are segregated by sex. Even the Academy Awards are segregated by sex. But in a campaign, men and women go head to head, winner-take-all. Once women decide to enter the arena, they are as strategic as men in their decisions about where to run, whether to pursue a long career in the House, or whether to seek higher office. For both men and women, these strategic choices are fundamentally shaped by the power of incumbency. But even incumbency status is not equal among men and women in Congress. While female incumbents are reelected at slightly higher rates than male incumbents, they face more competition and have to work harder to maintain their seats.

Because of the overwhelming effect of incumbency on the political opportunity structure, open seats are obviously one avenue of change. The problem is, of course, that there are relatively few of these in a given election cycle. Moreover, as we have shown, not all open seats are alike. Women are more likely to run and be successful in districts that are women-friendly. And there

---

[51] *Biographical Directory of the United States Congress*, http://bioguide.congress.gov/scripts/bio-display.pl?index+F000450 (accessed July 2, 2005).

[52] Quoted from "Robinson Accuses Arrested Pakistani of Terrorism in New Ad," Associated Press State and Local Wire, August 15, 2004, BC cycle.

[53] Quoted from Rob Christensen, "Candidate's Zeal Divides," *(Raleigh, N.C.) News and Observer*, August 13, 2004, A1.

[54] Bledsoe and Herring, 1990, 213.

are a handful of House districts currently held by male Democrats that, under the right circumstances, would elect a woman of either party. These are the kinds of opportunities that have been, for the most part, overlooked in each election cycle. The political glass ceiling is not simply a function of incumbency: it is about districts and their receptivity to female candidates.

In her exploration of the paucity of women in elective office, Kirkpatrick called for a revolution in cultural expectations and sex role socialization, and clearly, attitudes about the role of women in politics have changed. Our analysis demonstrates, however, that cultural change is a necessary but not sufficient condition for accelerating the entry of women into Congress. The political glass ceiling is still unbroken and continues to slow the integration of women into the national political arena.

Bibliography

Abramson, Paul, John Aldrich, and David Rohde. "Progressive Ambition among United States Senators: 1972–1988." *Journal of Politics* 49 (1987): 335.

Alexander, C. Allen. "Interview with Beverly A. Moore." In *Social Changes in Western Michigan, 1930 to 1990: Alexander Oral History Project*, vol. 2, edited by Henry Vance Davis. Kalamazoo: Western Michigan University, 1997.

Alexander, Deborah, and Kristi Anderson. "Gender as a Factor in the Attribution of Leadership Traits." *Political Research Quarterly* 46 (1993): 527–45.

Alpern, Sara. "Center Stage: Helen Gahagan Douglas, a Life." *American Historical Review* 98 (1993): 967–68.

Ambrose, Stephen. *Nixon: The Education of a Politician, 1913–1962*. New York: Simon & Schuster, 1987.

Amer, Mildred. *Women in the United States Congress: 1917–2004*. Washington, D.C.: Congressional Research Service, 2004. http://www.senate.gov/reference/resources/pdf/RL30261.pdf.

———. *Membership of the 109th Congress: A Profile*. Washington, D.C: Congressional Research Service, 2005. http://www.senate.gov/reference/resources/pdf/RS22007.pdf.

Amundson, Kirsten. *The Silenced Majority: Women and American Democracy*. Englewood Cliffs, N.J.: Prentice-Hall, 1971.

Andersen, Kristi, and Stuart Thorson. "Congressional Turnover and the Election of Women." *Western Political Quarterly* 37 (1984): 143–56.

Ardoin, Phillip, and James Garand. "Measuring Constituency Ideology in U.S. House Districts: A Top-Down Simulation." *Journal of Politics* 65 (2003): 1165–89.

Associated Press. "Swift Steps Out of Race." *Worcester (Mass.) Telegram and Gazette*, March 20, 2002.

Atkeson, Lonna Rae. "Not All Cues Are Created Equal: The Conditional Impact of Female Candidates on Political Engagement." *Journal of Politics* 65 (2003): 1040–61.

Baker, Ross. *House and Senate*, 2nd ed. New York: W. W. Norton, 1995.

Barone, Michael, and Richard Cohen. *Almanac of American Politics, 2002*. Washington, D.C.: National Journal, 2001.

———. *Almanac of American Politics, 2004*. Washington, D.C.: National Journal, 2003.

Barone, Michael, and Grant Ujifusa. *Almanac of American Politics, 1986*. Washington, D.C.: National Journal, 1985.

———. *Almanac of American Politics, 1990*. Washington, D.C.: National Journal, 1989.

———. *Almanac of American Politics, 1992*. Washington, D.C.: National Journal, 1991.

———. *Almanac of American Politics, 1994*. Washington, D.C.: National Journal, 1993.

———. *Almanac of American Politics, 1996*. Washington, D.C.: National Journal, 1995.

————. *Almanac of American Politics, 1998*. Washington, D.C.: National Journal, 1997.

Barone, Michael, Grant Ujifusa, and Douglas Matthews. *Almanac of American Politics, 1980*. New York: E. P. Dutton, 1979.

"The Battle for America's Front Yard." *National Geographic*, June 2004.

Becker, Jo, and Spencer Hsu. "Credit Firm Gave Moran Favorable Loan Deal." *Washington Post*, July 7, 2002.

Beiler, David. "How to Defeat Women and Blacks." *Campaigns & Elections*, August–September 1990.

Benenson, Bob, Gregory Giroux, and Jonathan Allen. "Safe House: Incumbents Face Worry-free Election." *CQ Weekly*, May 17, 2002.

Berch, Neil. "The 'Year of the Woman' in Context: A Test of Six Explanations." *American Politics Quarterly* 24 (1996): 169–93.

————. "Women Incumbents, Elite Bias, and Voter Response in the 1996 and 1998 U.S. House Elections." *Women & Politics* 26 (2004): 21–33.

Bernstein, Robert. "Why Are There So Few Women in the House?" *Western Political Quarterly* 39 (1986): 155–64.

————. "Might Women Have the Edge in Open-Seat House Primaries?" *Women & Politics* 17 (1997): 1–26.

Bingham, Clara. *Women on the Hill*. New York: Times Books, 1997.

Biographical Directory of Congress. http://bioguide.congress.gov.

Biographical Directory of the American Congress. Washington, D.C.: U.S. Government Printing Office, 1971.

Biographical Directory of the United States Congress, http://bioguide.congress.gov/scripts/biodisplay.pl?index=M001092.

Black, Earl, and Merle Black. *The Vital South*. Cambridge, Mass.: Harvard University Press, 1992.

————. *The Rise of Southern Republicans*. Cambridge, Mass.: Harvard University Press, 2002.

Black, Gordon. "Conflict in the Community: A Theory of the Effects of Community Size." *American Political Science Review* 68 (1974): 1245–61.

Bledsoe, Timothy, and Mary Herring. "Victims of Circumstances: Women in Pursuit of Political Office." *American Political Science Review* 84 (1990): 213–23.

Boles, Janet. *The Politics of the Equal Rights Amendment*. New York: Longman, 1979.

Bond, Jon. "The Influence of Constituency Diversity on Electoral Competition in Voting for Congress, 1974–1978." *Legislative Studies Quarterly* 8 (1983): 201–17.

Bousquet, Steve, and Anita Kumar. "Castor, Martinez Keep Senate Race Attacks Coming." *St. Petersburg (Fla.) Times*, October 29, 2004.

Boxer, Barbara. *Strangers in the Senate: Politics and the New Revolution of Women in America*. Washington, D.C.: National Press Books, 1993.

Brace, Paul. "Progressive Ambition in the House: A Probabilistic Approach." *Journal of Politics* 46 (1984): 556–71.

Braden, Maria. *Women Politicians and the Media*. Lexington: University of Kentucky Press, 1996.

Brady, David, Kara Buckley, and Douglas Rivers. "The Roots of Careerism in the U.S. House of Representatives." *Legislative Studies Quarterly* 24 (1999): 489–510.

Brady, David, and Edward Schwartz. "Ideology and Interests in Congressional Voting: The Politics of Abortion in the U.S. Senate." *Public Choice* 84 (1995): 25–48.

Brady, Ruth, and Donna Cassata. "Ohio's Convicted Rep. Traficant May Campaign from Prison." *CQ Weekly*, August 3, 2002.

Brown, Clyde, Neil Heighberger, and Peter Shocket. "Gender-Based Differences in Perceptions of Male and Female City Council Candidates." *Women & Politics* 13 (1993): 1–17.

"Brown-Waite, Ginny." In *CQ's Politics in America, 2006, the 109th Congress*. Washington, D.C.: CQ Press, 2005. http://library.cqpress.com/congress/document.php?id=pia109-Brown-Waite.

Bryce, Herrington, and Alan Warrick. "Black Women in Electoral Politics." In *A Portrait of Marginality: The Political Behavior of American Women*, edited by Marianne Githens and Jewel Prestage. New York: David McKay, 1977.

Bullock, Charles. "House Careerists: Changing Patterns of Longevity and Attrition." *American Political Science Review* 66 (1972): 1295–3000.

———. "Affirmative Action Districts: In Whose Face Will They Blow Up?" *Campaigns and Elections* 16 (1995): 22–23.

Bullock, Charles, and David Brady. "Party, Constituency, and Roll-Call Voting in the U.S. Senate." *Legislative Studies Quarterly* 8 (1983): 29–43.

Bullock, Charles, and Patricia Lee Findley Heys. "Recruitment of Women for Congress: A Research Note." *Western Political Quarterly* 25 (1972): 416–23.

Burdick, Eugene. *The 480*. New York: McGraw-Hill, 1964.

Burdick, Eugene, and Harvey Wheeler. *Fail-Safe*. New York: McGraw-Hill, 1962.

Burrell, Barbara. "The Political Opportunity of Women Candidates for the U.S. House of Representatives in 1984." *Women & Politics* 8 (1988): 51–68.

———. "Women Candidates in Open-Seat Primaries for the U.S. House: 1968–1990." *Legislative Studies Quarterly* 17 (1992): 493–508.

———. *A Woman's Place Is in the House: Campaigning for Congress in the Feminist Era*. Ann Arbor: University of Michigan Press, 1994.

Bystrom, Diane, et al. *Gender and Candidate Communication*. New York: Routledge, 2004.

Cain, Bruce, John Ferejohn, and Morris Fiorina. *The Personal Vote: Constituency Service and Electoral Independence*. Cambridge, Mass.: Harvard University Press, 1987.

Cameron, Charles, David Epstein, and Sharyn O'Halloran. "Do Majority-Minority Districts Maximize Substantive Black Representation in Congress?" *American Political Science Review* 90 (1996): 794–812.

Campbell, Angus, et al. *The American Voter*. Chicago: University of Chicago Press, 1960.

Canon, David. *Actors, Athletes and Astronauts*. Chicago: University of Chicago Press, 1990.

———. *Race, Redistricting, and Representation: The Unintended Consequences of Black Majority Districts*. Chicago: University of Chicago Press, 1999.

Carmines, Edward, and James Stimson. *Issue Evolution: Race and the Transformation of American Politics*. Princeton, N.J.: Princeton University Press, 1989.

"Carnahan, Jean." In *CQ's Politics in America 2002, the 107th Congress*. Washington, D.C.: CQ Press, 2001. http://library.cqpress.com/elections/pia107-0453058594.

Carroll, Susan. "Political Elites and Sex Differences in Political Ambition: A Reconsideration." *Journal of Politics* 47 (1985): 1231–43.

———. *Women as Candidates in American Politics*. Bloomington: Indiana University Press, 1994.

———. "Women Voters and the Gender Gap." American Political Science Association, 2005. http://www.apsanet.org/content_5270.cfm.

Carroll, Susan, and Ronnee Schreiber. "Media Coverage of Women in the 103rd Congress." In *Women, Media, and Politics*, edited by Pippa Norris. New York: Oxford University Press, 1997.

Castillo, Jaime. "Words Such as 'Gringo,' 'Smear' Flying in Doggett-Klein Race." *San Antonio (Tex.) Express-News*, July 24, 2004.

Center for American Women and Politics. *Women in State Legislatures, 2002*. New Brunswick, N.J.: Rutgers University, 2002.

———. *Women in Elective Office, 2005*. New Brunswick, N.J.: Rutgers University, 2005.

———. *Women in the U.S. Senate 1922–2005*. New Brunswick, N.J.: Rutgers University, 2005.

———. *Women of Color in Elective Office, 2005*. New Brunswick, N.J.: Rutgers University, 2005.

———. *Woman versus Woman Fact Sheet, 2004*. New Brunswick, N.J.: Rutgers University, 2005.

Chamberlin, Hope. *A Minority of Members: Women in the United States Congress.* New York: Praeger, 1973.

Chaney, Carole. "Running against a Woman: Advertising Strategies in Mixed-Sex Races for the United States Senate and Their Impact on Candidate Evaluation." Paper presented at the Western Political Science Association Annual Meeting, 1998, Los Angeles.

Chaney, Carole, and Barbara Sinclair. "Women and the 1992 House Elections." In *The Year of the Woman: Myths and Reality,* edited by Elizabeth Adell Cook, Sue Thomas, and Clyde Wilcox. Boulder, Colo.: Westview Press, 1994.

Chisholm, Shirley. *Unbought and Unbossed: An Autobiography.* New York: Houghton Mifflin, 1970.

Christensen, Rob. "Candidate's Zeal Divides." *(Raleigh, N.C.) News and Observer,* August 13, 2004.

Clark, Janet, Charles Hadley, and Robert Darcy. "Political Ambition among Men and Women State Party Leaders." *American Politics Quarterly* 17 (1989): 194–207.

Cleaver, Eldridge. *Soul On Ice.* New York: McGraw Hill, 1968.

Clift, Eleanor, and Tom Brazaitis. *Madam President.* New York: Scribner, 2000.

———. *Madam President,* 2nd ed. New York: Scribner, 2003.

Congress and the Nation, 1948–1964. Washington, D.C.: CQ Press, 1965.

Congress and the Nation, 1973–1976. Washington, D.C.: CQ Press, 1977.

Constantini, Edmond. "Political Women and Political Ambition." *American Journal of Politics* 34 (1990): 741–70.

Conway, M. Margaret. *Political Participation in the United States,* 3rd ed. Washington, D.C.: CQ Press, 2000.

Conway, M. Margaret, Gertrude Steuernagel, and David Ahern. *Women and Political Participation.* Washington, D.C.: CQ Press, 1997.

Cook, Elizabeth Adell. "Voter Reactions to Women Candidates." In *Women and Elective Office: Past, Present and Future,* edited by Sue Thomas and Clyde Wilcox. New York: Oxford University Press, 1998.

Cook, Elizabeth Adell, and Clyde Wilcox. "Women Voters in the Year of the Woman." In *Democracy's Feast: Elections in America,* edited by Herbert Weisberg. Chatham, N.J.: Chatham House, 1995.

Cooperman, Rosalyn, and Bruce Oppenheimer. "The Gender Gap in the House of Representatives." In *Congress Reconsidered,* 7th ed., edited by Lawrence Dodd and Bruce Oppenheimer. Washington, D.C.: CQ Press, 2001.

Copeland, Gary. "Choosing to Run: Why House Members Seek Election to the Senate." *Legislative Studies Quarterly* 14 (1989): 549–65.

Costain, Anne. *Inviting Women's Rebellion: A Political Process Interpretation of the Women's Movement.* Baltimore: Johns Hopkins University Press, 1992.

Cox, Gary, and Jonathan Katz. *Elbridge Gerry's Salamander: The Electoral Consequences of the Reapportionment Revolution.* New York: Cambridge University Press, 2002.

"CQ's Guide to Committees." *CQ Weekly,* April 11, 2005.

CQ's Guide to 1990 Congressional Redistricting. Washington, D.C.: CQ Press, 1993.

Crawford, Craig. "Ultimate Glass Ceiling Could Be Tested in 2008." *CQ Weekly,* March 7, 2005.

Cummings, Milton, and Robert Peabody. "The Decision to Enlarge the Committee on Rules: An Analysis of the 1961 Vote." In *New Perspectives on the House of Representatives,* 2nd ed., edited by Robert Peabody and Nelson Polsby. Chicago: Rand McNally, 1969.

Dahl, Robert, and Edward Tufte. *Size and Democracy.* Stanford, Calif.: Stanford University Press, 1973.

Darcy, R., and James Choike. "A Formal Analysis of Legislative Turnover: Women Candidates and Legislative Representation." *American Journal of Political Science* 30 (1986): 237–55.

Darcy, R., and Charles Hadley. "Black Women in Politics: The Puzzle of Success." *Social Science Quarterly* 69 (1988): 629–45.

Darcy, R., and Sarah Slavin Schramm. "When Women Run against Men." *Public Opinion Quarterly* 41 (1977): 1–12.

Darcy, R., Susan Welch, and Janet Clark. *Women, Elections, and Representation*, 2nd ed. Lincoln: University of Nebraska Press, 1994.

Darling, Marsha. "African-American Women in State Elective Office in the South." In *Women and Elective Office: Past, Present and Future*, edited by Sue Thomas and Clyde Wilcox. New York: Oxford University Press, 1998.

Davidson, Roger, and Walter Oleszek. *Congress and Its Members*, 5th ed. Washington, D.C.: CQ Press, 1996.

———. *Congress and Its Members*, 9th ed. Washington, D.C.: CQ Press, 2004.

Davis, Flora. *Moving the Mountain: The Women's Movement in America since 1960*. New York: Simon & Schuster, 1991.

Deber, Raisa. "The Fault Dear Brutus: Women as Congressional Candidates in Pennsylvania." *Journal of Politics* 44 (1982): 463–79.

Deering, Christopher, and Stephen Smith. *Committees in Congress*, 3rd ed. Washington, D.C.: CQ Press, 1997.

"Deficit-Reduction Bill Narrowly Passes." In *Congressional Quarterly Almanac, 1993*. Washington, D.C.: CQ Press, 1994.

deFiebre, Conrad. "Janklow Case: He Did Politics His Way; Roughshod Style Made Him SD Icon." *Minneapolis Star Tribune*, December 14, 2003.

Delli Carpini, Michael, and Ester Fuchs. "The Year of the Woman? Candidates, Voters, and the 1992 Elections." *Political Science Quarterly* 108 (1993): 29–36.

Delli Carpini, Michael, and Scott Keeter. *What Americans Know about Politics and Why It Matters*. New Haven, Conn.: Yale University Press, 1996.

Dewar, Helen. "NY Senate Primary Gets Muddy Near the Wire." *Washington Post*, August 30, 1992.

Diamond, Irene. *Sex Roles in the State House*. New Haven, Conn.: Yale University Press, 1977.

Dickenson, James, and Paul Taylor. "Widow of Burton Will Seek Election to His House Seat." *Washington Post*, April 19, 1983.

"Dingell, John D." In *CQ's Politics in America 2006, the 109th Congress*. Washington, D.C.: CQ Press, 2005. http://library.cqpress.com/congress/pia109-Dingell-John-D.

Dolan, Julie. "A Decade after the Year of the Woman: Female Candidates' Success Rates in the 2002 Elections." Paper presented at the Southern Political Science Association Annual Meeting, January 2005, New Orleans.

Dolan, Kathy. "Voting for Women in the 'Year of the Woman.'" *American Journal of Political Science* 42 (1998): 272–93.

———. "Electoral Context, Issues, and Voting for Women in the 1990s." In *Women and Congress: Running, Winning and Ruling*, edited by Karen O'Connor. New York: Haworth Press, 2001.

———. *Voting for Women: How the Public Evaluates Women Candidates*. Boulder, Colo.: Westview Press, 2004.

Dolan, Kathleen, and Lynne Ford. "Change and Continuity among Women State Legislators: Evidence from Three Decades." *Political Research Quarterly* 50 (1997): 137–51.

———. "Are All Women State Legislators Alike?" In *Women and Elective Office: Past, Present and Future*, edited by Sue Thomas and Clyde Wilcox. New York: Oxford University Press, 1998.

Drinkard, Jennifer. "The Disparity of Women Running for Congress." American University Washington Semester Program, Washington, D.C., 2003.

Duerst-Lahti, Georgia. "The Bottleneck: Women Becoming Candidates." In *Women and Elective Office: Past, Present and Future*, edited by Sue Thomas and Clyde Wilcox. New York: Oxford University Press, 1998.

Ehrenhart, Alan, ed. *Politics in America, 1982*. Washington, D.C.: CQ Press, 1981.

Elazar, Daniel. *American Federalism: A View from the States.* New York: Crowell, 1966.

"Electing to Carry On: Grief Fuels Matsui's Bid for Congress." Roberts, Alison. "Electing to Carry On: Grief Fuels Matsui's Bid for Congress." *Sacramento Bee,* January 22, 2005.

Epstein, Cynthia Fuchs. *Women in Law,* 2nd ed. Chicago: University of Illinois Press, 1993.

Epstein, David, and Sharyn O'Halloran. "A Social Science Approach to Race, Redistricting, and Representation." *American Political Science Review* 93 (1999): 187–91.

Erikson, Robert, Gerald Wright, and John McIver. *Statehouse Democracy: Public Opinion and Policy in the American States.* New York: Cambridge University Press, 1993.

Fears, Darryl. "On a Mission in a Political Second Act; Bush's Record Forced Her to Run, Braun Says." *Washington Post,* July 13, 2003.

"Federal Court Asked to Throw Out McKinney Defeat." Associated Press State and Local Wire. October 4, 2002.

Fenn, Jennifer. "Swift Sent Women a Bad Message." *Lowell (Mass.) Sun,* March 22, 2002.

Fenno, Richard. *Congressmen in Committees.* Boston: Little Brown, 1973.

———. *Home Style: House Members in Their Districts.* Boston: Little Brown, 1978.

———. *Senators on the Campaign Trail.* Norman: University of Oklahoma Press, 1996.

———. *Congress at the Grassroots: Representational Change in the South, 1970–1998.* Chapel Hill: University of North Carolina Press, 2000.

Fiorina, Morris. *Representatives, Roll Calls, and Constituencies.* Lexington, Mass.: D.C. Heath, 1974.

———. *Congress: Keystone of the Washington Establishment,* 2nd ed. New Haven, Conn.: Yale University Press, 1989.

———. *Culture War? The Myth of a Polarized America.* New York: Longman, 2005.

Fleisher, Richard. "Explaining the Change in Roll-Call Voting Behavior of Southern Democrats." *Journal of Politics* 55 (1993): 327–41.

Fleisher, Richard, and Jon Bond. "Polarized Politics: Does It Matter?" In *Polarized Politics: Congress and the President in a Partisan Era,* edited by Jon Bond and Richard Fleisher. Washington D.C.: CQ Press, 2000.

Florida, Richard. "The Rise of the Creative Class: Why Cities without Gays and Rock Bands Are Losing the Economic Development Race." *Washington Monthly* 34 (2002): 15–26.

Foerstel, Karen. *Biographical Dictionary of Congressional Women.* Westport, Conn.: Greenwood Press, 1999.

Foerstel, Karen, and Herbert Foerstel. *Climbing the Hill: Gender Conflict in Congress.* Westport, Conn.: Praeger Press, 1996.

Fowlkes, Diane, Jerry Perkins, and Sue Tolleson Rinehart. "Gender Roles and Party Roles." *American Political Science Review* 3 (1979): 772–80.

Fox, Richard. *Gender Dynamics in Congressional Elections.* Thousand Oaks, Calif.: Sage, 1997.

———. "Gender, Political Ambition and the Decision Not to Run for Office." Center for American Women and Politics, 2003. http://www.rci.rutgers.edu/~cawp/Research/Reports/Fox2003.pdf.

Fox, Richard, and Jennifer Lawless. "The Impact of Sex-Role Socialization on the Decision to Run for Office." Paper presented at the Southern Political Science Association Annual Meeting, January 2002, Atlanta.

Fox, Richard, Jennifer Lawless, and Courtney Feeley. "Gender and the Decision to Run for Office." *Legislative Studies Quarterly* 26 (2001): 411–35.

Fox, Richard, and Zoe Oxley. "Gender Stereotyping in State Executive Elections: Candidates Selection and Success." *Journal of Politics* 65 (2003): 833–50.

Francis, Wayne, and Lawrence Kenny. *Up the Political Ladder: Career Paths in U.S. Politics.* Thousand Oaks, Calif.: Sage, 2000.

Frankel, Bruce. "Anything Goes in NY Primary." *USA Today,* September 11, 1992.

Freeman, Jo. *The Politics of Women's Liberation*. New York: David McKay, 1975.

Freeman, Joanne. *Affairs of Honor: National Politics in the New Republic*. New Haven, Conn.: Yale University Press, 2001.

Friedman, Sally. "House Committee Assignments of Women and Minority Newcomers, 1965–1994." *Legislative Studies Quarterly* 21 (1996): 73–81.

Froman, Lewis. *Congressmen and Their Constituencies*. Chicago: Rand McNally, 1963.

———. *The Congressional Process*. Boston: Little, Brown, 1967.

Gaddie, Ronald Keith. "The Texas Redistricting, Measure for Measure." In *Extensions: Congressional Redistricting*, edited by Ronald Peters. Norman: University of Oklahoma, 2004.

Gaddie, Ronald Keith, and Charles Bullock. "Congressional Elections and the Year of the Woman: Structural and Elite Influences on Female Candidates." *Social Science Quarterly* 76 (1995): 749–62.

Gallagher, Jay, and Kyle Hughs. "Dirty Campaign Muddies Senate Contest in NY." *Chicago Sun-Times*, September 12, 1992.

Gallup Poll. Wilmington, Del.: Scholarly Resources, 1992.

Gallup Poll, 1935–1971. Wilmington, Del.: Scholarly Resources, 1973.

Gamarekian, Barbara. "'The Popular Burton' and Her Mission." *New York Times*, July 29, 1983.

Gelman, Andrew, and Gary King. "Enhancing Democracy through Legislative Redistricting." *American Political Science Review* 88 (1994): 541–59.

———. "A Unified Method of Evaluating Electoral Systems and Redistricting Plans." *American Journal of Political Science* 38 (1994): 514–54.

Geraghty, Jim. "Moranic Record." *National Review Online*, March 12, 2003. http://www.nationalreview.com/comment/comment-geraghty031203.asp.

Gerber, Larry. "Dornan Loses Solidly, Not Quietly." Associated Press, November 4, 1998.

Gertzog, Irwin. "The Matrimonial Connection: The Nomination of Congressmen's Widows for the House of Representatives." *Journal of Politics* 42 (1980): 820–33.

———. *Congressional Women: Their Recruitment, Integration, and Behavior*, 2nd ed. Westport, Conn.: Praeger Press, 1995.

Gertzog, Irwin, and Michele Simard. "Women and 'Hopeless' Congressional Candidacies: Nomination Frequency, 1916–1978." *American Politics Quarterly* 9 (1991): 449–66.

Giles, Kevin. *Flight of the Dove: The Story of Jeanette Rankin*. Beaverton, Ore.: Touchstone Press, 1980.

Gillon, Steven. *That's Not What We Meant to Do: Reform and Its Unintended Consequences in Twentieth-Century America*. New York: W.W. Norton, 2000.

Giroux, Gregory. "California Democrats' Remap Puts Two of Their Own in Tough Spots." *CQ Weekly*, September 22, 2001.

———. "Remaps' Clear Trend: Incumbent Protection." *CQ Weekly*, November 3, 2001.

Goodman, Ellen. "Racing All Out to Win Maine." *Boston Globe*, October 13, 2002.

"Grand Jury Indicts Espy on 39 Counts." *CQ Weekly*, August 30, 1997.

Greenblatt, Alan, and Jonathan D. Salant. "Retirement: Out with the Old and the New: Myers, LincolnWill Retire." *CQ Weekly*, January 13, 1996.

Grofman, Bernard, Robert Griffin, and Amihai Glazer. "The Effect of Black Population on Electing Democrats and Liberals to the House of Representatives." *Legislative Studies Quarterly* 17 (1992): 365–79.

Grofman, Bernard, and Lisa Handley, "Minority Population Proportion and the Black and Hispanic Congressional Success in the 1970s and 1980s." *American Politics Quarterly* 17 (1989): 436–45.

Gruberg, Martin. *Women in Politics: A Source Book*. New York: Academic Press, 1968.

———. "Defeated Rep. Franks Accused of 'Uncle Tomism.'" *Washington Post*, November 21, 1996.

Gugliotta, Guy. "In a Republican Redoubt, Doubts on Senate Hopeful: Conservative in Tight Race for Kansas Seat." *Washington Post*, October 29, 1996.

Guinier, Lani. "Don't Scapegoat the Gerrymander." *New York Times Magazine*, January 8, 1995.

Haga, Chuck. "'Come Home,' Coya Dies." *Minneapolis Star Tribune*, October 11, 1996.

Hain, Paul, Philip Roeder, and Manuel Avalos. "Risk and Progressive Candidacies: An Extension of Rohde's Model." *American Journal of Political Science* 25 (1981): 188–92.

Handley, Lisa, and Bernard Grofman. "The Impact of the Voting Rights Act on Minority Representation: Black Office Holding in Southern State Legislatures and Congressional Delegations." In *Quiet Revolution in the South: The Impact of the Voting Rights Act, 1965–1990*, edited by Chandler Davidson and Bernard Grofman. Princeton, N.J.: Princeton University Press, 1994.

Hansen, Susan. "Talking about Politics: Gender and Contextual Effects on Political Proselytizing." *Journal of Politics* 59 (1997): 73–103.

Hardy, Michael, and Karen McCurdy. "Representational Threshold: Women in Congressional Committees." Paper presented at the Southern Political Science Association, January 2005, New Orleans.

Harrison, Cynthia. *On Account of Sex: The Politics of Women's Issues, 1945–1968*. Berkeley: University of California, 1988.

Henry, Mark. "Bono's Mother Doesn't Want His Widow Elected." *Riverside (Calif.) Press Enterprise*, March 28, 1998.

———. "Phone Call Discouraged Election Run." *Riverside (Calif.) Press Enterprise*, March 31, 1998.

Herrnson, Paul. *Congressional Elections: Campaigning at Home and in Washington*. Washington, D.C.: CQ Press, 1998.

———. *Congressional Elections: Campaigning at Home and in Washington*, 4th ed. Washington, DC: CQ Press, 2004.

Herrnson, Paul, and James Gimpel. "District Conditions and Primary Divisiveness in Congressional Elections." *Political Research Quarterly* 48 (1995): 117–34.

Herrnson, Paul, J. Celeste Lay, and Atiya Kai Stokes. "Women Running 'as Women': Candidate Gender, Campaign Issues, and Voter-Targeting Strategies." *Journal of Politics* 65 (2003): 244–55.

High-Pippert, Angela. "Female Empowerment: The Influence of Women Representing Women." *Women & Politics* 19 (1998): 53–67.

Hill, David. "Political Culture and Female Political Representation." *Journal of Politics* 43 (1981): 159–68.

Hill, Kevin. "Do Black Majority Districts Aid Republicans?" *Journal of Politics* 57 (1995): 384–401.

Hoffman, Kim, Carrie Palmer, and Ronald Keith Gaddie. "Candidate Sex and Congressional Elections: Open Seats before, during, and after the Year of the Woman." In *Women and Congress: Running, Winning and Ruling*, edited by Karen O'Connor. New York: Haworth Press, 2001.

Hole, Judith, and Ellen Levine. *Rebirth of Feminism*. New York: Quadrangle Books, 1971.

Holtzman, Elizabeth, with Cynthia Cooper. *Who Said It Would Be Easy? One Woman's Life in the Political Arena*. New York: Arcade Press, 1996.

Hook, Janet. "Will the Flood of Retirements Arrive in 1992? Maybe Not." *CQ Weekly*, January 12, 1991.

Hotakainen, Rob. "McCollum Passes on Senate Bid, Will Seek 4th Term to U.S. House." *Minneapolis Star Tribune*, March 8, 2005.

Huddy, Leonie, and Nayda Terkildsen. "The Consequences of Gender Stereotypes for Women Candidates at Different Levels and Types of Office." *Political Research Quarterly* 46 (1993): 503–25.

———. "Gender Stereotypes and the Perception of Male and Female Candidates." *American Journal of Political Science* 37 (1993): 119–47.

Inskip, Leonard. "A Revival of Sorts for Minnesota's Knutson." *Minneapolis Star Tribune*, February 4, 1997.

Iyengar, Shanto, et al. "Running as a Woman: Gender Stereotyping in Political Campaigns." In *Women, Media, and Politics*, edited by Pippa Norris. New York: Oxford University Press, 1997.

Jacobson, Gary. *The Politics of Congressional Elections*, 4th ed. New York: Harper-Collins, 1997.

Jamieson, Kathleen Hall. *Beyond the Double Bind: Women and Leadership.* New York: Oxford University Press, 1995.

"Janklow Trial Begins, Could Shake Up State's Political Scene." *Bulletin's Frontrunner*, McClean, Virginia, December 2, 2003.

Jaynes, Jerald David, and Robin Williams, eds. *A Common Destiny: Blacks and American Society.* Washington, D.C.: National Academy Press, 1989.

Jenkins, Chris, and R. H. Melton. "Contrite, Combatative Moran on the Ropes: Congressman Fights to Survive." *Washington Post*, March 16, 2003.

Jennings, M. Kent, and Norman Thomas. "Men and Women in Party Elites: Social Roles and Political Resources." *Midwest Journal of Political Science* 12 (1968): 462–92.

Johnson, Dirk. "Race for Dole's Senate Seat Provokes Ideological Split." *New York Times*, August 5, 1996.

Jones, Allison North, and Ellen Gedalius. "Martinez 'Humbled to Be' U.S. Senator." *Tampa Tribune*, November 4, 2004.

Jones, Woodrow, and Albert Nelson. "Correlates of Women's Representation in Lower State Legislative Chambers." *Social Behavior and Personality* 1 (1981): 9–15.

Jost, Kenneth. "Redistricting Disputes." *CQ Researcher*, March 12, 2004.

Judis, John, and Ruy Teixeira. *The Emerging Democratic Majority.* New York: Scribner, 2002.

Kafka, Joe. "Herseth Feeling More Settled in Washington." Associated Press State and Local Wire, January 30, 2005.

Kahn, Kim Fridkin. "Characteristics of Press Coverage in Senate and Gubernatorial Elections: Information Available to Voters." *Legislative Studies Quarterly* 20 (1995): 23–35.

———. *The Political Consequences of Being a Woman.* New York: Columbia University Press, 1996.

Kahn, Kim Fridkin, and Edie Goldenberg. "Women Candidates in the News: An Examination of Gender Differences in U.S. Senate Campaign Coverage." *Public Opinion Quarterly* 55 (1991): 180–99.

Kaplan, Dave. "Louisiana: Redrawn Map Still Features Two Minority Districts." *CQ Weekly*, April 20, 1994.

Kaptur, Marcy. *Women of Congress: A Twentieth-Century Odyssey.* Washington, D.C.: CQ Press, 1996.

Kardiner, Abram. *Sex and Morality.* Indianapolis, Ind.: Bobbs-Merrill, 1954.

Katz, Jonathan, and Brian Sala. "Careerism, Committee Assignments, and the Electoral Connection." *American Political Science Review* 90 (1996): 21–33.

Kaufman, Karen, and John Petrocik. "The Changing Politics of American Men: Understanding the Sources of the Gender Gap." *American Journal of Political Science* 43 (1999): 864–87.

Kernell, Samuel. "Toward Understanding 19th Century Congressional Careers: Ambition, Competition, and Rotation." *American Journal of Political Science* 21 (1977): 669–93.

Kessel, John. "Review of Candidates, Issues and Strategies." *Midwest Journal of Political Science* 10 (1966): 515–18.

Key, V. O. *Southern Politics in State and Nation.* New York: A. A. Knopf, 1949.

Kincaid, Diane. "Over His Dead Body: A Positive Perspective on Widows in the U.S. Congress." *Western Political Quarterly* 31 (1978): 96–104.

King, David, and Richard Matland. "Sex and the Grand Old Party: An Experimental Investigation of the Effect of Candidate Sex on Support for a Republican Candidate." *American Politics Research* 31 (2003): 595–612.

King, Gary, Michael Tomz, and Jason Wittenberg. "Making the Most of Statistical Analyses: Improving Interpretation and Presentation." *American Journal of Political Science* 44 (2000): 341–55.

King, Gary, and Langche Zeng. "Logistic Regression in Rare Events Data." *Political Analysis* 9 (2001): 1–27.

Kirkpatrick, Jeane. *Political Woman*. New York: Basic Books, 1974.

Koch, Jeffrey. "Do Citizens Apply Gender Stereotypes to Infer Candidates' Ideological Orientations?" *Journal of Politics* 62 (2000): 414–29.

———. "Gender Stereotypes and Citizens' Impression of House Candidates' Ideological Orientations." *American Journal of Political Science* 46 (2002): 453–62.

Koetzle, William. "The Impact of Constituency Diversity upon the Competitiveness of U.S. House Elections, 1962–1996." *Legislative Studies Quarterly* 23 (1998): 561–73.

Komarovsky, Mirra. "Cultural Contradictions and Sex Roles." *American Journal of Sociology* 52 (1946): 184–89.

Koszczuk, Jacki. "Proof of Illegal Voters Falls Short, Keeping Sanchez in House." *CQ Weekly*, February 7, 1998.

Koszczuk, Jacki, and H. Amy Stern, eds. *CQ's Politics in America, 2006*. Washington, D.C.: CQ Press, 2005.

Kropf, Martha, and John Boiney. "The Electoral Glass Ceiling? Gender, Viability, and the News in U.S. Senate Campaigns." In *Women and Congress: Running, Winning and Ruling*, edited by Karen O'Connor. New York: Haworth Press, 2001.

Kuntz, Phil. "Uproar over Bank Scandal Goads House to Cut Perks." *CQ Weekly*, October 5, 1991.

———. "Overdrafts Were a Potent Charge." *CQ Weekly*, November 7, 1992.

Lamson, Peggy. *Few Are Chosen*. Boston: Houghton Mifflin, 1968.

Lane, Robert. *Political Life*. Glencoe, Ill.: Free Press, 1959.

Lau, Richard, and David Redlawsk. "Advantages and Disadvantages of Cognitive Heuristics in Political Decision Making." *American Journal of Political Science* 45 (2001): 951–71.

Lau, Richard, and David Sears, eds. *Political Cognition*. Hillsdale, N.J.: L. Erlbaum Associates, 1986.

Lawless, Jennifer, and Richard Fox. *It Takes a Candidate: Why Women Don't Run for Office*. New York: Cambridge University Press, 2005.

Lederer, William, and Eugene Burdick. *The Ugly American*. New York: Norton, 1958.

Leeper, Mark. "The Impact of Prejudice on Female Candidates: An Experimental Look at Voter Inference." *American Politics Quarterly* 19 (1991): 248–61.

Lengel, Allan. "Discovery May Alter Questions for Condit." *Washington Post*, May 24, 2002.

Lengel, Allan, and Petula Dvorak. "Condit Offers Long-Awaited Comment Tonight." *Washington Post*, August 23, 2001.

Lublin, David. *The Paradox of Representation: Racial Gerrymandering and Minority Interests in Congress*. Princeton, N.J.: Princeton University Press, 1997.

———. "Racial Redistricting and African-American Representation: A Critique of 'Do Majority-Minority Districts Maximize Substantive Black Representation in Congress?'" *American Political Science Review* 93 (1999): 183–86.

Lucas, Greg. "Matsui Wins Election to Late Husband's Seat." *San Francisco Chronicle*, March 9, 2005.

Luce, Clare Boothe. *Stuffed Shirts*. New York: Liveright, 1933.

Maisel, Sandy, and Walter Stone. "The Politics of Government-Funded Research: Notes from the Experience of the Candidate Emergence Study." *PS: Political Science and Politics* 31 (1998): 811–17.

Mandel, Ruth. *In the Running: The New Woman Candidate.* New Haven, Conn.: Ticknor and Fields, 1981.

Mandel, Ruth, and Katherine Kleeman. *Political Generation Next: America's Young Elected Leaders.* Rutgers, N.J.: Eagleton Institute of Politics, 2004.

Mansbridge, Jane. *Why We Lost the ERA.* Chicago: University of Chicago, 1986.

March, William, and Keith Epstein. "Bile Flows as Tight Senate Race Heads to End." *Tampa Tribune*, October 29, 2004.

Margolies-Mezvinsky, Marjorie. *A Woman's Place: The Freshmen Women Who Changed the Face of Congress.* New York: Crown, 1994.

Matland, Richard, and David King. "Women as Candidates in Congressional Elections." In *Women Transforming Congress*, edited by Cindy Simon Rosenthal. Norman: University of Oklahoma Press, 2002.

Matthews, Donald. *U.S. Senators and Their World.* Chapel Hill: University of North Carolina Press, 1960.

Matthews, Jay. "California's GOP Primary a Free-for-All." *Washington Post*, June 1, 1986.

Matthews, Joe. "Maybe Anyone Can Be President." *Los Angeles Times*, February 2, 2005.

Mayer, William. *The Changing American Mind.* Ann Arbor: University of Michigan Press, 1992.

Mayhew, David. *Congress: The Electoral Connection.* New Haven, Conn.: Yale University Press, 1974.

McCurdy, Karen. "The Institutional Role of Women Serving in Congress: 1960–2000." In *Representation of Minority Groups in the U.S.*, edited by Charles Menifield. Lanham, Md.: Austin and Winfield, 2001.

McDermott, Monika. "Voting Cues in Low-Information Elections: Candidate Gender as a Social Information Variable in Contemporary U.S. Elections." *American Journal of Political Science* 41 (1997): 270–83.

———. "Race and Gender Cues in Low-Information Elections." *Political Research Quarterly* 51 (1998): 895–918.

McGlen, Nancy, and Karen O'Connor. *Women, Politics and American Society,* 2nd ed. Upper Saddle River, N.J.: Prentice Hall, 1998.

McGlen, Nancy, et al. *Women, Politics, and American Society,* 3rd ed. Upper Saddle River, N.J.: Prentice Hall, 2002.

McKinney, Joan. "Reapportionment Reaction." *The Advocate*, Baton Rouge, Louisiana, December 1, 1996.

Melton, R. H. "Byrne Strikes a Nerve in Richmond: Fairfax Senator Says Colleagues Are Trying to Force Out Democratic Women." *Washington Post*, April 15, 2001.

Merrion, Paul. "Martin Campaign Lags; Gaffes Raise GOP Doubts, May Imperil Fund-Raising," *Crain's Chicago Business*, October 2, 1989.

Mikulski, Barbara, et al. *Nine and Counting: The Women of the Senate.* New York: William Morrow, 2000.

Miller, Clem. *Member of the House: Letters of a Congressman*, edited by John Baker. New York: Scribner, 1962.

Mills, Paul. "Mr. Vacationland and Why We Can't Forget the Lady from Rumford." *Lewiston (Maine) Sun Journal*, September 3, 2000.

"Miss Rankin—Sobbing—Votes No." *New York Times*, April 6, 1917.

Mitchell, Greg. *Tricky Dick and the Pink Lady: Richard Nixon vs. Helen Gahagan Douglas: Sexual Politics and the Red Scare, 1950.* New York: Random House, 1998.

Molinari, Susan. *Representative Mom: Balancing Budgets, Bill, and Baby in the U.S. Congress.* New York: Doubleday, 1998.

Moncrief, Gary, Joel Thompson, and Robert Schuhmann. "Gender, Race and the State Legislature: A Research Note on the Double Disadvantage Hypothesis." *Social Science Journal* 28 (1991): 481–87.

Moore, J. L. "Majority-Minority District." In *Elections A to Z*. Washington, D.C.: CQ Press, 2003. http://library.cqpress.com/elections/elaz2d-156-7490-402760.

Morris, Celia. *Storming the Statehouse: Running for Governor with Ann Richards and Dianne Feinstein*. New York: Charles Scribner's Sons, 1992.

Mueller, Melinda, and Barbara Poole. "A New Year of the Woman? Women Candidates for U.S. House Seats in 2004." Paper presented at the Southern Political Science Association Annual Meeting, January 2005, New Orleans.

Nechemias, Carol. "Geographic Mobility and Women's Access to State Legislatures." *Western Political Quarterly* 38 (1985): 119–31.

———. "Changes in the Election of Women to U.S. State Legislative Seats." *Legislative Studies Quarterly* 12 (1987): 125–42.

"New House Member Profile: Russ Carnahan." *CQ Weekly*, November 6, 2004, 2644.

"New Member Profile: Elijah E. Cummings, D-Md. (7)." *CQ Weekly*, April 20, 1996, 1070.

Newport, Frank. "Update: Hillary Rodham Clinton and the 2008 Election." *Gallup Poll News Service*, June 7, 2005.

Niven, David. "Party Elites and Women Candidates: The Shape of Bias." *Women & Politics* 19 (1998): 57–80.

Niven, David, and Jeremy Zilber. "'How Does She Have Time for Kids and Congress?' Views on Gender and Media Coverage from House Offices." In *Women and Congress: Running, Winning and Ruling*, edited by Karen O'Connor. New York: Haworth Press, 2001.

Norman, Michael. "Mrs. Fenwick and Lautenberg Meet in Final Debate." *New York Times*, November 1, 1982.

———. "Rep. Fenwick Tries to Figure Out Why She Lost." *New York Times*, November 4, 1982.

Norrander, Barbara, and Clyde Wilcox. "The Geography of Gender Power." In *Women and Elective Office: Past, Present and Future*, edited by Sue Thomas and Clyde Wilcox. New York: Oxford University Press, 1998.

Norris, Pippa. "Women Leaders Worldwide: A Splash of Color in the Photo Op." In *Women, Media, and Politics*, edited by Pippa Norris. New York: Oxford University Press, 1997.

Novak, Robert. "Showdown in Kansas a Major Test for GOP." *Chicago Sun-Times*, August 6, 1996.

Nuwer, Deanne Stephens. "Southern Women Legislators and Patriarchy in the South." *Southeastern Political Review* 28 (2000): 449–68.

O'Connor, Karen. *Women's Organizations' Use of the Courts*. Lexington, Mass.: Lexington Books, 1980.

———. *No Neutral Ground? Abortion Politics in an Age of Absolutes*. Boulder, Colo.: Westview Press, 1996.

Oleszek, Walter. *Congressional Procedures and the Policy Process*, 6th ed. Washington, D.C.: CQ Press, 2004.

Open Secrets, "The Big Picture: 2002 Cycle, Most Expensive Races." http://www.opensecrets.org/bigpicture/topraces.asp?cycle=2002.

———. "New Jersey Senate Race: 2000 Campaign Money Profile." http://www.opensecrets.org/races/summary.asp?ID=NJS1&Cycle=2000.

———. "2004 Election Overview: Stats at a Glance." http://www.opensecrets.org/overview/stats.asp?cycle=2004&type=A&display=A.

Ornstein, Norman, ed. *Congress in Change: Evolution and Reform*. New York: Praeger, 1975.

Ornstein, Norman, Thomas E. Mann, and Michael Malbin, eds. *Vital Statistics on Congress*. Washington, D.C.: CQ Press, 1998.

Page, Benjamin, et al. "Constituency, Party, and Representation in Congress." *Public Opinion Quarterly* 48 (1984): 741–56.

Page, Susan, and Mimi Hall. "Verdict Could Kill Law That Made Case Possible: Espy Acquittal Puts Heat on Independent Counsel Statute." *USA Today*, December 3, 1998.

Palmer, Barbara, and Dennis Simon. "Breaking the Logjam: The Emergence of Women as Congressional Candidates." In *Women and Congress: Running, Winning, and Ruling*, edited by Karen O'Connor. Binghamton, N.Y.: Haworth Press, 2001.

———. "Political Ambition and Women in the U.S. House of Representatives, 1916–2000." *Political Research Quarterly* 56 (2003): 127–38.

———. "When Women Run against Women: The Hidden Influence of Female Incumbents in Elections to the U.S. House of Representatives, 1956–2002." *Politics and Gender* 1 (2005): 39–63.

Patrick, Steven. "Traficant Refuses to Go Quietly Despite Calls for His Resignation." *CQ Weekly*, April 13, 2002.

Peabody, Robert, Norman Ornstein, and David Rohde. "The United States Senate as Presidential Incubator: Many Are Called but Few Are Chosen." *Political Science Quarterly* 9 (1976): 237–58.

Pearson, Kathryn, and Eric McGhee. "Strategic Differences: The Gender Dynamics of Congressional Candidacies, 1982–2002." Paper presented at the American Political Science Association Annual Meeting, September 2004, Chicago.

Perine, Keith. "Specter Diagnosed with Hodgkin's, Vows to Stick to Judiciary Agenda." *CQ Weekly*, February 21, 2005.

Perkins, Jerry, and Diane Fowlkes. "Opinion Representation versus Social Representation: Or Why Women Can't Run as Women and Win." *American Political Science Review* 74 (1980): 92–103.

Peterson, Bill. "Alabama Senate 'Sleeper' Catches Political Experts Dozing." *Washington Post*, October 3, 1978.

Petrocik, John. "Issue Ownership in Presidential Elections, with a 1980 Case Study." *American Journal of Political Science* 40 (1996): 825–50.

Phillips, Kevin. *The Emerging Republican Majority.* New York: Anchor House, 1969.

Phillips, Frank. "Shake-up in the Governor's Race: Swift Yields to Romney Saying 'Something Had to Give,' Exits Race for Governor." *Boston Globe*, March 20, 2002.

Pitt, Leonard. "Mrs. Deeds Goes to Washington." *Reviews in American History* 21 (1993): 477–81.

Polsby, Nelson. "The Institutionalization of the U.S. House of Representatives." *American Political Science Review* 52 (1968): 124–43.

Pool, Ithiel de Sola, Robert Abelson, and Samuel Popkin. *Candidates, Issues, and Strategies: A Computer Simulation of the 1960 and 1964 Presidential Elections.* Cambridge, Mass.: MIT Press, 1965.

Prestage, Jewel. "Black Women State Legislators: A Profile." In *A Portrait of Marginality: The Political Behavior of American Women*, edited by Marianne Githens and Jewel Prestage. New York: David McKay, 1977.

———. "The Case of African American Women and Politics." *PS: Political Science and Politics* 27 (1994): 720–21.

Price, H. Douglas. "Congress and the Evolution of Legislative Professionalism." In *Change in Congress*, edited by Norman Ornstein. New York: Praeger, 1975.

Quinn, Sally. "Maryon Allen: The Southerngirl in the Senate." *Washington Post*, July 30, 1978.

Rahn, Wendy. "The Role of Partisan Stereotypes in Information Processing about Political Candidates." *American Journal of Political Science* 37 (1993): 472–96.

Ratcliffe, R. G. "Hutchison to Run for Senate, Not Governor." *Houston Chronicle*, June 18, 2005.

Reed, John Shelton. *The Enduring South: Subcultural Persistence in Mass Society.* Chapel Hill: University of North Carolina Press, 1986.

Reyes, B. J. "Case Wins Hawaii's 2nd Congressional District." Associated Press State and Local Wire, January 5, 2003.

"Robinson Accuses Arrested Pakistani of Terrorism in New Ad." Associated Press State and Local Wire, August 15, 2004.

Rodine, Sharon. "How to Beat Bubba." *Campaigns & Elections*, October–November 1990.

Roddy, Dennis. "Admission of Guilt: Waldholtz Admits Financial Violations, Apologizes to All but Ex-Wife." *Pittsburgh Post Gazette*, June 6, 1996.

Rohde, David. "Risk-Bearing and Progressive Ambition: The Case of Members of the United States House of Representatives." *American Journal of Political Science* 23 (1979): 1–26.

Rosenstone, Steven, and John Hansen. *Mobilization, Participation, and Democracy in America.* New York: Macmillan, 1993.

Ross, Shelly. *Fall from Grace: Sex, Scandal, and Corruption in American Politics from 1702 to the Present.* New York: Ballantine Books, 1988.

Rozell, Mark. "Helping Women Run and Win: Feminist Groups, Candidate Recruitment and Training." *Women & Politics* 21 (2000): 101–16.

Rule, Wilma. "Why Women Don't Run: The Critical and Contextual Factors in Women's Legislative Recruitment." *Western Political Quarterly* 34 (1981): 60–77.

———. "Why More Women Are Legislators: A Research Note." *Western Political Quarterly* 43 (1990): 437–48.

Rusk, Jerrold. "The Effect of the Australian Ballot on Split Ticking Voting: 1876–1908." *American Political Science Review* 64 (1970): 1220–38.

Rutenberg, Jim. "An Idea, with 4 Words, That Was Supposed to Soothe the Tone of Ads but Did Not." *New York Times*, October 30, 2004.

Sabato, Larry. *Feeding Frenzy: How Attack Journalism Has Transformed American Politics.* New York: Free Press, 1991.

Sanbonmatsu, Kira. "Gender Stereotypes and Vote Choice." *American Journal of Political Science* 46 (2002): 20–34.

———. "Political Parties and the Recruitment of Women to State Legislatures." *Journal of Politics* 64 (2002): 791–809.

"Sanchez Claims Victory in Nation's Most Expensive Race." Associated Press, November 4, 1998.

Sapiro, Virginia. "Private Costs of Public Commitments or Public Costs of Private Commitments? Family Roles versus Political Ambition." *American Journal of Political Science* 26 (1982): 265–79.

———. *The Political Integration of Women.* Urbana: University of Illinois Press, 1983.

Savodnik, Peter. "Capito, Dole Discuss Senate Bid." *The Hill*, June 27, 2005.

Saye, Albert. "Georgia's County Unit System of Election." *Journal of Politics* 12 (1950): 93–106.

Scammon, Richard, and Ben Wattenberg. *The Real Majority.* New York: Coward-McCann, 1970.

Scammon, Richard, A. V. McGillivray, and R. Cook. "Analysis of the Elections of 2002." In *America Votes, 25.* Washington, D.C.: CQ Press, 2003. http://library.cqpress.com/elections.amvt25-181-9622-602649.

Schlesinger, Joseph. *Ambition and Politics: Political Careers in the United States.* Chicago: Rand McNally, 1966.

Schroeder, Pat. *Twenty-four Years of House Work and the Place Is Still a Mess.* Kansas City, Mo.: Andrews McMeel, 1999.

Scobie, Ingrid Winther. *Center Stage: Helen Gahagan Douglas, a Life.* New York: Oxford University Press, 1992.

Seligman, Lester. "Political Recruitment and Party Structure: A Case Study." *American Political Science Review* 5 (1961): 77–86.

Seltzer, Richard, Jody Newman, and Melissa Voorhees Leighton. *Sex as a Political Variable.* Boulder, Colo.: Lynne Rienner Publishers, 1997.

Shames, Shauna. "The 'Un-Candidates': Gender and Outsider Signals in Women's Political Advertisements." *Women & Politics* 25 (2003): 115–47.

Sheckels, Theodore, Jr.. "Mikulski vs. Chavez for the Senate from Maryland in 1986 and the 'Rules' for Attack Politics." *Communication Quarterly* 42 (1994): 311–26.

Sidlow, Edward. *Challenging the Incumbent: An Underdog's Undertaking.* Washington, D.C.: CQ Press, 2004.

Simon, Dennis. "Electoral and Ideological Change in the South: The Case of the U.S. House of Representatives, 1952–2000." Paper presented at the Southern Political Science Association Annual Meeting, January 2004, New Orleans.

Simon, Dennis, and Barbara Palmer. "Gender, Party, and Political Change: The Evolution of a Democratic Advantage." APSAnet eSymposium, "An Open Boundaries Workshop: Women in Politics in a Comparative Perspective." *PS Online* 37 (2004): http://www.apsanet.org/imgtest/EvolutionDemocraticAdvan-Palmer.pdf.

———. "The Political Geography of Women-Friendly Districts, 1972–2000." Paper presented at the Southern Political Science Association Annual Meeting, January 2005, New Orleans.

Simon, Dennis, Barbara Palmer, and David Peterson. "Women in the Political Hierarchy: A Time Series Analysis." Paper presented at the Southern Political Science Association Annual Meeting, January 2004, New Orleans.

"Simon, Martin File Campaign Funding Data." *Crain's Chicago Business*, August 7, 1989.

Sinclair, Barbara. *Unorthodox Lawmaking.* Washington, D.C.: CQ Press, 1997.

Solowiej, Lisa, and Thomas Brunell. "The Entrance of Women to the U.S. Congress: The Widow Effect." *Political Research Quarterly* 56 (2003): 283–92.

Stanley, Alessandra. "In Primary Race for Senate, Ads Are Costly and Caustic." *New York Times*, September 13, 1992.

Stanley, Harold, and Richard Niemi. *Vital Statistics on American Politics 2003–2004.* Washington, D.C.: CQ Press, 2003.

Stanley, Jeanie. "Gender and the Campaign for Governor." In *Texas Politics: A Reader*, 2nd ed., edited by Anthony Champagne and Edward Harpham. New York: W.W. Norton, 1998.

Stevens, Allison. "The Strength of These Women Shows in Their Numbers." *CQ Weekly*, October 25, 2003.

Struble, Robert. "House Turnover and the Principle of Rotation." *Political Science Quarterly* 94 (1979): 649–67.

Sullivan, Bartholomew. "Safe Territory: Redrawing of Congressional District Lines Puts Incumbents in Driver's Seat." *Memphis (Tenn.) Commercial Appeal*, October 27, 2004.

Sullivan, John. "Political Correlates of Social, Economic and Religious Diversity of the American States." *Journal of Politics* 35 (1973): 70–84.

Sullivan, Joseph. "U.S. Senate Race Tops Jersey Elections." *New York Times*, October 31, 1982.

Swain, Carol. *Black Faces, Black Interests: The Representation of African-Americans in Congress.* Cambridge, Mass.: Harvard University Press, 1993.

Swers, Michelle. "Research on Women in Legislatures: What Have We Learned, Where Are We Going?" In *Women in Congress: Running, Winning, Ruling*, edited by Karen O'Connor. Binghamton, N.Y.: Haworth Press, 2001.

Swift, Elaine, Robert Brookshire, David Canon, Evelyn Fink, and John Hibbing, comps. *Database of Congressional Historical Statistics.* Interuniversity Consortium for Political Research Study 3371. Ann Arbor, Mich.: Interuniversity Consortium for Political Research, 2004.

"Thompson, Fred." In *CQ's Politics in America 2002, the 107th Congress.* Washington, D.C.: CQ Press, 2001. http://library.cqpress.com/congress/pia107-0453055379.

Thompson, Joan Hulce. "Career Convergence: Election of Women and Men to the House of Representatives, 1916–1975." *Women & Politics* 5 (1985): 69–90.

Thompson, Seth, and Janie Steckenrider. "The Relative Irrelevance of Candidate Sex." *Women & Politics* 17 (1997): 71–92.

Tolchin, Susan, and Martin Tolchin. *Clout: Womanpower and Politics.* NewYork: Coward, McCann & Geoghegan, 1974.

Tolleson-Rienhart, Sue, and Jeanie Stanley. *Claytie and the Lady: Ann Richards, Gender, and Politics in Texas.* Austin: University of Texas Press, 1994.

Tomz, Michael, Gary King, and Langche Zeng. *RELOGIT: Rare Events Logistical Regression, Version 1.1.* Cambridge, Mass.: Harvard University Press, 1999.

Tomz, Michael, Jason Wittenberg, and Gary King. *Clarify: Software for Interpreting and Presenting Statistical Results.* Cambridge, Mass.: Harvard University, 2001.

Torry, Jack. "From His Cell, Traficant Still a Force in Election." *Columbus Dispatch*, November 2, 2002.

"Traficant, James A., Jr." In *CQ's Politics in America 2002, The 107th Congress.* Washington, D.C.: CQ Press, 2001. http://library.cqpress.com/congress/pia107-0453055393.

Turner, Wallace. "Burton's Widow among 4 Considering Race for Congress Seat." *New York Times*, April 18, 1983.

U.S. Bureau of the Census. *Historical Statistics of the United States.* Washington, D.C.: U.S. Department of Commerce, Bureau of the Census, 1975.

———. *Statistical Abstract of the United States, 2004–2005.* http://www.census.gov/prod/www/statistical-abstract-04.html.

U.S. Congress Handbook. Washington, D.C.: Votenet Solutions, 2005.

Wayne, Stephen. *The Road to the White House, 2000: The Politics of Presidential Elections.* Boston: St. Martin's Press, 2000.

Welch, Susan. "Recruitment of Women to Public Office." *Western Political Quarterly* 31 (1978): 372–80.

———. "Are Women More Liberal than Men in the U.S. Congress?" *Legislative Studies Quarterly* 10 (1985): 125–34.

Welch, Susan, and Lee Sigelman. "Changes in Public Attitudes toward Women in Politics." *Social Science Quarterly* 63 (1982): 312–21.

Welch, Susan, and Donley Studlar. "The Opportunity Structure for Women's Candidacies and Electability in Britain and the United States." *Political Research Quarterly* 49 (1996): 861–74.

Welch, Susan, et al. "The Effect of Candidate Gender on Election Outcomes in State Legislative Races." *Western Political Quarterly* 38 (1985): 464–75.

Welch, William. "Ideology Rocks the Vote in Kansas." *USA Today*, August 2, 1996.

Werner, Emmy. "Women in Congress: 1917–1964." *Western Political Quarterly* 19 (1966): 16–30.

———. "Women in the State Legislatures." *Western Political Quarterly* 19 (1968): 40–50.

Whitby, Kenny. *The Color of Representation: Congressional Behavior and Black Interests.* Ann Arbor: University of Michigan Press, 1997.

White, Theodore H. *The Making of the President, 1972.* New York: Atheneum Publishers, 1973.

Whitney, David. "Freshman Matsui Learns Life in Congress Is Hectic." *Sacramento Bee*, March 20, 2005.

———. "Matsui Has Money in Bank for '06 Race." *Sacramento Bee*, April 27, 2005.

"Widow of Rep. Burton Is Elected in California Congressional Race." *New York Times*, June 23, 1983.

Wilcox, Clyde. "Why Was 1992 the 'Year of the Woman'? Explaining Women's Gains in 1992." In *The Year of the Woman: Myths and Reality*, edited by Elizabeth Adell Cook, Sue Thomas, and Clyde Wilcox. Boulder, Colo.: Westview Press, 1994.

Wilkerson, Isabel. "Black Woman's Senate Race Is Acquiring a Celebrity Aura." *New York Times*, July 29, 1992.

"Will Byrd Run?" *The Journal*, Martinsburg, West Virginia, May 1, 2005.

Williams, Christine. "Women, Law and Politics: Recruitment Patterns in the Fifty States." *Women & Politics* 10 (1990): 103–23.

Williams, Joan. *Unbending Gender: Why Family and Work Conflict and What to Do about It.* Oxford: Oxford University Press, 2000.

Williams, Leonard. "Gender, Political Advertising, and the 'Air Wars.'" *Women and Elective Office: Past, Present and Future*, edited by Sue Thomas and Clyde Wilcox. New York: Oxford University Press, 1998.

Wilson, Marie. *Closing the Leadership Gap: Why Women Can and Must Help Run the World.* New York: Viking, 2004.

Winkler, Robert, and William Hays. *Statistics: Probability, Inference and Decision*, 2nd ed. New York: Holt, Rinehart, and Winston, 1975.

Witt, Linda, Karen Paget, and Glenna Matthews. *Running as a Woman: Gender and Power in American Politics.* New York: Free Press, 1995.

Wolbrecht, Christina. *The Politics of Women's Rights: Parties, Positions, and Change.* Princeton, N.J.: Princeton University Press, 2000.

Wolfinger, Raymond, and Steven Rosenstone. *Who Votes?* New Haven, Conn.: Yale University Press, 1980.

Women in History: Living Vignettes of Notable Women in U.S. History. http://www.lkwdpl.org/wihohio/luce-cla.htm.

Woodward, Bob. *The Agenda: Inside the Clinton White House.* New York: Simon & Schuster, 1994.

Yamamura, Kevin. "Matsui Set to Be Sworn in Today and Cast First Vote as a Congressman's Widow and Washington Veteran." *Sacramento Bee*, March 10, 2005.

Young, James Sterling. *The Washington Community 1800–1828.* New York, Columbia University Press, 1966.

Index